STRUCTURAL ECONOMIC POLICIES

IN WEST GERMANY

AND THE UNITED KINGDOM

BY

ALAN PEACOCK

IN COLLABORATION WITH

ROB GRANT
MARTIN RICKETTS
G.K. SHAW
ELAINE WAGNER

The research for this publication was financed by the
ANGLO-GERMAN FOUNDATION FOR THE STUDY OF INDUSTRIAL SOCIETY
as part of its programme of study of social and economic
policy issues

St. Stephen's House, Victoria Embankment, London SW1A 2LA

The opinions expressed in this report are entirely those of the authors.

ISBN 0 905492 26 9

Price £15.00
inc. postage and packing

STRUCTURAL ECONOMIC POLICIES

IN WEST GERMANY

AND THE UNITED KINGDOM

CONTENTS

FOREWORD

The purpose of this study is to throw light on an important question in contemporary discussion of economic policy:

How far do accepted macroeconomic policy objectives, notably promotion of economic growth and of a high level of employment require the use not only of widely fiscal and monetary instruments but also what may be called a 'structuralist' approach?

The starting point in seeking an answer to this question must be a closer look at what is meant by a 'structuralist' approach. Its policy components are far from clear in economics literature. Broadly speaking, structural policies (what is called in West Germany 'Strukturpolitik') require that macro-economic objectives are promoted by micro-economic policies which may alter the balance between different industrial groupings in the economy. To take a familiar example from the economic discussion of the 1960s, if it is believed that economic growth is 'export-led', the structural policies should concentrate on diverting resources by tax and subsidy measures, for example, towards export markets. The range of structuralist measures is very wide-ranging from government influence on the demand for the output of particular sectors, e.g. subsidies to consumers, discriminatory public purchasing, import controls, to influence on the supply of factors of production, e.g. discriminatory labour subsidies, investment allowances, subsidised interest rates, subsidies to technical innovation and so on. In Chapter 1 a case is made for concentrating on a particular range of such micro-economic measures which constitute selective aid in the form of direct subsidies or 'soft' loans to individual firms or firms within a designated industrail grouping. One important practical reason for doing so, apart from resource constraints, is to be able to make effective comparisons between the Bundesrepublik Deutschland (BRD) and the United Kingdom (UK).

Any study of structuralist measures must be prefaced by an analysis of the incidence of structural changes in the two economies. Clearly, if it is thought that altering the balance of industrial sectors affects economic growth and employment, then evidence is needed about the relation between these variables and structural change. Chapter 2 considers a variety of measures of structural change. What emerges is that there is little evidence to support the view that recent differences in growth between the BRD and the UK can be accounted for by structural disparities. The rationale of structural policies must therefore be based on other considerations; for example, the extent to which improvements in efficiency require government action at the sectoral level.

The evolution of structural economic policies requires an understanding of the interplay between the economic experience of each country and the diagnosis and prescriptions of economic analysts. What is interesting is that if one attempts to dilineate the 'median' position of writers on economic policy who have considered structuralist measures, in both countries little support is found for such measures. This lack of support is all the more interesting, considering both the different economic problems which each country has had to face and also the different 'trade-offs' of policy objectives (Cf. Chapter 3.).

Whatever the degree of scepticism of economists, selective aid, as a prime example of structuralist intervention, has grown in size and scope in both the BRD and UK, as Chapter 4 indicates. One important point, taken up in later discussion, that emerges is the extent to which selective aid policies create an administrative structure which entails continuing contact and discussion between officials and business management, not to speak of the amount of Parliamentary attention devoted to the scrutiny of the regional and industrial pattern of aid. These 'feedback' effects of selective aid measures are of major importance in any assessment of their effectiveness.

In order to understand the way in which structural measures are devised in response to policy objectives and the economic environment in which those objectives are pursued, it is necessary to examine particular cases in some depth. Fortunately, there are two industrial fields in which both the BRD and the UK have developed elaborate schemes of selective assistance, as well as other structural measures. The policies towards the computer industry in both countries have been very similar though they have had some markedly different effects (Cf. Chapter 5). On the other hand, shipping and shipbuilding (Cf. Chapter 6) though beset in each country by similar economic problems, have been subjected to very different policy treatment reflecting a whole range of factors such as the relative efficiency of the industries, the differing outlook regarding the efficacy of state 'takeover' of shipbuilding, and the relative importance of long-term efficiency objectives as against short-term employment objectives.

Chapters 4, 5 and 6 provide, it is hoped, important background material for the study of the appraisal of structural policies. In Chapter 7 particular emphasis is put on the very great technical difficulties facing appraisal of structural policies, once it is decided to extend appraisal beyond the relatively simple matter of checking on the costing of proposals, the preparation and authorisation of budgets and a system of budget control for selective assistance. While standard methods of economic appraisal are expected to be undertaken by economists — within government in the UK but not necessarily so in the BRD — the technical problems offer the opportunity to politicians, administrators and other technical branches of government (accountants, scientists, lawyers) to dispute the economist's claim to pronounce on the success or otherwise of structural aid policies. The fact that economic appraisals frequently lead to the result that selective aid policies, judged by standard economic criteria, are rarely justified gives an added incentive to politicians and others to obfuscate objectives or at least to stress non-economic objectives (e.g. national prestige), and to question the economist's competence to assess intangible factors governing aid policy such as the management capability of firms offered support.

The strong likelihood that Western industrial countries will resist the use of expanding aggregate demand as a method of stimulating industrial output, obviously because of the fear of inflation, has concentrated their attention on improving factor efficiency as the clue to maintaining what they request as a satisfactory growth rate and satisfactory level of employment. This appears all the more necessary given the growing importance of international trade in manufactures relative to the size of their gross national products, and therefore the growing intensity of international competition. In Chapter 8, this prospect is shown to be the governing influence in the UK on contemporary industrial policy but strong doubts are expressed about the possibility of improving UK industrial efficiency by tripartite (government, management and labour) involvement in the evolution of structural policies. In both countries, more radical proposals originating with the unions are likely to be brought into the arena of serious discussion, notably control over the allocation of private investment, alongside the development of more selective employment policies designed to cope with groups of the working population most at risk from long-term employment. At the same time the proliferation of structural policies may be self-defeating in a world in which international trade plays an important part as industrial countries try to counteract each other's attempts to improve their international competitiveness by selective aids. In sum, the growth of selective aids has opened a Pandora's box and saddled industrial countries with immense problems in counteracting the vested interests which demand their continuance though this may defeat the purpose for which policies were originally designed.

This report represents close collaboration between its authors over a period of two years in the form of frequent joint discussions, distribution of draft chapters for comment and criticism and joint authorship of certain sections. It is still possible to assign broad responsibility for each part of the report as follows: Martin Ricketts — Chapter 2; Rob Grant — Chapter 4; Rob Grant and Keith Shaw — Chapters 5 and 6. Elaine Wagner supplied a number of draft reports on BRD policies and a major one on 'Investitionslenkung' which merits separate publication. She was also our main contact with the various government departments in Bonn. I am responsible for the general editing and for the final drafting of Chapters 1, 3, 7 and 8, though I used freely material supplied by others, notably Keith Shaw.

I would like to express my gratitude to my co-authors not only for supplying expertise but also for tolerating work conditions which imposed a strict deadline. I must finally make it clear that they are in no way committed to my summing up in Chapter 8.

Alan Peacock

August 1979

A NOTE ON CONTRIBUTORS

ROB GRANT is Lecturer in Economics at
the City University, London

ALAN PEACOCK is the Principal of the
University College at Buckingham

MARTIN RICKETTS is Lecturer in Economics at the
University College at Buckingham

G. K. SHAW is Reader in Economics at the
University of East Anglia

ELAINE WAGNER is a free-lance Research Economist
who lives in Andernach, Federal
Republic of W. Germany.

ACKNOWLEDGMENTS

This report was sponsored by the Anglo-German Foundation and undertaken by the Economists Advisory Group of which I am a former Director. Mr. Peter McGregor, Secretary General, and Mr. Hans Wiener, Projects Director of the Foundation have been most helpful at all stages in the production process in arranging contacts and offering advice and in the steering of the Report to its completion.

I am grateful to Mr. Graham Bannock, Managing Director of EAG, for professional advice and for organising, through his secretarial staff, the production of the various drafts of this Report.

I owe a personal debt to three German academic colleagues who gave generously of their time in the early stages of preparation. These were Professor Dieter Biehl, Berlin, Professor Kurt Schmidt, Mainz, and Professor Norbert Kloten, Tübingen. Likewise it is a great pleasure to thank Herr Kornel Wager, husband of one of the contributors, not only for his professional advice as an economist and business executive but also for the generous hospitality offered by him and his wife. I also benefitted considerably from discussions with Mr. Nicholas Plessz, Economics Division, OECD, Paris.

I must mention the considerable help received, particularly by Elaine Wagner and G. K. Shaw, from a number of senior German Government officials notably in the Economics and Finance Ministries in Bonn and the Federal German shipping offices in Hamburg. Finally, I must thank Mr. Hans Liesner CB, my successor as Chief Economic Adviser to the Departments of Trade and Industry, for some useful suggestions which bore fruit in Chapters 4 and 7. Of course, none of these officials in the BRD or the UK bear any responsibility for our use of their advice and help.

Alan Peacock

CHAPTER 1

APPROACHES TO AN EXAMINATION OF STRUCTURAL ECONOMIC POLICIES

A. Introduction

1.1   The purpose of this report is to describe and to analyse economic policy measures in the UK and BRD that attempt to reach policy goals by their influence on the structure of the economy. These measures are collectively described by German economists as 'Strukturpolitik', which we shall translate as 'structural economic policies', though this is not a term found in Anglo-Saxon literature. Therefore, before considering the rationale of such policies a definitional excursus is inevitable.

1.2   As the term 'Strukturpolitik' has been the subject of extensive discussion in the BRD it is fitting to consider how it is defined there. An important distinction is made in German economics literature between 'Global-steuerung' (global control) of the economy where the object is to influence the level of broad economic aggregates, particularly the level of aggregate demand, and 'Wirtschaftslenkung' (sectoral control of the economy) in which the government deliberately influences the balance between broad aggregates (e.g. between public and private consumption and investment) and the balance within the aggregates themselves.

1.3   There are three preliminary points which need to be made about this distinction. The first is that each set of policy measures is associated in the BRD with an ideological position which also colours the view taken about the efficacy of global or selective measures in achieving policy objectives. The nature of this controversy about ends and means in economic policy and its bearing on structural policies in practice is considered later (see Chapter 3, below). It is sufficient to say at this stage that supporters of global measures believe that structural policies are neither necessary nor desirable. They are unnecessary because the market is considered to be the best method for promoting the sectoral change which policy demands, it being explicitly or implicitly assumed that the purpose of economic policy is to ensure that consumers get what they want. They are undesirable because sectoral policies call for co-ordinated, centralised direction of the economy which, apart from being characterised by bureaucratic inefficiency which is difficult to eliminate, is incompatible with the freedom of the individual. The reply in recent debate of those who support 'Wirtschaftslenkung' is couched in Galbraithian terms. The technocratic base of industrial life is such that large firms dominate the market and 'corrupt' consumer choice, so that this choice is an 'irrational' basis for the allocation of resources. 'Too much' is spent on 'inessential' goods, and firms control the social and physical environment in 'undesirable' ways and impose costs on the community which are not reflected in the market. Sectoral intervention is essential if the economy is to be made to conform with society's objectives.

1.4   There are clear parallels in the contemporary debate in the UK but the only purpose in anticipating later discussion is simply to warn the reader that the terminology used may contain hidden biases of meaning. Thus in a recent German publication [Besters (Editor) (1978)] the sub-title reads 'Technokratischer Interventionismus versus marktwirtschaftliche Ordnungspolitik' (technocratic intervention *against* the social market economy) and suggests an irreconcilable conflict between structural economic policy and the system of economic freedom supported by prominent German liberal thinkers.

1.5   The second point concerns the impact of global and structural policies on the sectoral balance. Virtually all economic policies will influence decision making in the private sector and in a way which will alter that balance. Thus a global measure such as an alteration in the exchange rate will exert a differential effect on firms which are either export-oriented or highly import intensive. A change in the level of aggregate demand is almost certain to alter the personal and factor distribution of incomes and, in consequence, the composition of demand and therefore of supply of goods and services. Equally, measures designed to alter the structure of the economy may have effects on global aggregates. Thus a regional policy designed to reduce disparities in employment opportunities through differential regional support can, through inter-regional 'multiplier' effects, influence the level of aggregate demand.

1.6   The difficulty of identifying measures which are exclusively structural in effect can only be resolved in an arbitrary way. We shall assume that the structural impacts of global measures are regarded as side-effects, intentional or unintentional, and are not the primary aim of such measures. Structural change is only implicit in the operation of such measures. In contrast, explicit structural change is associated with policies specifically designed to achieve this end.

1.7   The third preliminary point concerns the question: structural change for what? Such change is clearly not desired for itself alone but because it achieves some ultimate policy goal. Further, policy intervention implies that the structural change arising from the process of economic development without such intervention, i.e. through market forces, is in some sense undesirable. Leaving aside the ideological debate briefly referred to, a rather different approach is followed here than is normally found, at least in the textbook literature. It is common practice to assume that measures designed to alter the structural balance have as their object the 'correct' allocation of resources, the optimal position conforming with the canons of Paretian welfare economics with their emphasis on consumer sovereignty. Even supporters of the 'social market economy' have recognised one important exception to 'global measures' in pursuing the policy aim of ensuring consumer sovereignty, namely in the operation of enforcing competion through anti-monopoly provision. (They might claim that a 'competition enforcement law' is a global measure in the sense that it admits of few, if any, exceptions, but it must be selective if only because investigations of particular cases and subsequent enforcement edicts require advance selection of the *order* in which cases are handled.)

1.8   Though structural policy is undoubtedly closely bound up with allocational objectives, the emphasis in this report is shifted to a more recent phenomenon in both UK and BRD policy, the use of structural policy to achieve *macro-economic goals* of a dynamic and long-term character. In particular, interest centres in the level of employment, the rate of economic growth and balance of payments goals all of which are closely interrelated and all of which, rightly or wrongly, are of contemporary importance. As will become clear in later discussion, promotion of efficiency is an important dimension of structural policies designed to promote macro-economic goals but policy-makers are less concerned with the 'right' structure of output to conform with consumer wishes and more with reducing the costs of production.

B.   The choice of structural policies for study

1.9   The choice of structural policies for study is therefore conditioned by this emphasis on the achievement of macroeconomic goals and to understand the process of selection used in this Report more needs to be said about this relationship between ends and means.

The maintenance of employment. The major objective of selective industrial support to UK industry has been to maintain employment by financial backing for otherwise failing firms. While such measures have become frequent only since 1971, structural policies aimed at the planned contraction of industries date back to the inter-war period. Selective intervention to maintain employment has been less evident in the BRD for obvious reasons, though such support has been given to the coal and textile industries.

Encouragement of exports and import substitution. In the UK subsidies to companies competing in international markets has been particularly important in the support given to the motor vehicle, shipbuilding and aluminium industries. In the BRD, support for import-substituting industries has been for strategic rather than balance of payments reasons, as in the case of the support given to the domestic coal and oil producing industries.

Encouraging of investment in fixed capital and research and development. In both countries selective intervention in private industry has been used to stimulate long term economic growth by the support of 'high technology' industries such as aerospace, computers and electronics.

1.10   The three objectives have coalesced in recent policy discussion at both the national and international level into one — the prevention of the 'de-industrialisation' of major advanced economies, including particularly the UK and, to a lesser extent, the BRD. This coalescence highlights a particular problem affecting the choice of structural policies for study and the method of analysis. The meaning and measurement of 'de-industrialisation' is a disputed area of discourse (c.f. Chapter 2 below) but the fears are real enough in official thinking for selective aid to be given in a form not only to make a positive contribution towards the growth of a particular sector (ignoring the present opportunity cost of any such aid) but also in forms which have been designed to maintain inefficient and over-manned industrial sectors. The reasoning behind these fears are considered in much more detail later in this Report and it is sufficient to say that it has been widely believed that the objective of improving the balance of payments position and also growth can only be achieved in the long run if decreasing cost industries (manufacturing) are able to expand at the expense of service sectors and agriculture. If our selection of structural measures for study is to take account of this view, and of the official policies which have been based on it, then we must look at measures which are in essence 'negative' as well as those which are 'positive' in their aims.

1.11   The identification of objectives and how they are traded off against one another may narrow down the number of relevant selective measures but tells us little about the character of the structural policies which would repay study. Considering the following, admittedly arbitrary, taxonomy of forms of selective measures [on the awkward problems of classification of subsidy measures in particular, see Prest (1976) and Wiseman (1977)] :

Financial/Non-Financial Measures: Selective measures are commonly thought of as forms of direct subsidy designed to alter the product or factor mix of a particular industry of group of concerns which can be identified in the government accounts. However, many selective measures designed for the same proximate aim cannot be identified in this way, examples being import controls or internationally negotiated restrictions on import volumes.

— *Open/Concealed Measures:* Explicit subsidies to industry which appear as an item in the government accounts presumably receive legislative sanction and are, in principle at least, public knowledge. However, selective aid may easily be 'hidden', as instanced in government procurement policies where the conditions and terms of contracting amount to discrimination in favour of particular suppliers. Similarly, the imposition of safety and environment controls which effectively curb imports could be regarded as a concealed form of non-financial aid.

— *Direct/Indirect Aid:* For some purposes it might be convenient to distinguish between aid given directly to a selected firm or industry from indirect aid which subsidises the consumers of a given firm or industry. A recent UK example of indirect aid to shipbuilding was the provision of grants and extremely favourable credits to the Polish government which then placed contracts for ships to be built in British yards. A further example of indirect aid to support a specific industry is provided by the United Kingdom experience of improvement grants whereby existing householders were subsidized to improve their dwellings. That this measure was directed towards the maintenance of employment in the construction industry and was not merely one aspect of social policy may be gathered from the fact that such grants were considerably greater in the so-called development (high unemployment) regions. Theoretically, the distinction is one drawn between costs and revenue. Direct aid lowers firms' cost curves whilst indirect aid operates by raising firms' revenue curves. Both measures promote an extension of output and hence employment and are thus identical in their effects. Nevertheless, the distinction is not without significance in view of the fact that programmes of fiscal harmonization, trading agreements, GATT conventions and so forth progressively outlaw the more blatant forms of direct selective intervention in the interests of preventing distortions to competition in world trade.

1.12 While it is clearly desirable, particularly in a study which must investigate policies which have a sectoral impact, to keep a broad definition of the tools of structural policy, pragmatic considerations dictate that attention should be focussed on 'open' selective measures which are quantifiable, i.e. are translatable into and identifiable money flow from government to the relevant sector. There are several reasons for this:

— It is easier to establish the connexion between such measures and the macro-economic policies which they are intended to promote;

— it is easier to pursue the problem of the appraisal of particular selective measures. Given that the true cost of a selective aid programme is measured in terms of the resources foregone to finance such aid, an explicit figure for the aid programme greatly facilitates appraisal;

It may make it easier to pursue the question of the relative effectiveness of selective aid programmes in one country as compared with another provided these programmes for particular sectors are roughly similar. At the same time, one must not under-estimate the difficulties of such comparisons, and ample illustration of them is given in Chapters 6 and 7.

1.13 A final consideration governing the choice of policies for study is whether to concentrate on examining particular instruments and their effects on a number of industries or whether to take the industry itself as the frame of reference and consider the range of structural policies which affect it. The two approaches are not mutually exclusive but in seeking to throw light on the practical operation of structural policies it seems sensible to look at particular industries, particularly if comparisons are to be made between the treatment of particular sectors on a comparative basis. It so happens that whereas the range and scope of selective aids to industry in the BRD and UK has differed considerably, and while the issue of de-industrialisation has been more important in the UK than in the BRD, the same *sectors* have been the subject of influence by structural policy, e.g. computers, textiles and shipping and shipbuilding and for roughly the same reasons. Accordingly, a special feature in this Report is the detailed study of particular industry cases, notably shipping and shipbuilding as the example of a sector subject to contradictory forces and computers which is generally assumed to be a sector of potential expansion with important 'spin-offs' for the rest of the economy.

1.14 To summarise: While the aims of an explicit structural economic policy obviously require us to examine the rationale of the policy in general and to offer an explanation for the range of policies actually adopted, and an assessment of their impact on macroeconomic objectives, the very emphasis on altering the sectoral balance as a means of achieving those objectives offers strong support for backing up the general analysis with a case study approach.

C. The 'political economy' of structural economic policies

1.15 The approach to the analysis of structural economic policies suggested so far fits very closely with what may be called the 'economist's paradigm' of the theory of economic policy. A 'welfare function' for the government is dilineated, which we have associated with macro-economic aims. A particular policy measure is identified, in our case some selective aid project designed to affect growth of a particular sector. An examination is made of the direct and indirect impact of the policy measure during a specific period of intervention using some 'policy-on'/'policy-off' or alternative policies comparison — an approach subject to much controversy as studies of regional policy impacts will indicate [c.f. Moore and Rhodes (1976) and Mackay (1976)]. Perhaps a re-appraisal of the measure is then undertaken and possible improvements in the measure suggested.

1.16 The problem with this paradigm is that it implies that the government-industry interface is one of a dominant policy maker influencing the activities of passive adjusters. However, the implementation of such policies, particularly if they called upon private concerns to make radical adjustments in their activities, relies on the co-operation of those subjected to such policies. Governments anxious to survive, even those in centralist democracies such as the UK, need to test the reactions of the electorate and the 'feedback' on their voting strength of sectoral policies which are more open and obvious in their impact than more global measures. Government departments have to seek the advice of industrial experts in management and technology in developing selective aid policies and the source of recruitment must be industry itself. When selective aid policies are in operation they have to be monitored by bureaucrate who are in consequence no longer able to execute policies 'at arm's length'. It is no accident therefore that the development of a structural and therefore sectoral approach is associated with the evolution of a system of negotiation of a tri-partite kind — industry, labour and government — formally if not firmly embodied in the governmental administrative structure, as instanced in the foundation of the National Economic Development Council in the UK in 1962. What Walter Eucken [Eucken (1955)] in another context called 'eine eigenartige Verschmelzung von privater Macht aund Zentralverwaltungswirtschaft' (an unusual fusion of private power and central economic planning) takes place in which a complicated bargaining structure between government and industry at both industry and national level makes it incumbent upon economists to recognise the naive nature of a theory of economic policy which ignores 'feedback' problems [c.f. Peacock (1979)].

1.17 There is considerable controversy among economists as to whether economic analysis can be extended in order to take account of the 'feed-back' problem. There are those who maintain that the political and administrative consequences of policies directed towards economic objectives are neither their concern nor are economists competent to analyse them. There are others who argue that political and administrative behaviour is just as amenable to economic analysis as the behaviour of firms and households in the private sector and that examinations of this behaviour and how it modifies the pursuit of policy objectives must be an integral part of any study of economic policy, particularly if interest centres in what is feasible as distinct from what economists may think is desirable. Again a pragmatic reason is the determining factor in this Report. It is that the problem of the evolution of 'Wirtschaftsordnung' (the politico-economic system) in response to changing policy aims and their implementation through 'Strukturpolitik' is an issue of considerable importance in BRD contemporary economic discussion, which permeates not only academic discussion but official documents such as the annual reports of the *Sachverständigerrat zur Begutachtung der gesamtwirtschaftlichen Entwicklung*. (The Council of Economic Advisers). The possibility that alongside the failure of the market to meet macro-economic objectives there may be a corresponding 'bureaucratic failure' in trying to correct the market's deficiencies is constantly presented as an important issue of economic policy. It could hardly be denied that the correct comparison in examining the relative merits of the free market and structural policies is between two imperfect systems and that this comparison is a relevant one to pursue for the UK as well.

D. Plan of the report

1.18 It remains in this Chapter to outline the topics which will be covered in the rest of the report. Chapter 2 offers a detailed study of structural change in both the BRD and UK which provides necessary background material and highlights the structural problems which governments have sought to solve. Chapter 3 traces the general influences which have governed the evolution of structural policies in both countries such as the severity of the economic problems, 'trade-off' between objectives in both countries and how this has changed through time, the view taken of the performance of the economy and how all these factors determine the choice of structural measures. Chapter 4 offers a short account of the evolution of structural policies in both countries. Chapters 5 and 6 exemplify the issues raised in Chapter 4 and 5, through detailed studies of the computer industry and shipping and shipbuilding industries respectively. Chapter 7 analyses the problems encountered in appraising and monitoring structural policy. A final chapter considers the lessons which may be learnt from the policy experiences of the UK and BRD and their bearing on the 'policy scenarios' for the future.

REFERENCES

Resters, Hans (Editor) (1978) *Strukpolitik—wozu?* Gespräche der List Gesellschaft E. V.N.F. Band 3., Nomos Verlagsgesellschaft Baden-Baden.

Eucken, Walter (1955) *Grundsätze der Wirtschaftspolitik* (Edited by Edith Eucken and K. P. Hensel), Second Edition, Tübingen.

Moore, B. and Rhodes, J. (1976) 'A Quantitative Analysis of the Effects of the Regional Employment Premium and Other Regional Policy Instrument', in Alan Whiting (Editor). *Economics of Industrial Subsidies*, Her Majesty's Stationery Office, London. Also Discussant's Comment in the same volume by R. R. Mackay.

Peacock, Alan (1979) *The Economic Analysis of Government and Related Themes*, Martin Robertson London, Chapter 1.

Prest, A. R. (1976) 'The Economic Rationale of Subsidies' in Whiting (Editor) op. cit.

Wiseman, J. (1977) 'The Economics of Subsidies: Some Taxonomic and Analytical Problems' University of York Reprint Series: Economics Number 256.

CHAPTER 2

THE ANALYSIS OF STRUCTURAL CHANGE IN POST-WAR UK AND BRD

A. **Introduction**

2.1   In this chapter the statistical background to the study of structural policies is presented, which entails an examination of the major structural changes in the UK and BRD. A fully comprehensive study of structural change would entail a detailed and exhaustive analysis of every major feature of each economy but, apart from taking much more time to complete than is available, it might confuse rather than enlighten the reader. A selection of the major features of structural change must be made and its basis must first of all be explained.

2.2   It has been indicated in Chapter 1, that the rationale for the emphasis on economic structure as a determinant of economic policy depends on the view taken about how the economy is supposed to work as well as on the choice of policy objectives. However, whatever the results of the technical debate — which we shall re-examine in another context (Chapter 3) — the development of structural policy has clearly been influenced by the 'structuralist approach' to the study of the economy. An examination of this approach can provide a useful shopping list of factors which illustrate structural change and the illustration itself will enable us to make some assessment of the 'structuralists' claims.

B. **Structuralist Economic Thought**

2.3   Broadly speaking there are two ways of looking at structural change. There are those who see structural change as the outcome of a growth process in the economy largely determined by 'exogenous' forces such as the changes in the quantity and quality of labour, the changes in capital stock, the influence of technological change on both the previous factors, and the terms of exchange with other economies. On the other hand, there are those who believe that the growth process is highly dependent on the change in the structure of the economy itself and that the importance of structural influences on growth is sufficient reason why governments should exploit and improve their ability to influence the structure of the economy. This latter view is the one which requires further elaboration. It has a long intellectual history particularly in the context of development economics but the arguments used in that context are paralleled in the study of advanced industrial economies.

2.4   These two views of structural change are not completely incompatible, and they may both give rise to demands for an active government policy towards industrial structure. But the nature of government intervention is likely to differ considerably between the two cases. A government which regards structural developments as reflecting exogenous forces will be mainly concerned to give what the West Germans term 'adjustment aid' or possibly 'maintenance aid' in order to facilitate structural changes with as little disruption to employment as possible. That is, the major objective would be to reduce the inevitable frictions which the continual growth and decline of various sectors entails. The alternative 'structuralist' view implies sectoral intervention designed not to accommodate change but to initiate it. Examples would include assistance specifically designed to assist 'high technology' industries such as electronics and computers, to favour manufacturing over service industries (or vice versa), to encourage investment rather than consumption, to assist in the establishment of large firms or to discourage size and support small ventures.

2.5   Central to 'structuralist' thinking is the notion that, for any given country at a particular stage of development, there will exist an 'appropriate' relationship between the various sectors of the economy. Departure from this relationship, it is argued, may create intractable problems of economic management making it impossible to achieve macro-economic policy goals through the use of conventional fiscal or monetary instruments. These arguments can be illustrated by the controversy in the early 1960's between 'monetarist' and 'structuralist' explanations of inflation in certain South American countries.

2.6   The essence of the 'structuralist' argument was that certain basic structural characteristics of the economies concerned make it exceptionally difficult to contain inflation by monetary methods. In particular they emphasised the dependence of many developing countries on exports of one or a few primary products much subject to price fluctuation. As incomes rise in years of high export prices, it was argued, expectations of future trends and government commitments to projects including large expenditures are formed which are very difficult to reverse when export prices fall. Such a fall in export prices will result in balance of payments deficits unless imports are cut, but declining imports will reduce government revenue in countries heavily dependent upon tariff receipts. Further, price of imported commodities. Fear of social unrest in the event of expenditure cuts or tax increases, in these circumstances make resort to inflationary finance inevitable.

2.7 A further structural characteristic militating against price stability, it was argued, was the relatively slow rate of output growth of the agricultural sector[1]. With incomes in the urban manufacturing centres growing but static output (even if higher labour productivity) in agriculture, there would be inevitable upward pressure on agricultural prices and again a political tendency to accomplish the relative price readjustments within the context of a higher general price level.

2.8 The argument applied to developing countries has re-appeared in much the same form in developed countries. Much of the discussion of the consequences of the high rate of inflation experienced in the mid-1970's centred on the influence of primary product prices and particularly the marked rise in oil prices. Though the impact on the balance of payments of western countries was on the marked rise in the value of imports, rather than in a fall in the value of exports, the same kind of structuralist explanations and associated remedies were deployed in considering the balance of payments effects. Thus, in the specific case of the UK, the failure of currency devaluation and of monetary and fiscal policy to produce a 'virtuous circle' of high productivity and high growth has led to the development of 'structuralist' explanations for their lack of success. It has been suggested that expansionary policies will not work because of structural maladjustments which must always thwart their operation. In particular it is asserted that the propensity to import foreign manufactured goods is too high. Stated crudely, if the income elasticity of demand for imports is twice the foreign income elasticity of demand for British exports the balance of payments constraint will prevent the British economy from growing at a rate faster than half the rate of overseas countries. The conclusion is then drawn that a restructuring of the economy is required with the emphasis on 'growth industries' i.e. those with a high income elasticity.

2.9 We noted above the argument that sectoral imbalance between agriculture and industry gave rise to inflationary pressure in the less developed countries. Recently a similar argument has been adduced, particularly in the UK, with attention focused not on agriculture but on the public sector. The public sector is regarded as a sector of low productivity growth involved primarily in the provision of non-marketed services such as defence, health, education, police and fire services. The demands of this sector for marketed consumption and investment goods must be met primarily from the private sector or from imports. Too rapid an expansion of the public sector, it is argued, therefore, has three important effects. If consumption and investment demands from those in the public sector are taken from private investment expenditure, growth will suffer. If they are satisfied from imports, the balance of payments will deteriorate. If they make inroads into private sector consumption there is a strong chance of 'tax-backlash' and a high level of wage inflation. In the 1970's the UK has, of course, suffered from all three of these problems — low growth, balance of payments deficits, and historically high levels of wage inflation and the argument outlined above, particularly associated with Bacon and Eltis (1975), was developed as 'a basic explanation of a structural kind of the underlying deterioration in Britain's economic performance'.[2]

2.10 Bacon and Eltis emphasise that the structural maladjustment they have identified is in the relative size of the market goods sector vis-a-vis the non-market goods sector. Although the public sector is clearly the major provider of non-marketed services it may also provide marketed goods and services, e.g. the nationalised industries, so that the distinction drawn is not strictly between the public and private sectors as usually defined.

2.11 Since their views have become influential in political circles, it is important to understand the mechanisms by which the suggested structural imbalance results in low growth and inflation. The market sector, it is argued, must provide for the demands of the non-market sector. However, it is equally true that the non-market sector must provide sufficient services to meet the demands of those in the market sector. What is so special, it might be asked, about non-marketed goods and services which requires that the size of this sector be considered as of crucial structural importance? The answer harks back to one of the oldest problems in Public Finance. If goods and services are not marketed they must be paid for by taxation and there is the utmost difficulty in ensuring that individual taxpayers are satisfied with the 'fiscal package' they are offered. If individuals voluntarily purchase a good in the market there is some reason to suppose that they gain by the transaction. If the same individuals are given services at a zero price and pay in the form of taxation there is no assurance that they are satisfied with the distribution of benefits received and the 'tax/price' paid. Indeed there will usually exist an incentive to the individual to accept the non-marketed goods and services while contributing as little as possible to the costs of their provision — the 'free-rider problem'. Growth in the non-market sector is therefore harmless enough in so far as individual taxpayers are willing to acquiesce. A problem arises only if it becomes 'too large' or grows 'too fast', a situation which is easily recognisable by high levels of wage inflation as workers attempt to maintain post-tax income. The Bacon-Eltis view is therefore not so radically different from earlier structuralist theorising about the public sector. In particular Colin Clark's rule of thumb, put forward in the 1940's, that a tax share in excess of 25 per cent of net national product would set up inflationary pressures is based upon similar reasoning[3].

2.12 So far structuralist thought is the field of the over-seas trade sector and the public sector have been briefly considered. The more conventional emphasis, however, is on three major sectors — primary, secondary and tertiary. These correspond basically with agriculture and mining, manufacturing, and services respectively. Economic development has traditionally been seen as a process involving the relative decline of the primary sector in terms of labour employed and the rise of manufacturing industry. Attitudes to the tertiary or service sector differ markedly. In one view, the development of a large service sector is a mark of the 'post-industrial society' and high per capita income. Another view regards service employment as relatively 'unproductive' when compared with manufacturing, and therefore as something to be discouraged.

2.13 A major criticism of structuralist analysis is that, however persuasive it sounds in the context of a given country and given circumstances, it is very difficult to generalise from it. Even some of the simplest hypotheses concerning the growth of the service sector as income rises are open to dispute. Larger numbers of people employed in service occupations may result from increasing division of labour and not necessarily from a rise in the service component of total value added. Thus conceptual problems associated with defining a 'sector' and statistical problems of measuring its size can be exceptionally important.

2.14 Opponents of structuralist thinking tend to emphasise the diversity of development methods. Some countries may concentrate on the export of a particular raw material, others such as Japan may have none. Some may develop a dominant industry (cotton in the UK is a common example, used in economic history teaching), others may specialise less in the early stages. Some may utilise international trade extensively (e.g. Hong Kong) while others with larger internal markets may be less dependent on trade (e.g. the United States). The finance for capital investment may be borrowed from foreign countries or in some cases provided from internal sources. In some cases a rapidly growing population fuels development, in others where social conventions and factor proportions differ population growth is seen as a plight to be conquered before growth can be achieved. If generalisations about economic structure of this broad type are impossible it may be justifiably doubted how far more detailed observations can give a clue to economic performance.

2.15 Nevertheless structuralist ideas are not confined to speculations about the impact of the relative size of major sectors on growth or inflation. The scale of research and development effort, the quality of education, the growth of technologically advanced industries, and the size of individual firms have all been considered at various times important structural factors requiring intervention in the interests of employment, balance of payments or growth objectives. A case can be made out for intervention in these areas on conventional 'market failure' grounds, but much discussion is based on the 'structuralist' premise that particular industries or production methods are of special significance and that it is impossible to develop a modern high income economy without them.

2.16 In the following pages evidence is presented on these structural characteristics of the UK and the BRD discussed above. Section C provides information on certain 'performance indicators' particularly those concerning growth, inflation, balance of payments and employment objectives. Section D charts sectoral change in the two countries in some detail and includes an investigation of changes in employment and output within the manufacturing or 'secondary' sector. Attention is also focused, in accordance with the structuralist reasoning outlined earlier, on the development of international trade in the two countries and on various measures of public sector size. Some brief comments are included on concentration and firm size in each economy. Although of considerable importance to public policy only a small amount of basic information is provided on regional economic structure. A full discussion of this aspect of structural policy would clearly require a paper to itself. Section E presents a brief summary and conclusions.

C. Performance indicators

Table 2.1

REAL GROSS DOMESTIC PRODUCT — PER CENT RATE OF CHANGE

	BRD	UK
1951—1955	9.5	3.0
1956—1960	6.5	2.4
1961—1965	5.1	3.3
1966—1970	4.7	2.4
1971—1975	1.7	1.7

Source: Oppenländer, K. (1977), Table 1. Calculated in 1962 prices.
UK Data calculated from *The British Economy. Key Statistics* 1900—1970. Table B (1963 prices). For periods 1966—1970 and 1971—1975, National Income and Expenditure 1966—1976, Table 2.1 (1970 prices).

2.17 The following six tables provide summary information on some of the most important areas of policy interest growth, price stability, the balance of payments, trade, productivity and unemployment. More detailed appraisal of sectoral growth rates, international trade flows, and employment trends follows in section D below. However, the information contained in this section is sufficient to indicate the major differences in performance between the UK and the BRD. In each of these major policy areas, the economic performance of the BRD is shown to be consistently superior to that of the UK.

Table 2.2

INFLATION. ANNUAL PER CENT RATE OF INCREASE IN PRICE DEFLATOR[1]

	BRD	UK
1951—1955	2.0	4.5
1956—1960	1.8	2.4
1961—1965	2.9	3.3
1966—1970	2.6	4.0
1971—1976[2]	6.0	14.5

Notes:1. For the UK 1951—1970 the index used is the Consumers' expenditure average value index (not the RPI). Similarly for the BRD over the same period the index is the private consumption deflator.

2. For 1971—1976 the recorded figures are the rate of increase of the index of consumer prices.

Sources: OECD Economic Survey, Germany, July 1977, Table J.
OECD Economic Survey, United Kingdom, March 1968, International Comparisons.
The British Economy, Key Statistics (op. cit), Table 1.

Growth rates in West Germany have been higher than in the UK throughout the period since 1950 although there has also been a long run tendency for the rate of growth to decline in the former. Both countries were, of course, adversely affected by the recession of the early 1970's and in the period 1971—1975 both experienced rather similar rates of growth of real GDP.

2.18 The West German authorities also appear to have been more successful in controlling the rate of inflation than their UK counterparts. This observation applies to the entire period since 1950 but is especially noticeable in the years since 1970. (Cf. Table 2.2.) Not perhaps surprisingly, the balance of payments responded in rather different ways in the two countries during this time. (Cf. Table 2.3)

Table 2.3

CURRENT BALANCE AS PER CENT OF GROSS NATIONAL PRODUCT

	BRD	UK
1950	-:0.4	2.6
1955	+1.2	- 0.9
1960	+1.7	- 1.2
1965	- 1.4	- 0.1
1970	+0.5	+1.7
1971	+0.4	+2.2
1972	+0.3	+0.3
1973	+1.2	- 1.1
1974	+2.5	- 4.4
1975	+0.9	- 1.8
1976	+0.7	- 1.1

Note: The Gross National Product figures for the UK were at factor cost. Those for the BRD at market prices.
Sources: Calculated from:
OECD, Economic Survey, Germany. July 1977, Tables B and E.
British Economy, Key Statistics, op. cit., Tables A and N (figures for 1950, 1955, 1960).
Economic Trends, CSO, February 1977, p. 46 (1965—1975).
OECD, Economic Survey, UK March 1978, Table F. National Income and Expenditure 1977, Table 1.

Table 2.4

UNEMPLOYMENT

	BRD % of dependent labour force	UK % of total employees	
1965	0.7	1.5	(1966)
1970	0.7	2.6	
1971	0.8	3.4	
1972	1.1	3.8	
1973	1.2	2.7	
1974	2.6	2.6	
1975	4.8	4.2	
1976	4.7	5.8	

Source: OECD Economic Survey, Germany. July 1977, Table 1. Annual Abstract of Statistics (1977), Table 6.8, p. 164.

2.19 The West German balance of payments has tended to be stronger and less volatile than that of the UK, at least since about 1955. However, the difference is especially marked once more in the early 1970's. The current balance in the BRD strengthened from around 0.4 per cent of GNP in 1971 to 2.5 per cent in 1974. The UK, however, experienced an enormous reversal from a surplus of 2.2 per cent of GNP in 1971 to a deficit of -—4.4 per cent in 1974.

2.20 British trade performance has been especially poor in the field of manufacture and the sharp deterioration in the balance of payments during the years following 1971 is mirrored in the 'trade ratio' for the same period in manufactures. The trade ratio is defined as (exports — imports)/(exports + imports), and is often used as a measure of comparative advantage or 'competitiveness'. If exports are zero the ratio has a value of minus one, indicating a total lack of competitiveness. If imports are zero the value will be plus one, indicating a 'complete' trade advantage.

Table 2.5

TRADE RATIOS IN MANUFACTURES

	UK	BRD
1965		0.31
1966	0.31	
.	.	.
.	.	.
.	.	.
1970	0.23	0.27
1971	0.25	0.27
1972	0.16	0.27
1973	0.11	0.31
1974	0.09	0.37
1975	0.14	0.32
1976	—	0.30

Source: UK figures from A Singh (1977), Table 1.
BRD figures calculated from OECD Survey (1977), Table G.
'Manufactures' is taken to mean sections 5, 6, 7 and 8, of the SITC.

2.21 As seen from Table 2.5 the UK has experienced a large fall in the trade ratio for manufactures between the years 1966 and 1975. The West German ratio on the other hand exhibits greater stability with the exception of a sudden jump in 1974 from 0.31 to 0.37.

2.22 A high rate of output growth in Germany has also been reflected in very low levels of unemployment — less than 1 per cent before the beginning of this decade, compared with rates around 2.5 per cent in the UK in the later 1960's. World recession and a slower growth rate have tended to result in unemployment rates becoming higher, reaching similar levels in both countries. However, by 1976 the West German unemployment rate had levelled off and was considerably below that of the UK. (Cf. Table 2.4).

2.23 Comparisons of the *level* of labour productivity between countries presents enormous conceptual and practical difficulties associated with measuring output either in physical or value terms (see Dravia 1976). A recent study by Jones (1977) however, presents data on labour productivity for several European countries using both official rates of exchange and specially calculated 'purchasing power parity' rates of exchange to measure real output. His results are recorded in Table 2.6.

2.24 As can be seen, the level of labour productivity in the UK has been well below that of the BRD, and indeed of other selected European countries in each sub-sector of manufacturing. Care should be exercised in the interpretation of the data since, as Jones emphasises, rather different results can be obtained using different methods. The enormous disparity in labour productivity in the field of basic metals, for example, is greatly reduced when output is measured in physical terms, e.g. liquid steel tonnes per man. However, the broad finding of a relatively low level of labour productivity in the UK has been confirmed by many studies over a long period of time using differing measures, and is universally accepted.

Table 2.6

LEVELS OF GROSS VALUE ADDED PER PERSON EMPLOYED IN SUB-SECTORS OF MANUFACTURING, 1970

	Food, Drink and tobacco	Textiles Leather & Clothing	Chemicals	Basic Metals	Metal Products	Other Manufacturing
Belgium	163	129	160	271	156	131
France	197	109	164	268	177	141
Italy	120	82	133	215	138	95
Netherlands	184	141	188	272	178	156
Germany	153	120	147	258	153	175
UK	100	100	100	100	100	100

Source: D. T. Jones, 'Output, Employment and Labour Productivity in Europe since 1955', NIER, No. 77, August 1976, Table 2, p. 74.

2.25 This evident relative failure of the UK to achieve common policy objectives has stimulated considerable interest in the German economy and, as explained in Section B has given rise to several 'structuralist' theories as to the causes of Britain's economic problems. In section D a more detailed appraisal of structural trends in the two economies is presented.

D. **Structural trends in industry**

2.26 *Population and employment:* In terms of simple population size and employment the BRD and the UK are very similar. Total population in 1976 was 61.5 million in Germany compared with 56 million in the UK. Total civilian employment was respectively 24.6 million and 24.4 million. It may also be of some interest to note that land area is also remarkably similar in the two cases, 249 thousand km^2 for Germany and 244 thousand km^2 for the UK. Population in the BRD however, has had a tendency to increase more rapidly since the war. Thus between the years 1950 and 1970 the German population grew from 50.7 million to 60.6 million. For the UK the corresponding figures are 50.2 million and 55.3 million, a yearly compound rate of 0.90 per cent in West Germany and 0.48 per cent in the UK.

2.27 This superficial similarity between the BRD and the UK of total employment and land area has made the comparative study of the two economies particularly attractive to analysts attempting some explanation of the relatively poor performance of the UK. Tables 2.7 to 2.11 which follow in the text and Tables 2.A2 in the Appendix to this chapter present some basic data on employment trends. At the broad sectoral level it is seen from Table 2.7 that the service sector has grown in relative size in both countries during the period 1960–1975. In the BRD the proportion of employment in this sector rose by 8.2 percentage points compared with 8.9 percentage points in the UK. However, throughout the period the service share in total employment has always been greater in the UK (by between 9 and 10 percentage points).

Table 2.7

PER CENT MANUFACTURING AND SERVICES EMPLOYMENT IN TOTAL EMPLOYMENT, SELECTED YEARS

| | Manufacturing | | | Services | |
	BRD	UK		BRD	UK
1960	34.7	35.8		38.5	47.5
1965	36.3	35.0		40.5	49.6
1970	37.4	34.7		42.7	52.0
1975	35.9	30.9		46.7	56.4

Source: OECD Labour Force Statistics 1960–1971 and 1964–1975

Table 2.8

EMPLOYMENT BY SECTOR PER CENT — BRD

	Primary[1]	Secondary[2]	Tertiary[3] plus State
1951–1955	20.4	44.8	34.8
1956–1960	16.0	47.3	36.7
1961–1965	11.9	48.5	39.6
1966–1970	9.7	48.1	42.2
1971–1975	7.5	47.5	45.0

Notes: 1. Agriculture, forestry and fishing
2. Energy, mining, manufacturing and construction
3. Other, i.e. numbers 4–9 (see Table 3).
Source: Table 5, Oppenländer, K. (1977), op. cit.

Table 2.9

SHARES IN TOTAL EMPLOYMENT BY ECONOMIC BRANCH (BRD)

		1960	1973	Change
		%	%	%
0.	Agriculture, Forestry and Fishing	13.2	7.33	−6.39
1.	Energy, Water and Mining	2.90	1.84	−1.06
2.	Manufacturing	37.17	37.95	0.78
3.	Construction	7.83	8.08	0.25
4.	Distribution	12.64	12.71	0.07
5.	Transport and Communication	5.60	5.69	0.09
6.	Banking and Finance	1.47	2.52	1.05
7.	Other Commercial, Private Services[1]	7.66	8.90	1.24
8.	Non-Commercial Private Services[2]	2.93	2.48	−0.45
9.	State Services	8.09	12.50	4.41

Notes: 1. Including stock broking and insurance broking.
2. Including domestic service.
Sources: Beiträge zur Arbeitsmarkt − und Berufsforschung. 3.1 Institut für Arbeitsmarkt − und Berufsforschung der Bundes-samt für Arbeit, Nürnberg 1975. Table 2.1.2.

Table 2.10

SHARES IN TOTAL EMPLOYMENT BY INDUSTRY GROUP (UK)

	1961	1973	Change
	%	%	%
Agriculture, Forestry and Fishing	4.6	2.9	−1.7
Mining and Quarrying	3.0	1.5	−1.5
Manufacturing	36.0	32.3	−3.7
Construction	6.9	7.4	+ 0.5
Gas, Electricity and Water	1.6	1.4	−0.2
Transport and Communication	7.2	6.5	−0.7
Distributive Trade	13.8	13.0	−0.8
Other Services	26.9	35.0	+ 8.1

Source. Appendix Table 2, C. J. F. Brown and T. D. Sheriff, op. cit. (1978)

Table 2.11

INDUSTRIAL EMPLOYMENT BY SECTOR[1], BRD (%)

	1960	1974
Mining	7.63	3.10
Basic Production Goods[2]	21.30	21.08
Investment Goods[3]	40.00	47.80
Consumer Goods[4]	24.81	22.01
Food and Tobacco[5]	6.26	6.01
	100.0	100.0

Notes: 1. Includes firms with 10 or more employees.
2. Consists of industries such as iron and steel; non-ferrous metals; chemicals; mineral oil; wood, paper and pulp, etc.
3. Steel products (including railway wagons), vehicles, shipbuilding, aircraft, electronics, industrial machinery.
4. Glass, wood products, ceramics, printing and duplicating, clothing, jewellery, toys, artificial films, textiles, leather, musical instruments.
5. Including brewing.
Source: Beitrage. Leupoldt and Ermann (op. cit.), Table 2.10.2

2.28 In the sphere of manufacturing, trends appear to have diverged considerably. Over the period 1960–1975 the share of manufacturing to total employment in the UK fell from 35.8 per cent to 30.9 per cent. In contrast, the manufacturing share of the BRD increased by 1.2 per cent and in 1975 was at a level almost the same as that of the UK in 1960. It is also of some importance to note that the trends have not been consistent throughout the period. Until 1970 the relative decline in manufacturing in the UK was rather slow while in Germany the upward trend was more marked (a rise of 2.7 percentage points). After 1970 both economies experienced a relative fall in manufacturing employment, this fall being more pronounced in the UK (almost 4 percentage points in 5 years). It was this acceleration in the downward trend of manufacturing employment in the early 1970.s that resulted in considerable concern in the UK and produced the heightened interest in 'structuralist' theorising reviewed in Section B.

2.29 Presenting employment data in terms of proportions can present a misleading picture of trends in *absolute* levels of employment. Further, a particularly important consideration which reflects on the figures is the rapid fall of employment in the primary sector in Germany, a fall which, as is well known, could not occur in the UK. As is indicated in Table 2.8 the growth in tertiary employment in the BRD was mainly at the expense of the declining numbers in agriculture. Secondary sector employment as a share of total employment remained very stable from the mid-1950's to the mid-1970's. This general impression of the service sector growing primarily at the expense of primary employment in the BRD, but to some extent at the expense of manufacturing in the UK, is confirmed by Table 2.9 and 2.10. These give a more detailed breakdown of employment by industry group. (The German and UK figures are not strictly comparable and they are used here not for detailed analysis but for investigating broad trends over more than a decade).

2.30 Once again the comparative stability of manufacturing in the BRD is apparent from Table 2.9. The major areas of employment growth (especially system numbers 6, 7 and 9) did not result in a decline in secondary employment because of a large fall in the agricultural sector's share. In the UK on the other hand (Table 2.10) an 8 percentage points rise in service employment (excluding transport and distributive trends) could be accommodated only by a relative decline in almost every other industry group, but especially in manufacturing.

2.31 Employment trends within the manufacturing sector alone are recorded in Tables 2.A1 and 2.42. It is necessary to emphasise again that each table adopts the conventions of the country concerned and no attempt has been made at standardisation. However, some general conclusions are possible. In the first place, the period up to 1966 saw an *absolute* increase in manufacturing employment in both countries. Indeed, the increase seems to have been about ½ million employees in each case. Further, although the information presented does not permit a very specific analysis of the destination of these employees the main growth areas appear to have been in engineering and metal manufactures.

2.32 In contrast, the period following 1966 reveals quite divergent experience. While manufacturing in the BRD continued to grow in absolute size in terms of employment, albeit at a slower rate, the manufacturing sector in the UK lost ¾ million employees, a large proportion from metal manufacture, engineering and textiles. All industries were involved in this decline, however, so that in terms of employment *share*, engineering and vehicles gained somewhat in spite of lower levels of employment. Since 1973 the labour shake-out has continued in the UK, total employment in manufacturing being 7,246,000 in 1976. How much of this decline represents a continuing trend away from manufacturing, and how much is the result of economic depression is not clear.

2.33 The general picture emerges of a manufacturing sector in the UK declining in terms of total employment and relative to the size of other sectors, while in Germany a smaller relative decline is compatible with the maintenance of the absolute size of the manufacturing sector. Both economies have had to contend with the decline of certain industries, particularly textiles and shipbuilding, throughout the period, but the greater stability of manufacturing employment in the BRD, and, as Table 2.11 indicates, a move towards higher employment in investment goods compared with consumer goods industries, have probably created a more favourable environment for the reallocation of labour involved.

2.34 *Capital inputs.* It is a commonplace observation that relative to other major industrialised countries UK labour is 'backed up' by less capital (i.e. techniques of production tend to be relatively labour intensive) and that the percentage of GNP is lower than in other countries. Estimates by Elliott and Hughes (1976) suggest that throughout the period 1954–1972 the capital stock in German manufacturing industry grew at slightly less than twice the rate attained in the UK (7.4 per cent per annum compared with 3.9 per cent). These figures involve some 'catching up' after the war and the excess of the German over the UK rate of capital accumulation seems to have narrowed somewhat in more recent periods. However, the general conclusion is well established that 'in virtually all sectors and sub-periods, West German industries outstripped their UK counterparts in their rate of capital formation. . .'.[4]

2.35 An interesting and perhaps more surprising aspect of their analysis concerns the allocation of the capital stock between manufacturing industries in the two countries. The percentage distribution of the stock is remarkably similar. Indeed in 1972 the rank correlation coefficient was as high as 0.92, i.e. the rank order of industries in terms of share in total capital stock was virtually identical in both countries. It is not possible to argue therefore that differing performance is the result of a greatly differing industrial structure, at least at the 'industry order' level of the UK Standard Industrial Classification.

2.36 *Output and labour productivity.* A comparison of trends in manufacturing output as a percentage of GNP reveals a situation very similar to that outlined above with respect to employment. In the UK the ratio of manufacturing output to GDP at current prices has fallen from 36.1 per cent in 1960 to 28.9 per cent in 1975. In West Germany the ratio remained stable at around 41 per cent until 1970, declining thereafter to 37.8 per cent (see Table 2.12). At a more disaggregated level the distribution of output within manufacturing is indicated in Table 2.14. These figures taken from Maroof (1976) have been arranged so that the German statistics are roughly comparable with the UK Standard Industrial Classification.[5]

2.36 A glance at the table reveals considerable similarity between the structure of manufacturing output in the two countries. The UK has a higher proportion of output in Food, Drink and Tobacco, while the BRD is well represented in the field of chemicals and metal manufacture. However, the overall structure is very similar, the correlation coefficient between the two sets of data being 0.83. A linear regression line computed for the data yields

$$BRD = 0.41 + 0.94 \, UK$$
$$(0.24)$$

The standard error, in parenthesis, indicates that the coefficient is significantly greater than zero and not significantly different from unity.

2.38 Similar conclusions can be drawn when considering the rate of growth of output. In general those industries experiencing relatively high output growth in the BRD were the same as those experiencing high output growth in the UK. George and Ward (1975), for example, calculate a Spearman rank correlation coefficient of 0.88 for rates of growth between 1953–1969, but Maroof argues that the strong association over the long period obscures the fact that much weaker correlation coefficients are obtained in certain sub-periods, especially 1968–1972. The major difference between the two countries is in the *absolute* level of output growth, the UK as already noted in Section C growing at a considerably lower rate than the BRD.

2.39 Tables 2.A3 and 2.A4 in the Appendix provide more detail on productivity changes within the manufacturing sector itself. Output per person employed rose by 5.1 per cent per annum over the period 1960–1973 in West Germany but by rather less in the UK. Brown and Sheriff estimate the UK figure to be about

3.1 per cent. Although the figures are again presented according to the statistical convention of the two countries, some comparison of broad features is possible. In particular it is interesting to note the similarity in the *ranking* of productivity changes. In both countries, chemicals and petroleum products are top of the list whereas ferrous and non-ferrous metals are at the bottom. In both countries, textiles rank high in the order of productivity growth and highest in terms of the rate of employment decline.[6]

Table 2.12

MANUFACTURING OUTPUT AS PER CENT GDP AT CURRENT PRICES

	BRD	UK
1960	41.3	36.1
1965	41.2	34.0
1970	41.8	32.4
1975	37.8	28.9

Source: National Accounts Statistics of OECD Member Countries, OECD.

Table 2.13

DISTRIBUTION OF NET OUTPUT IN MANUFACTURING IN THE UK AND WEST GERMANY, 1972

	Per cent	
	UK	BRD
Food, Drink and Tobacco	11.2	7.1
Chemicals	12.3	16.4
Metal Manufacturing	6.3	11.2
Engineering and electrical goods	24.4	23.2
Mechanical engineering	11.6	9.8
Instrument engineering	1.4	1.2
Electrical engineering	11.6	12.3
Shipbuilding and marine engineering	1.3	0.8
Vehicles and aircraft	9.7	9.1
Metal goods	5.4	5.5
Textiles	7.5	4.8
Leather, fur, clothing and footwear	3.6	3.7
Bricks, pottery, glass and cement	4.3	6.0
Timber and furniture	2.8	3.4
Paper, printing and publishing	7.5	4.5
Other manufacturing	3.9	4.3
Total manufacturing	100.0	100.0

Source: Maroof (1976), Table 1.9.

2.40 This last observation leads to a more general point concerning employment trends. If employment is to be maintained in the face of productivity growth, output must rise faster than productivity. The textile industry is a classic case, of course, of an industry in which this has not happened and which has been compelled to shed large numbers of its workforce. However, in the BRD, the rate of growth of manufacturing output over the period (6.0 per cent) was sufficiently high to allow a rise in employment in the sector as a whole. In the UK on the other hand, a rate of growth of output of 2.1 per cent implied that rising productivity was accompanied by a loss of employment as was demonstrated earlier in the paper. It was this phenomenon that led Bacon and Eltis to conclude that the UK has been suffering from productivity increases instead of benefiting from them.[7]

2.41 The relationship between the growth of output and the growth of productivity has been the subject of lively interest in recent years. 'Verdoorn's law', as it has been termed, states that high rates of output growth will be associated with high rates of growth of productivity and employment. It is not the place here to enter the debate on the precise causal mechanisms involved although Kaldor, the most prominent advocate of Verdoorn's law in the UK, argues strongly that a high rate of output growth is likely to stimulate productivity, enabling firms to benefit from 'dynamic economies of scale' [e.g. Kaldor (1966), (1977)].

2.42 Recent comparative studies of West Germany and the UK have sought to confirm the existence of Verdoorn's relationship within the industry groups of each country. Elliott and Hughes (1976), for example, found that for the whole period 1954—1972 and for five sub-periods within it 'labour productivity growth was significantly and positively related to output growth' in each country.[8] However, the relationship was noticeably weaker in West Germany compared with the UK and indeed another study by George and Ward (1975) found the correlation coefficient between the two variables to be 'virtually zero' in Germany. Their tentative suggestion is that there exists a 'threshold level' of output growth which enables productivity to advance rapidly, a level which most industries reached in the BRD but which only a few, such as electrical machinery and chemicals, attained in the UK.[9]

2.43 Of all the sources of 'effective demand' for industrial products (the rate of growth of which, according to the Verdoorn thesis, determines productivity growth) the greatest emphasis in the UK has been placed on exports. Kaldor, in particular, has argued that all the countries which have failed to develop in the postwar era — some in Latin America, India and Pakistan — have a 'single common characteristic' in that 'they failed to develop a significant volume of exports in manufactured goods'. Conversely 'the growth of all fast-growing countries appears to have been "export led" '[10]. The following section therefore continue a brief comparison of structural trends in the field of international trade in the UK and BRD.

2.44 *International Trade.* The increasing importance of international trade to both the BRD and UK is indicated in Table 2.14. This simply records the value of exports of goods and services as a proportion of GNP in the two countries in selected years since 1960. In both countries this proportion rose over the period by nine percentage points and in 1976 was around 30 per cent of GNP.

Table 2.14

EXPORTS OF GOODS AND SERVICES, PER CENT OF GNP (CURRENT PRICES)

	BRD Per cent GNP at market prices	UK Per cent GNP at factor cost
1960	20.7	22.5
1965	19.7	21.0
1970	23.1	26.0
1976	29.4	31.6

Sources: National Income and Expenditure, 1977, Table 1.6. OECD Economic Survey, Germany, Table B, p. 59.

2.45 The structural similarity displayed in Table 2.13 is not mirrored, however, in the performance of the two countries in international trade. Taking as an indicator, the share of world manufacturing exports, the BRD has held its position or perhaps slightly improved it. The UK on the other hand has experienced a much slower rate of growth of exports than that of world trade generally, and consequently her share has fallen substantially as shown in Table 2.15. Between 1955 and 1977 the share of the UK in world exports of manufacturers fell from 19.8 per cent to 9.3 per cent while that of the BRD rose from 15.5 per cent to 20.8 per cent.

Table 2.15

SHARES IN THE VALUE OF WORLD EXPORTS OF MANUFACTURES

	BRD	UK	JAPAN	USA
1955	15.1	19.8	5.1	24.5
1960	19.3	16.5	6.9	21.6
1965	19.1	13.9	9.4	20.3
1970	19.8	10.8	11.7	18.5
1975	20.8	9.3	15.4	15.9

2.46 As with other indicators of poor performance on the part of the UK, explanations of this declining share have been sought in structural characteristics. Low labour productivity in the UK relative to the BRD cannot be explained by industrial structure, and neither can trade performance. In Table 2.16 the imports and exports of each economy are recorded by Standard International Trade Classification Section. The percentage of total imports accounted for by each section are uncannily similar while the percentage of manufactured goods (sections 5-8) in total imports is almost identical for each country (54.9 per cent in the BRD, 54.5 per cent in the UK). The share of manufactured exports is 6 percentage points lower for the UK relative to Germany however, and there does appear to be a tendency for the BRD to export a larger proportion of machinery and transport equipment (section 7) compared with manufactured goods classified by materials (section 6).

Table 2.16

FOREIGN TRADE BY SITC SECTION, PER CENT TOTAL, 1976

		BRD			UK		
		Imports cif		*Exports fob*	*Imports cif*		*Exports fob*
0.	Food and live animals	12.6		3.5	14.2		3.9
1.	Beverages and Tobacco	1.1		0.4	1.5		2.5
2.	Crude materials except fuels	9.5		2.2	9.6		2.7
3.	Mineral fuels, lubricants etc.	17.9		2.9	17.9		4.8
4.	Animal and vegetable oil and fat	0.5		0.4	0.6		0.1
5.	Chemicals	7.3		12.3	6.1		11.5
6.	Manufactured goods classified by material	18.7		20.3	19.2		22.3
			54.9	88.8		54.5	82.6
7.	Machinery and transport equipment	17.9		47.5	21.4		39.7
8.	Miscellaneous manufactures	11.0		8.7	7.8		9.1
9.	Other	3.4		1.7	1.5		3.3
		100.0		100.0	100.0		100.0

Sources: Monthly Digest of Statistics, CSO, August 1978, Tables 14.5 and 14.6. OECD Economic Survey, Germany, Table G, p.66.

2.47 In 1976 there remained some significant differences in the origin and destination of imports and exports. Although EEC trade is becoming increasingly important for the UK, exports to and imports from other EEC members represent a larger portion of the total trade of the BRD. Exports to other EEC countries represent 45.7 per cent of total West German exports compared with 35.6 per cent for the UK. The share of exports going to the oil and non-oil developing countries on the other hand is considerably higher in the UK (25.4 per cent compared with 16.3 per cent), a reflection no doubt of the UK's continuing Commonwealth connections.

2.48 Since the later 1960's, UK trade flows have been subjected to fairly detailed study. In particular, interest has centred on income elasticities of demand following the study by Houthakker and Magee (1969) which showed the UK as having a high income elasticity of demand for imports relative to the foreign income elasticity of demand for her exports. Most subsequent studies have tended to confirm these conclusions [e.g. Taplin (1973), Panic (1975), Stout (1978)]. Structuralist explanations of this phenomenon are not easy to devise for, as we have seen in 2.47, the structure of trade flows is not substantially different, at least at section level, while both countries have experienced increasing import penetration and a rising share of exports in GNP.

2.49 Tables 2.A5 and 2.A6 in the Appendix concerning import and export quotas by industry group give more detail. Virtually every industry in each country has experienced both higher import and export ratios between 1968 and 1976. Indeed many German analysts regard the growth of intra-industry trade and competition between advanced industrial economies as the major factors leading to structural adjustment problems [e.g. Scholz (1977)]. Care should be taken in interpreting the data in 2.A5 and 2.A6 and more confidence can be placed in the general trends recorded for each country than in specific cross-country comparisons of a particular industry year-by-year. Figures for the UK taken from Wells and Imber (1977) record a rise in the import quota (total imports/home demand) for manufacturing as a whole – from 17 per cent in 1968 to 23 per cent in 1976. German data from IFO reveal a similar rise from 17.1 per cent to 24.6 per cent between the same dates. In the field of exports, however, the figures indicate a somewhat lower export ratio for manufacturing in the UK compared with the BRD. A rise in the export ratio from 23.5 per cent to 29.8 per cent in the BRD compares with a rise from 17 per cent to 23 per cent in the UK for the period 1968-1976.

2.50 The general tendency for import and export quotas to increase over time and the observation that much international trade involves the exchange of similar products, i.e. it is intra-industry rather than inter-industry trade, has led to the development of new models of international trade. Trade flows are seen as stemming not from differing production functions between countries or from differing factor endowments but from demand side consideration such as a desire for increasing variety as incomes rise [e.g., Barker(1977)]. Building on Lancaster's (1966) re-appraisal of consumer theory it is argued that goods produced in each country offer a bundle of 'characteristics' to the purchaser, that economies of scale limit the number of varieties of any particular good produced withing the confines of a given country, and that increasing per capita incomes and a consequent rise in the desire for variety will result in higher levels of imports relative to domestic demand.

2.51 It is evident that such reasoning provides not only an explanation of the phenomenon of rising import and export ratios but some insight into possible causes of the UK's relatively poor export performance. The bundle of 'characteristics' offered by UK export goods it is asserted, are simply not attractive to foreign buyers. In particular the analysts supporting this view have in mind 'characteristics' such as product design, technical specification, delivery dates, reliability, service etc. which are often seen as being of poor standard relative to foreign competitors [e.g. Singh (1977), Panic (1975)]. Differences in these factors between the UK and BRD cannot be revealed by the structural breakdown provided in the Appendix Tables. They may, however, be indicated by the larger share of machinery in total German exports compared with the UK, and by the former's greater reliance on exports to other EEC countries to which reference has already been made. Evidence reported by Stout (1979) that unit values of UK manufactured goods were generally much lower than those of BRD goods in equivalent product groups also suggests that, with notable exceptions, such as radio, radar and electronic goods, UK exports have served less sophisticated markets — markets in which price-elasticities may be greater but income elasticities of demand may be lower.[11]

2.52 *Concentration.* The analysis of aggregate and market concentration and the comparison of firm and plant size between countries can be considered of considerable structural importance for two reasons. Firstly, the degree of market concentration may be of relevance in determining the 'competitiveness' of a particular industry, and secondly the relative size of firm or plant may indicate the extent to which economies of scale have been achieved. These 'structuralist' propositions are both open to dispute. The 'degree of competition' is an elusive concept and will not necessarily be closely related to market concentration as conventionally measured. Much will depend here on the definition and measurement of market size. The existence of many close substitutes may make it difficult to tell where one market ends and another begins, while international trade may make the number and concentration of firms in the domestic market, e.g. as measured by sales, a misleading indicator of competitive pressure. Similarly, the assumption that increasing size of firm permits the use of more efficient production processes and results in declining costs of production is questionable. As is well known, statistical studies indicate a wide range of output subject to constant costs in many industries. The use of accounting data in these studies can be criticised on methodological grounds[12] however, while studies using engineering data find it difficult to incorporate factors such as the impact on labour relations of increasing plant size.

2.53 Recent comparative studies of concentration and plant size in the UK and BRD [George and Ward (1975), Hughes (1976)], confirm earlier impressions that UK industry is more concentrated but that plant size tends to be smaller. The study by George and Ward uses 1963 data and concludes that industries which are relatively highly concentrated in the UK (by reference to the 4-firm employment concentration ratio) also tend to be relatively highly concentrated in West Germany. However, the absolute levels of UK concentration tend to be substantially higher than West Germany. Table 2.17 reveals that the excess of the UK over the West German concentration ratios is greatest in the most concentrated industries, whereas in the least concentrated industries the concentration ratios are roughly comparable between the two countries.

Table 2.17

AVERAGE 4-FIRM EMPLOYMENT CONCENTRATION RATIOS UK AND BRD, 1963

Industry Group	UK	West Germany
A (11)	62	28
B (10)	39	24
C (10)	22	16
D (10)	13	12

Note: 41 industries are arranged in descending order of their concentration ratio in the UK and divided into groups.
Source: From Table 3.3 George and Ward (1975), p.17.

2.54 The period since 1963 has seen considerable merger activity both in the UK and in West Germany. The relative effect of this merger activity on concentration is still an open question although it appears that the character of mergers differed between the two countries. In the UK a greater proportion of the firms acquired were small, whereas in the BRD merger activity 'tended to involve relatively larger companies'.[13]

2.55 For analysts interested in technological efficiency the size of plant is probably of more relevance than the size of firm. Further, it is not so much concentration of plants or their size relative to each other in a given country, but their absolute size which will be related to productive efficiency if production functions are similar between countries. Unfortunately statistical analysis in this area yields little result for a large amount of effort. There is clearly no summary statistic which can provide a measure of relative size for a whole distribution of firms which will not in some respects be misleading. A simple average may be suggestive but tells us nothing about the importance of plants much larger or smaller than the average. A measure of dispersion such as the variance is not very helpful since *inequality* in plant size is not the issue. Most studies overcome this problem by looking at a part of the distribution of plants, i.e. 'large plants' usually defined as those with over 1,000 employees. Even this procedure can give rise to problems however, for the definition of what constitutes a 'large plant' is ultimately arbitrary. Further, a 'large' plant in the motor industry may be enormously different from a 'large' plant in (say) textiles. if 'large' is defined in terms of the upper quartile or upper decile size.

2.56 Table 2.18 provides information from the NEDO study by Hughes on plants with over 1,000 employees in the UK and BRD. It is clear that there is no very marked numerical superiority of large plants in the BRD. Numbers differ most markedly in the Food, Drink and Tobacco industry in which the UK possesses more large plants, and perhaps rather surprisingly in the field of Vehicles and Aircraft in which the UK has a similar numerical superiority. West Germany tends to have more large plants than the UK in engineering and metal manufacture.

Table 2.18

LARGE PLANTS IN WEST GERMAN AND UK MANUFACTURING, 1968

	Number of large plants		Ratio of UK to BRD average size of large plants	Per cent total employment in large plants	
	UK	BRD		UK	BRD
Food, Drink and Tobacco	134	46	118	32.0	13.8
Chemicals	90	103	60	41.4	61.2
Engineering and electrical goods	384	425	83	39.8	46.2
Shipbuilding and Marine Engineering	35	15	85	63.3	76.8
Vehicles and Aircraft	168	86	65	73.7	82.8
Metal Goods n.e.s.	53	43	82	16.0	12.9
Metal manufacturing	105	154	90	53.2	58.4
Textiles	61	57	106	15.6	17.3
Leather, fur etc.	21	17	115	6.4	4.3
Bricks, pottery, glass, cement	35	35	90	20.6	15.4
Timber and furniture	3	8	80	1.4	4.1
Paper, printing, publishing	69	33	106	20.5	12.2
Other manufacturing	40	43	92	27.5	30.9
All manufacturing	1198	1065	85	34.5	36.5

Source: From Table 4.26, Hughes (1976), p.112.

2.57 From column 3 of Table 2.18 it appears that 'large' plants in the UK tend to be smaller on average than large plants in the BRD. In the field of vehicles and aircraft for example the average 'large' UK plant was 65 per cent of the average in the BRD in terms of employment. As an illustration of the difficulties of this type of analysis it is instructive to look more closely at a particular industry. George and Ward in their study of industrial structure note that if, in the field of vehicles, a comparison is made between the average size of the largest 86 plants in each country, the result is an identical average size of plant in 1968.[14] Hughes even notes that 'if the 70 largest UK vehicle plants are compared with the 80 largest West German vehicle plants, the UK plants turn out to be 10 per cent bigger'.[15] A more detailed study of relative plant size in the motor industry by Jones and Prais (1978) indicates how misleading these 'large plant' averages can be. The median German car plant in 1970 was nearly three times the size of the corresponding UK plant in terms of employment (See Table 2.19). One quarter of the German labour force in vehicles were employed in plants of over 32,000 people.

Table 2.19

MEDIAN AND QUARTILE PLANT-SIZES IN VEHICLES, BRITAIN AND GERMANY

	Britain	Germany
Lower Quartile	560	1,500
Median	2,300	7,600
Upper Quartile	7,200	32,000

Note: Median and quartile sizes relate to number of employees not the number of plants, i.e. one half of all employees are employed in plants that are bigger than the median size.
Source: From Table 1, Jones and Prais (1978), p.132.

2.58 Large plant averages can evidently be misleading when industry data are insufficiently disaggregated, so that no distinction is made between, for example, motor component plants which tend to be relatively small and car assembly plants which are very large, and when even very small plants by the standards of the industry are nevertheless considered 'large' for the purposes of statistical analysis.

2.59 Although it would therefore seem dangerous to put too much faith in the magnitudes involved, there does not seem much doubt that plants in the BRD tend to be larger than those in the UK for equivalent industries, but that firm concentration ratios tend to be larger in the UK. Thus there appears to be some evidence to support the contention that if British industry suffers from small scale, it is not because of a lack of large firms but rather a deficiency in the size of plants.

E.   Structural trends and the public sector

2.60 A central problem involved in all studies of public sector size and growth is one of measurement. Public sector 'influence' in modern Western economics is so pervasive and may take so many diverse channels that appropriate measures of 'size' will depend crucially on the objectives of any particular study. If the *output* of non-marketed goods and services is of interest the usual solution is to measure *inputs*, i.e. public current plus capital expenditure (excluding the expenditure of the nationalised industries) on goods and services. If a measure of more general influence on resource allocation is required it may be decided to include industrial and other subsidies but not income transfers. Subsidies would have to include so-called tax-expenditures, e.g. accelerated depreciation allowances, the valuation of which can be problematical, while the existence of loan 'guarantees', or cheap credit from the state may make it impossible to devise a single measure to permit comparison between time periods or countries. If the relationship between public sector size and inflation is the issue, interest may centre on the Public Sector Borrowing Requirement (PSBR), the rate of expenditure growth, the total tax share in GDP, or the share of direct taxes in GDP, depending on the theoretical model being tested [See Panic (1978), Peacock and Ricketts (1978)]. If the structure of property rights is considered to be of great importance in determining incentives and efficiency (e.g. whether assets are privately or publicly owned) the size and growth of public sector employment may be of relevance — the growth of employment in nationalised industries, public utilities, central and local bureaucracy etc. Finally, if an explanation is sought for public sector activity itself, e.g. within the context of a model of public choice, attention may be focussed on constitutional rules, the importance of direct compared with representative democracy, the power of regional and local relative to national assemblies, the extent of 'earmarked' taxation compared with general fund taxation and so forth.

2.61 In terms of conventional expenditure and tax-share measures of public sector size, Tables 2.20 and 2.21 indicate that there is little difference between BRD and the UK. Both the tax share and government consumption expenditure share tend to be very slightly higher in the UK (by about one to two percentage points) and from 1965-1975 the tax figures seem to have behaved more erratically in the UK. In 1970, for example, total tax revenue as a percentage of GDP reached 37.9 per cent in the UK compared with 32.4 per cent in the BRD. The addition of capital expenditure and transfers to government current expenditure does not greatly alter this picture. In 1975 total public expenditure defined in this way amounted to 43.3 per cent of GDP in the UK compared with 40.5 per cent in the BRD. Clearly slightly different (and higher) percentages would be obtained if GDP were measured at factor cost instead of market prices, so that the comparative results for the UK and BRD will be influenced by the structure of indirect taxes and subsidies in the two countries.

Table 2.20

GOVERNMENT CONSUMPTION EXPENDITURE AS PERCENTAGE OF GDP (CURRENT PRICES)

	UK	BRD
1965	16.8	15.3
1966	17.2	15.6
1967	18.0	16.3
1968	17.7	15.6
1969	17.3	15.8
1970	17.7	15.9
1971	18.0	17.1
1972	18.5	17.4
1973	18.4	18.1
1974	20.2	19.6
1975	22.1	21.0
1976	21.8	20.4

Source: National Accounts of OECD Countries, 1976, Vol. 1, pp.66-67 and 118-119.

Table 2.21

TOTAL TAX REVENUE[1] AS A PERCENTAGE OF GDP (MARKET PRICES)

	BRD	UK
1965	31.41	31.08
1966	31.95	32.27
1967	32.07	33.41
1968	31.72	35.20
1969	33.43	37.02
1970	32.40	37.86
1971	32.87	35.76
1972	34.30	34.49
1973	35.86	32.61
1974	35.80	36.04
1975	35.22	36.77

Note 1: Including Social Security
Source: Revenue Statistics of OECD Member Countries, 1965-75, Table 3, p.80.

2.62 A closer inspection of revenue flows suggests that there are areas of contrast between the tax structure of each country, although the economic significance is debatable. In particular Table 2.22 reveals a somewhat greater reliance on property taxation in the UK and a considerably higher proportion of total taxation made up from taxes on profits and income. On the other hand OECD statistics distinguish between social security contributions and income taxes and the former are of much greater importance in the BRD as a percentage of total taxation.

Table 2.22

TAX REVENUE BY MAIN HEADINGS AS PER CENT OF TOTAL TAXATION, 1975

	BRD	UK
Income and Profit	34.54	44.08
Social Security	34.16	18.26
Property	3.09	12.36
Goods and Services	26.61	25.12
Other	1.60	0.18
	100.00	100.00

Source: Revenue Statistics of OECD Member Countries 1966-1975, Table 7.

2.63 Much of the popular discussion of tax systems is concerned with rates of personal taxation and the consequent effects on 'incentives' or, in the context of discussions on inflation, on 'tax backlash' and wage bargaining. Table 2.23 shows taxes on personal income and the employees' share of social security contribution as a proportion of GDP. It can be seen that in both countries the percentage has been rising (from 11.8 per cent to 15.9 per cent in the BRD between 1965 and 1975 and from 12.0 per cent to 17.1 per cent in the UK). Again, the UK proportion is marginally greater than that in the BRD but this cannot be said to represent a marked structural divergence between the two countries. Nevertheless, a rise of five percentage

Table 2.23

TAXES ON PERSONAL INCOME AND EMPLOYEES' SOCIAL SECURITY CONTRIBUTIONS PER CENT GDP

	BRD			UK		
	Personal Income	*Social Security*	*Total*	*Personal Income*	*Social Security*	*Total*
1965	8.15	3.67	11.82	9.58	2.44	12.02
1966	8.60	3.87	12.47	9.89	2.40	12.29
1967	8.44	3.83	12.27	10.28	2.39	12.67
1968	8.46	3.95	12.41	10.63	2.49	13.12
1969	8.85	4.09	12.94	11.44	2.40	13.84
1970	8.63	4.39	13.02	11.91	2.59	14.50
1971	9.23	4.56	13.79	11.66	2.48	14.14
1972	10.04	4.70	14.74	10.84	2.66	13.50
1973	10.93	5.00	15.93	10.78	2.68	13.46
1974	11.41	5.04	16.45	12.43	2.82	15.25
1975	10.60	5.29	15.89	14.29	2.78	17.07

Source: Revenue Statistics of OECD Member Countries 1965-1975. Tables 10 and 16.

points in an economy experiencing relatively slow growth of GDP may have a much greater political impact than a rise of four percentage points in a fast growing economy. If GDP is growing quickly enough, a rising tax share is quite compatible with rapidly rising personal disposable income. Resistance to higher tax shares, it might be argued, is likely to be greater where the rate of income growth is lower. Certainly a cross-section analysis of OECD countries between the years 1965-1972 revealed a significant inverse re-lationship between the growth of GDP per head and the rate of inflation [Peacock and Ricketts (1978)].

2.64 Perhaps the major differences between the public sectors of the BRD and the UK concern the federal political structure of the West German State and the comparatively small amount of state enterprise. As can be seen from Table 2.24, a much greater proportion of total tax revenue accrues to the Länder in the BRD compared with the Local Authorities in the UK. Further, the method of financing regional or local expendi-ture differs between the two cases. Apart from local property 'rates' the Local Authority in the UK receive 'rate support grants' from the central government. In 1976 these current grants amounted to 55 per cent of Local Authority current receipts, the remainder mainly consisting of rates, rent and interest payments. By contrast the Länder governments in the BRD receive a larger proportion of their revenue through 'local government taxes' as defined by the OECD. A tax is defined as a 'local government tax' if it is collected by the local governments themselves (as with the UK local rates); if it consists of an extra rate on central government taxes the proceeds of which are then distributed to the local governments; or if it consists of a particular tax 'collected by central government accruing automatically and unconditionally to local govern-ments'.[16] Within the BRD, the Länder governments receive revenues from property tax; inheritance tax and motor vehicle tax. They also receive a share in the income and corporation taxes. In 1974 the Länder re-ceived 58 per cent of the yield of taxes on individual incomes and 60 per cent of the yield of corporate taxes.[17]

Table 2.24

PER CENT OF TAX REVENUES ACCRUING TO DIFFERENT LEVELS OF GOVERNMENT, (1974)

	BRD	*UK*
Central/Federal	34	73
Local/State	33	11
Social Security Funds	32	16
Supernational bodies	1	1

Source: Revenue Statistics of OECD Member Countries 1965-1975 p.206, Annex 1.

Table 2.25

PUBLIC SECTOR EMPLOYMENT, UK. PER CENT OF TOTAL EMPLOYED LABOUR FORCE

	1960	*1963*	*1970*	*1975*
Total Public Sector	24.2	23.7	26.2	29.0
Central Government	8.9	7.1	7.7	9.0
HM Forces	2.1	1.7	1.5	1.3
Civilians	6.8	5.4	6.2	7.7
Local Authorities	7.5	8.5	10.3	12.0
Public Corporations	7.7	8.0	8.1	8.0

Source: 'Employment in the Public and Private Sectors, 1959-1974'. *Economic Trends*, February 1976.
'Employment in the Public and Private Sectors, 1971-1975', *Economic Trends*, February 1977.

2.65 A general survey such as this is not the place to speculate upon the possible implications of differing political systems. However, modern public choice theory might lead us to expect constitutional rules to exert an important influence on public sector activity and hence, possibly, on economic performance. If government actions are seen as the outcome of a political system, rather than the rational responses of a despot (benevolent or otherwise) pursuing specified objectives, certain characteristics of that system, e.g. voting rules, the power of local versus national assemblies, constitutional limitations on the government's power to legislate in certain areas, and so forth, may be regarded as a legitimate aspect of a study of 'economic structure'.[18]

2.66 As pointed out in section B, much recent discussion in the UK has concerned employment levels in the public sector. Table 2.9 records that employment in the State Services sector of the BRD rose from 8.1 per cent to 12.5 per cent between 1960 and 1973. The UK also experienced a substantial rise over the same period although precisely comparable data are not easily available. The figures given in Table 2.25 indicate a rise between 1960 and 1975 from 24.2 per cent to 29.0 per cent of the employed labour force. However, these figures include employment in the Public Corporations which, apart from the German post office and railways, are less important in the BRD. Further, central government employment comprises the service, the Atomic Energy Authority, and the Forestry Commission in addition to employment in central government departments. Similarly, Local Authority employment includes education services and construction departments as well as the more usual 'local government services' such as refuse collection, police and fire protection etc.[19] Thus the major contributor to public sector employment growth in the UK was the local authority sector which grew from 7.5 per cent to 12 per cent of the employed labour force, primarily as a result of expansion in education.

F. Regional structure

2.67 Brief mention must also be made to regional economic structure in the BRD and UK. The following tables give a brief indication of the regional problem in each country using the conventional indicators — unemployment rates, participaton rates and income differentials. It should be emphasised that Tables 2.26 and 2.27 are not suitable for comparisons between countries and are included to show the relative performance of regions within each country. In addition the spread of unemployment rates, or other indicators, will depend to a great extent on the way the regions are defined. The German data refer to the Länder, whereas the UK data refer to economic planning regions and correspond to no particular level of government.

2.68 It is evident that both the BRD and UK face similar problems in terms of regional variations in unemployment and participation rates. Calculations by Biehl[20] using European Community Regional Statistics suggest a range of unemployment rates from 0.1 per cent to 2.7 per cent in West Germany compared with a range from 1.1 per cent to 4.9 per cent in the UK in 1973. This might suggest a somewhat more severe problem in the UK although such a conclusion depends crucially upon how the 'regional problem' is perceived. For example the income per capita figures of Table 2.28 show a considerably small regional range in the UK compared with the BRD, while the general impression of a somewhat smaller regional dispersion of income per capita in the UK compared with the BRD is confirmed by more sophisticated measures such as the coefficient of variation.[21]

Table 2.26

UNEMPLOYMENT AS PER CENT OF EMPLOYEES IN EMPLOYMENT (1972), BRD

Schleswig-Holstein	1.65
Hamburg	0.52
Schleswig-Holstein/Hamburg	1.05
Niedersachsen	1.68
Bremen	1.74
Niedersachsen/Bremen	1.69
Nordrhein-Westfalen	1.17
Hessen	0.93
Rheinland-Pfalz	1.11
Saarland	1.44
Rheinland-Pfalz/Saarland	1.19
Baden-Wurttemburg	0.44
Nordbayern	1.35
Sübayern	1.15
Bayern	1.24
Berlin (West)	1.27
BRD	1.10

Source: Beiträge (op. cit.), Tables 2.6 and 2.18.

Table 2.27

UNEMPLOYMENT AS PER CENT ESTIMATED EMPLOYEES (1972), UK

England	3.3
North	6.3
Yorkshire and Humberside	4.2
East Midlands	3.1
East Anglia	2.9
South East	2.1
South West	3.5
West Midlands	3.6
North West	4.8
Wales	5.2
Scotland	6.4
Northern Ireland	7.8
UK	3.8

Source: Annual Abstract of Statistics (1977), CSO Table 6.8

Table 2.28

LABOUR FORCE PARTICIPATION RATES AND INCOME PER CAPITA, 1973

Participation Rates	National Average	Lowest	Highest
BRD	42.4	35.6	46.9
UK	44.8	39.7	47.1

Income per capita (in DM)		Regional IPC	
BRD	10 880	6 680	17 480
UK	7 650	6 270	8 790

Source: 'The Impact of Enlargement on Regional Development and Regional Policy in the European Community', Dieter Biehl, Technische Universität, Berlin.

G.   Summary and conclusions

2.69   There are clearly some structural differences between the two economies which may be listed as follows:

i.   Whether measured in terms of employment or output there has been a somewhat greater concentration in manufacturing activity in the BRD than in the UK, at least taking the mid-1970's as a benchmark. The concentration was much the same in both countries in the early sixties and what has happened is that the *relative* share of manufacturing output and employment in total output and employment has remained roughly constant in the BRD whereas it has fallen in the UK.

ii.   The greater dependence of the UK on the service sector has been mirrored in international trade. West Germany runs a considerable net deficit in services mainly as a result of foreign travel, whereas the UK has a substantial surplus. The trade ratio for services in the UK indicates a continuing comparative advantage in this area compared with manufacturing [Singh (1977)].

iii.   There is some evidence that, in the field of manufactures, the BRD exports rather more sophisticated equipment with low price-elasticities of demand compared with the UK.

iv.   Plant size in the UK in vehicles and, if large plant averages are to be trusted, in most other manufacturing industries, tend to be smaller than in the BRD.

v.   In comparisons of public sector activity, account must be taken of the federal structure of West Germany and the relatively small area of public ownership.

2.70   Interpretation of these differences is less easy than describing them. A comparative advantage in services would, from the perspective of conventional economic analysis, hardly be a matter for surprise or for regret. A tendency for the UK to build smaller plants might be a reflection of a comparative disadvantage, perhaps for historical and social reasons, in large scale production. It could not be inferred from this that larger plants would permit the attainment of scale economies and greater factor productivity. Rather, a trend towards larger plants would, in these circumstances, be predicted to lower productivity. An observed trend towards the manufacture of vehicle components in relatively small plants on the other hand, and their export for final assembly abroad would seem quite consistent with established trade theory.

2.71 Whatever structural differences we observe between the two economies it is the structural similarities rather than the differences which are so striking. The distribution of employment and output within industrial sectors is similar, there are no marked differences in the balance of exports and imports by sector, and, in global terms at least, the ratio of government expenditure and taxation to GDP in both countries is now very close. It might be argued that a finer breakdown of industrial sectors and closer examination of public sector activities would be necessary before any conclusive proof could be offered of the appearance of growing similarity between the two economies. However, the onus of proof must remain with 'structuralist' thinkers as to the degree of disaggregation which is appropriate to their argument and insofar as structuralists are clear on this matter there is no evidence that they have in mind as fine a breakdown of sectors as has been examined in this Chapter. It is therefore reasonable to conclude that differences between the performance, as conventionally measured, of both economies cannot be explained in structuralist terms.

2.72 This conclusion must not be taken to mean that an implicit technical recommendation has already been slipped into our analysis which necessarily runs counter to the actual structural policies which are to be examined in later Chapters, namely that improvement of performance of the economy cannot be obtained by measures designed to prevent 'de-industrialisation', to mention only current British preoccupations in the field of industrial policy. If, as has been indicated, there are pronounced differences in the efficiency with which factor inputs are used in both countries, this would suggest not only global measures designed to improve the allocation of labour and capital but also specific measures designed to improve productivity in particular sectors. Indeed, as such improvements rest upon action taken at the industry and even the plant level, insofar as government measures are to be effective they would have to be applied at the sectoral level. As the degree of success of such measures is likely to be at least partly a function of the prospects of individual sectors, they must embody a structuralist approach. Any evaluation of such measures must clearly wait until a detailed examination of selective economic policies in both countries has been carried out. This examination occupies the next four Chapters of this Report.

FOOTNOTES

1. This argument has recently been reiterated by Kaldor (1977), p.198.

2. Bacon and Eltis argue that the 'fine tuners' have failed to correct the economic problems of the UK and that 'the case for looking for a structural explanation of the deterioration of the British economy is therefore overwhelming'. (p.6).

3. See Clark (1977), *The State of Taxation*, Readings 16. Institute of Economic Affairs, London.

4. Elliott and Hughes (1976), p.21.

5. Elsewhere in this report, no attempt at standardisation of statistics has been made, but the procedures adopted by Maroof are recorded in Table A.7, and this may be of some assistance when comparisons are made between UK and West German import and export penetration recorded in Tables A.5 and A.6.

6. Comparisons in the field of textiles are particularly likely to be misleading because of classification differences between the two countries. Man-made fibres are included under 'textiles' for the UK but under 'chemicals" for the BRD. Hence the UK productivity growth in the more traditional areas is likely to be rather exaggerated by the reported figures.

7. Bacon and Eltis (op.cit.), p.20.

8. Elliott and Hughes, NEDO, Monograph 5, p.42-43, Chapter 2.

9. George and Ward (1975), Chapter 6, p.67.

10. Kaldor (1977), p.202 and p.204.

11. The Economist Intelligence Unit Review of West Germany (1st quarter 1978) comments for example, 'a very high proportion of exports consist of sophisticated high technology products where price is not a major consideration . . . .'

12. See, for example, Friedman (1955), reprinted in Archibald (1971).

13. Hughes, p.105. More recent trends in the BRD may have changed this situation. A recent spate of merger activity in the BRD which is concerning the West German Cartel office is reported as 'mostly involving small and medium sized enterprises as one of the partners'. 'In 1977, 554 mergers were notified of which about half were not covered by the 1976 merger control legislation which insists on controls above a certain size of turnover'. Economist Intelligence Unit. 3rd Quarter 1978. Review of BRD, p.14.

14. George and Ward, Table 4.12, p.41.

15. Hughes, p.113.

16. Revenue Statistics of OECD countries 1976-75, p.198.

17. Table 1 Annex 1, Revenue Statistics 1965-75.

18. The UK has no written constitution. In the BRD on the other hand the government cannot ignore constitutional constraints. A recent example concerns the West German borrowing requirement. The constitution lays it down that federal borrowing must not exceed the states' investment spending unless 'the overall economic balance is disturbed'.

19. For details see *Economic Trends*, February 1976.

20. Dieter Biehl, 'The Impact of Enlargement on Regional Development and Regional Policy in the European Community'. Technische Universität Berlin, p.2.

21. See Dieter Biehl (op. cit.) p.6. International comparisons of real income inevitably give rise to the familiar problems of index numbers — how to define the 'representative basket' of goods, how to include 'quality' changes (including environmental costs and benefits), how to deal with exchange rate changes, etc.

APPENDIX TO CHAPTER 2

Table A.1

THE MANUFACTURING SECTOR. EMPLOYEES, BRD (000s)

	1960	1966	1973	Change 1960-66	Change 1966-73
Chemicals and mineral oils 20/21	746 8.4	908 9.6	1024 10.7	+162	+116
Ceramics, glass etc. 22	451 5.1	451 4.8	432 4.5	0	-19
Ferrous and non-ferrous metals 23	969 10.9	935 9.9	840 8.8	-34	-95
Steel manufactures, machines and vehicles 24	2046 22.9	2344 24.8	2549 26.7	+298	+205
Electrical and instrument engineering[1] 25	1577 17.7	1769 18.7	1935 20.2	+192	+166
Wood, paper printing 26	937 10.5	911 9.6	944 9.9	-26	+33
Textiles 275	655 7.3	578 6.1	459 4.8	-77	-119
Leather and clothing (except 275) 27	737 8.3	716 7.6	555 5.8	-21	-161
Food and Drink 28/29	804 9.0	830 8.8	921 8.6	+26	-9
TOTAL MANUFACTURING	8922 100.0	9442 100.0	9559 100.0	+520	+117

Note: 1 = Includes optical and musical instruments
Source: Table 2.2.1. Beiträge. Leupoldt and Ermann 1975 (op.cit.).

Table A.2

THE MANUFACTURING SECTOR. EMPLOYEES, UK (000s)

	1959	1966	1973	Change 1959-66	Change 1966-73
Food, Drink and Tobacco	771	797	754	+26	-43
Coal and Petroleum Products	56 0.7	43 0.5	40 0.5	-13	-3
Chemicals and Allied Industries	429 5.3	453 5.3	427 5.4	+24	-26
Metal Manufacture	582 7.2	628 7.3	518 6.6	+46	-110
Engineering	1755 21.7	2099 24.4	1936 24.7	+344	-163
Shipbuilding and Marine Engineering	283 3.5	210 2.4	187 2.4	-73	-23
Vehicles	854 10.6	855 9.9	797 10.2	+1	-58
Metal goods not elsewhere specified	507 6.3	611 7.1	567 7.2	+104	-44
Textiles	839 10.3	757 8.8	594 7.6	-82	-163
Leather, leather goods and fur	58 0.7	55 0.6	45 0.6	-3	-10
Clothing and footwear	529 6.5	508 5.9	440 5.6	-21	-68
Bricks, pottery, glass and cement	313 3.9	335 3.9	305 3.9	+22	-30
Timber and Furniture	278 3.4	288 3.4	292 3.7	+10	+4
Paper, Printing and Publishing	553 6.8	623 7.3	574 7.3	+70	-49
Other	266 3.3	325 3.8	352 4.5	+59	+27
TOTAL MANUFACTURING	8071	8584	7828	+513	-756

Source: C.S.O. Annual Abstract of Statistics, Various Issues. A.R. Thatcher (op. cit.), Table 3.2.

Table A.3

GROWTH RATES OF OUTPUT PER PERSON AND EMPLOYMENT IN MANUFACTURING, 1960-1973.
PER CENT COMPOUND (BRD)

	Output/person	Employment
Chemicals and mineral oil	8.04	2.4
Ceramics, glass etc.	6.00	-0.5
Ferrous and non-ferrous metals	3.80	-1.1
Steel manufactures, machines and vehicles	3.80	1.6
Electrical and instrument engineering	5.12	1.5
Wood, paper, printing	4.77	-0.2
Textiles	5.23	-2.6
Leather and clothing	4.81	-2.2
Food and drink	4.43	-0.6
TOTAL MANUFACTURING	5.11	0.3

Growth rate of output in manufacturing 1960-1973 = 6.04 per cent.

Sources: Beiträge, Leupoldt and Ermann (op.cit.), 1975.
From Table 4.1.1., 4.2.1., and 2.1.1.

Table A.4

GROWTH RATES OF OUTPUT PER PERSON AND EMPLOYMENT IN MANUFACTURING' 1960-1975.
PER CENT COMPOUND. (UK).

	Output/person	Employment
Food	2.0	-0.3
Drink and Tobacco	4.2	-0.1
Coal and Petroleum Products	6.1	-2.3
Chemicals and Allied Industries	6.0	-0.2
Ferrous Metals	0.9	-1.6
Non-ferrous Metals	1.7	-1.2
Engineering and Allied Industries	3.6	0.3
Shipbuilding and Marine Engineering	3.1	-2.7
Vehicles	1.7	-1.0
Metal Goods, n.e.s.	0.8	0.2
Textiles	4.5	-2.8
Leather, Clothing, Footwear	2.8	-1.8
Bricks, Cement etc.	4.2	-1.0
Pottery and Glass	4.1	-0.3
Timber, Furniture etc.	2.7	0.3
Paper, Printing, Publishing	2.0	-0.1
Other Manufacturing	3.5	1.3
TOTAL MANUFACTURING	3.1	-0.6

Note: Growth rate of output in manufacturing 1960-1975 = 2.1 per cent.

Source: Brown, C.J.F. and Sheriff, T.D. NIESR (op. cit.). April 1978. Appendix Table 23.

Table A.5

IMPORT PENETRATION AND EXPORT SALES RATIOS, 1968, 1973 and 1976. BRD.

	Imports/Domestic Supply			Exports/Total Turnover		
	1968	1973	1976	1968	1973	1976
BASIC PRODUCTION GOODS	20.6	21.5	25.3	22.7	24.0	27.3
Stone and Earth	9.2	8.3	10.2	5.9	5.7	9.4
Iron and Steel	23.3	22.5	27.6	30.5	30.7	37.4
Non-ferrous metal	54.6	45.1	45.9	33.1	29.2	34.1
Mineral Oil	12.2	19.9	24.1	6.7	6.2	6.8
Chemicals	17.1	21.2	25.0	33.3	36.7	38.6
Saw Mills and Wood	23.3	26.2	26.2	9.9	9.9	14.5
Paper and Pulp	39.6	41.9	47.5	13.6	22.6	25.6
Rubber and Asbestos	14.7	19.0	24.3	20.0	25.4	29.2
INVESTMENT GOODS	13.6	16.4	20.7	37.5	37.2	42.8
Steel and light metal construction	2.5	3.8	5.3	12.9	8.7	17.8
Mechanical engineering	19.0	16.6	19.7	49.5	47.9	53.5
Vehicles	14.2	19.8	23.4	47.7	48.2	51.1
Shipbuilding	12.2	23.8	25.7	41.7	61.1	59.1
Aircraft	68.5	45.1	99.5	58.8	36.8	99.4
Electrical Engineering	11.0	14.1	19.4	25.5	25.8	32.7
Precision tools and optics (Instrument Engineering)	25.1	35.0	40.8	49.6	52.4	54.6
Iron, tin and metal goods	8.6	12.8	13.5	25.5	27.1	24.9
CONSUMER GOODS	13.7	18.7	23.2	13.9	16.2	20.8
Ceramics	15.0	24.3	29.0	34.0	34.2	39.1
Glass	12.7	16.8	19.9	20.7	19.1	22.8
Wood Products	5.0	8.1	9.7	8.8	8.7	12.3
Musical instruments, toys, etc.	36.9	43.3	48.8	42.1	42.2	49.3
Paper and cardboard	3.6	6.0	7.7	6.3	8.1	11.1
Artificial fibres	8.2	11.0	13.1	17.0	18.9	21.0
Leather producing	34.6	51.6	56.8	25.2	36.1	39.2
Leather goods	10.6	19.8	26.5	14.9	12.8	14.2
Shoes	19.0	29.3	39.7	8.3	10.1	13.9
Textiles	22.1	30.1	38.0	16.1	23.4	32.4
Clothing	11.3	22.6	31.6	7.7	10.9	16.5
Food and Tobacco	10.6	13.8	14.4	3.9	7.1	8.7
TOTAL INDUSTRY	17.1	19.6	24.6	23.5	25.5	29.8

Source: Strukturdaten über die Industrie, I.F.O., München, July 1978. Tables 5 and 7.

Table A.6

IMPORT PENETRATION AND EXPORT SALES RATIOS. 1968, 1973 and 1976. UK.

	Imports/Home Demand			Exports/Manufactures Sales		
	1968	*1973*	*1976*	*1968*	*1973*	*1976*
Food, drink and tobacco	21	21	18	4	6	6
Coal and petroleum products	22	17	(15)	13	15	(14)
Chemicals and allied industries	18	22	26	24	28	34
Metal manufactures	18	20	(21)	15	16	(17)
Mechanical engineering	20	27	30	32	37	46
Instrument engineering	30	45	54	33	47	56
Electrical engineering	14	27	32	20	24	37
Shipbuilding and marine engineering	[43]	57	(59)	[31]	30	(39)
Vehicles	14	24	31	34	37	44
Metal goods n.e.s.	5	9	12	12	13	17
Textiles	16	22	28	18	23	27
Leather, Leather goods and fur	21	25	29	25	24	28
Clothing and footwear	12	19	25	9	10	15
Bricks, pottery, glass and cement	5	7	8	9	11	14
Timber, furniture	27	29	28	2	3	6
Paper, printing and publishing	17	18	22	7	8	10
Other manufacturing	10	15	17	15	17	22
TOTAL MANUFACTURING	17	22	23	17	20	23

Note: [ ] Figure for 1969, ( ) Figure for 1975.

Source: 'The Home and Export Performance of UK Industries', J.D. Wells and J.C. Imber. *Economic Trends*, August 1977, HMSO.

Table A.7

RECLASSIFICATION OF BRD DATA SUGGESTED BY NEDO (1976)

UK	*BRD*
Food, drink and tobacco	Food and confectionery, brewing, malting and tobacco
Chemicals and Allied Industries	Chemicals (including coal products and chemical fibres) plus miner al oil
Metal Manufacturing	Iron and steel plus non-ferrous metal, plus steel and light metal construction
Engineering and electrical goods	Machine construction (mechanical engineering), plus electrical engineering, plus precision tools and optical industry (instrument engineering)
Shipbuilding and marine engineering	Shipbuilding
Vehicles and aircraft	Road vehicles plus aircraft
Metal goods n.e.s.	Iron, tin and metal goods industry
Textiles	Textiles
Leather, fur, clothing and footwear	Leather industry plus clothing
Bricks, pottery, glass and cement	Stone and earth, plus ceramics, plus glass
Timber and furniture	Sawmills and woodworking
Paper, printing and publishing	Pulp, paper and board, plus printing and duplicating
Other manufacturing	Rubber and asbestos, musical instruments, toys ornaments and sports equipment, plus plastic goods industry.

REFERENCES

Archibald, G.C. (ed.) (1971), *Theory of the Firm*, Penguin.

Bacon, R. and Eltis, W. (1976), *Britain's Economic Problem: Two Few Producers*, Macmillan

Barker, T. (1977), 'International Trade and Economic Growth: an alternative to the neoclassical approach', *Cambridge Journal of Economics*, pp.153-172.

Biehl, D. (1978), 'The Impact of Enlargement on Regional Development and Regional Policy in the European Community', Technische Universitat Berlin.

Blackaby, F. (ed.) (1979), *Deindustrialisation*, Economic Policy Papers 2, National Institute of Economic and Social Research, Heinemann.

Brown, C.J.F. and Sheriff, T.D. (1978), 'Deindustrialisation in the UK: a summary of empirical evidence and alternative explanations', in Blackaby, F. (ed.), *op. cit.*

Elliot, I. and Hughes, A. (1976), 'Capital and Labour: their growth, distribution and productivity'.

Friedman, M. (1955), 'The Theory and Measurement of Long Run Costs', in Archibald, G.C. (ed.) (1971), *op. cit.*

Gahlen, B. (1978), 'Strukturpolitik in der Marktwirtschaft', *Wirtschaftsdienst*.

George, K.D. and Ward T.S. (1975), *The Structure of Industry in the EEC, an International Comparison*, University of Cambridge Department of Applied Economics, Occasional Paper 43, Cambridge University Press.

Houthakker, H.S. and Magee, S.P. (1969), 'Income and Price Elasticities in World Trade', *Review of Economics and Statistics*.

Hughes, A. (1976), 'Company Concentration, size of plant, and merger activity', in Panic, M. (ed.) 1976, *op. cit.*

Jones, D.T. (1976), 'Output, Employment and Labour Productivity in Europe since 1955', *National Institute Economic Review*, (August), pp.72-85.

Jones, D.T. and Prais, S.J. (1978), 'Plant-Size and Productivity in the Motor Industry: Some International Comparisons' *Oxford Bulletin of Economics and Statistics*, pp. 131-151.

Kaldor, N. (1966), 'Causes of the Slow Rate of Economic Growth of the United Kingdom', Cambridge University Press.

Kaldor, N. (1977), 'Capitalism and Industrial Development: some lessons from Britain's experience', *Cambridge Journal of Economics*, pp. 193-204.

Kravis, I.B. (1976), 'A Survey of International Comparisons of Productivity', *Economic Journal*, March, pp.1-44.

Maroof, F. (1976), 'The Growth of Output' and 'UK and West German Trade in Manufactures' with (Amin Rajon), both in Panic, M. (ed.) 1976, *op. cit.*

Oppenländer, K. (1977), 'Der gesamtwirtschaftliche Strukturwandel in der Bundesrepublik Deutschland', IFO, Schnelldienst, Heft 11/12, pp.9-13.

Panic, M. (ed.) (1975), 'Why the UK Propensity to Import is High", *Lloyds Bank Review*, Jan.

Panic, M. (ed.) (1976), *The UK and West German Manufacturing Industry*, 1954-72, NEDO Monograph 5.

Panic, M. (1978) 'The Origin of Increasing Inflationary Tendencies in Contemporary Society', in Hirsch, F. and Goldthorpe, J.H. (eds.), *The Political Economy of Inflation*, Martin Robertson.

Peacock, A.T. and Ricketts, M.J. (1978), 'The Growth of the Public Sector and Inflation' in Hirsch, F. and Goldthorpe, J.H. (eds.), *The Political Economy of Inflation*, Martin Robertson.

Scholz, L. (1977), 'Ursachen and Ausmass sektoraler Strukturwandlungen in der verarbeitenden Industrie bis 1985', IFO Schnelldienst Heft 11/12, pp.31-45.

Singh, A. (1977), 'UK Industry and the World Economy: a case of de-industrialisation?' *Cambridge Journal of Economics,* June 1977, pp.13-136.

Stout, B.K. (1979), 'Deindustrialisation and Industrial Policy' in Blackaby, F. (ed.) 1979, *op. cit.*

Thatcher, A.R. (1979), 'Labour Supply and the Employment Trends' in Blackaby, F. (ed.) 1978, *op. cit.*

Wells, J.D. and Imber, J.C. (1977), 'The Home and Export Performance of United Kingdom Industries', *Economic Trends,* (August), pp.78-89, CSO.

CHAPTER 3

THE POLITICAL ECONOMY OF STRUCTURAL POLICY IN THE UK AND BRD

A.   Introduction

3.1   The evolution of policies is observed to be a function of three factors: the aims of government policy, the view taken by government of the economic environment in which policy aims have to be carried out and the view taken by government of the appropriate policy instruments, structural measures and any alternative measures, which appear to best fulfil these aims.

3.2   This method of comparison suggests that economic policy is formulated within the framework of the ruthless logic of the theory of economic policy, whereby policy aims are clearly identified in quantifiable form — a target rate of growth, target rate of price increases, etc — aims are 'traded off' against one another to some precise extent, the resultant 'objective function' containing precise details of aims and trade-offs is maximised subject to clearly discernible constraints represented in a computable macro-economic model, and the effects of policy measures designed to maximise the objective function are known for certain. Reference has already been made in Chapter 1, 1.16, to the temptations of simplification in policy discussion that such a model can engender. It should be stated in advance of our comparison that it takes account of the fact that governments may have good reasons for not stating aims and trade-offs in too specific terms, that there are pronounced technical disagreements amongst economists regarding the nature and the extent of the constraints on meeting policy aims and that in consequence the precise relation between structural policies and what they are designed to achieve may not be known and, even if claimed to be known, may not be fully revealed. Even if economics ministers, as is apparent in the UK have learned to pay lip-service to the logic of economic policy and employ its language in justifying policy changes, it would be misleading to give the impression that in either the BRD or UK economic policy is formulated in terms of a sophisticated optimal control model. Indeed, the very idea of economic planning embodied in this approach has been a prime target of attack by German economists who have played a major part in developing the reasoning underlying the approach to economic policy in the BRD. [For one recent example among many see Watrin (1978)].

3.3   Nevertheless, this trichotomy of aims and trade-offs, constraints and policy instruments can be turned into a taxonomic device which helps to avoid the making of snap judgements about the comparative success of structural policies in each country. The appraisal of structural policy cannot be judged by technical criteria. The appropriateness of specific measures will depend crucially on the extent to which structural change and economic growth are endogenously or exogenously determined (c.f. Chapter 2). Thus faster growing economies will find it easier to absorb labour displaced by the process of secular decline and will therefore require few interventionist measures to achieve a given employment goal. The judgement of the *comparative* efficiency of specific measures in both countries cannot be made solely with reference to economic circumstances for the range of feasible policy instruments may be determined by quite different political and even historical influences. Looking for some positive correlation between the nature and extent of structural policy and the perceived attainment of policy objectives may therefore prove to be chimerical.

3.4   A striking characteristic of the development of structural policies in both countries has been the interplay between their different economic experience and approaches to economic analysis of such policies. Thus sections B and C covering these matters prefaces an account of the evolution of policy aims (section D) within the different political and administrative framework of each country. Chapter 4 shows how the changing aims have manifested themselves in the growing amount and increasing complexity of aid structure.

B.   The severity of the economic problem

3.5   When as a consequence of structural change in some sectors resources become released at a rate greater than that which macro-economic policies of a conventional character (e.g. demand management policies) can permit absorption in other sections, there could be a *prima facie* case for specific selective intervention, if only because of pressure on government to prevent growing short-term unemployment. In the longer run, however, the perceived need for structural policies will depend on the capacity of the labour market to adjust in such a way as to bring about an allocation of labour which removes the short term barriers to absorption in growing sectors. The capacity for re-absorption will clearly depend not only on labour supply mobility but also upon the relation between expansion in the growing sectors and the derived demand for labour. The BRD has enjoyed a comparative advantage over the UK both in respect of supply and demand factors in the labour market. The capacity for re-absorption of displaced labour has been markedly affected by the high growth rate accompanying structural change, at least from the later 1950's until the world recession of 1974-77, as compared with the UK (cf. Chapter 2, Table 2.1) but the 'pull' of increased demand in growing sectors has also been accompanied by a considerable degree of inter-sectoral labour mobility of firms, so that structural unemployment has been much less severe than in the UK [Fels and Glisman (1975)].

3.6   The attendant adjustment problems are also more acute the greater the regional concentration of industry. Regional concentration is especially marked in the United Kingdom partly in consequence of its being the first nation to experience the process of industrialisation when natural regional advantages were particularly important. A graphic illustration is provided by the United Kingdom jute industry. Although only of minor significance to the UK economy, it is the largest jute industry in the EEC and is concentrated in Dundee and its immediate environs. Considerable localised unemployment followed from the partial replacement of jute (labour intensive) by the highly capital intensive substitute, polypropylene. The degree of regional concentration in the United Kingdom together with a disappointing post-war growth performance has been more important in dictating the need for selective intervention than the ability or otherwise of regional policies to transmit economic activity throughout the economy. Moreover, it is possible to argue that the BRD's adjustment problems have been eased by her dependence upon 4 million foreign workers (Gastarbeiter) who have not enjoyed the same residential rights as their United Kingdom counterparts.

3.7   Two other influences, again undoubtedly inter-related, point to the more severe adjustment problems confronting the UK economy. In the decade following the Second World War, the age structure of the capital stock was older and less efficient than its newly rebuilt counterpart in the BRD. In 1960, no less than 41 per cent of BRD industrial plant was less than five years old. By 1974, this figure had declined to approximately 30 per cent. This in itself might be sufficient to explain the comparative lack of technological change, but, in addition, any associated excess capacity might suggest that rationalisation to improve competitiveness would need to be accompanied by some form of government assistance and encouragement. There was therefore a greater disposition to promote schemes for positive selective intervention in those sectors where the age profile of the capital stock was relatively high.

3.8   By far the greatest economic influence, however, stemmed from the respective exchange rate policies pursued by the two countries. The peculiar position of sterling in the 1950s and 1960s and the attempt to maintain it as a reserve currency undoubtedly led to it being maintained at an overvalued rate of exchange for most of the post-war period. Equally, the W. German policy of counteracting the appreciation of the D. Mark, in the search for continuing export-led growth, has meant that the D. Mark has been undervalued over the bulk of the post-war period. Today, this comparative divergence between the respective exchange rates and the true purchasing parities of the respective currencies is maintained artificially by the appreciation of the pound induced by North Sea oil prospects together with considerable capital remittances on the part of migrant workers in the BRD. One result has been considerable inflows of venture capital into the German export sector whilst the British economy has experienced frequent balance of payments crises, a preference for domestic markets and frequent recourse to 'stop-go' policies. Moreover, this comparative undervaluation of the D. Mark served to delay the impact of third world export expansion, whereas in the UK the over-valuation of sterling encouraged the importation of cheaper textiles and eventually engendered strong political pressure for positive intervention in the textile industry. Not only did the German export sector enjoy the benefits of exchange rate undervaluation but German industry in general enjoyed a relatively high degree of protection. To a certain extent protectionist measures were necessary in the early post-war years as a means of employing the sizeable inflows of refugee labour but once that problem had been solved with the attainment of full employment, such measures nonetheless remained. In part, the explanation is to be found in the belief that such measures are consistent and compatible with the free functioning of the market economy — 'marktkonformes Mittel'. Although nominal tariff rates imposed by the BRD are not notably high, Fels had argued that with respect to iron, steel and non-ferrous metals the *effective* rate of protection has been three times as high as the nominal level [Fels and Glisman (1975)].

3.9   In short, the problems confronting the British economy were probably more acute (although occasionally self-imposed) and led to drastic measures, whereas in the BRD the re-allocation of resources proceeded in large degree according to the dictates of the market economy. To what extent this situation was compounded by vastly differing labour supply conditions in the immediate post-war period is difficult to judge. It is commonly suggested that the BRD's labour market flexibility was greatly enhanced by the combination of the influx of refugees from the East and the initial post-war prohibition of re-armament which produced a labour surplus economy. To what extent these factors influenced wage structure and trade union bargaining attitudes is problematical. There can be no doubt that West Germany succeeded in avoiding many pitfalls that beset British policy makers. In particular, in the Federal Republic the central government has been notably successful in financing its budget deficits by issue of new bonds at comparatively modest rates of interest owing to the high German average propensity to save — in the region of 14-17 per cent. Consequently, monetary expansion has been limited primarily to periods when the banking sector was unable to neutralise the impact of balance of payment surpluses. In contrast, in the United Kingdom, the public sector borrowing requirement has necessitated frequent recourse to significant increases in the money supply owing to the unwillingness of the authorities to jeopardise the capital values of existing bonds by making new issues more attractive. Such unwillingness, it may be noted, was misplaced. The resulting inflation increased the nominal value of real assets and thus depressed real values of assets payable in nominal terms, particularly long term government bonds, with consequential increases in interest rates.

3.10 One reason, therefore, for the comparative greater degree of selective intervention in the UK lies in the severity of the associated economic problems in the post-war period which have appeared less amenable to normal market processes, although it must be admitted that such difficulties have been compounded by particular misplaced economic policies — particularly in relation to sterling. However, as we shall see, quite apart from the immediate economic circumstances, there were other deeply rooted reasons to explain comparative attitudes to selective aid.

C.   The economic philosophy of intervention

3.11 It is often claimed that the attitudes of policy makers have been influenced to a considerable extent by the view taken of the performance of the economy by economic writers and structural policies would presumably offer no exception. In this respect the contrast between British and German experience is particularly marked, at least until the late 1960s. The discussion of this contrast could fill volumes and here we can only record the highlights as a prelude towards the examination of the evolution of structural policies in both countries. Another interesting feature of the intellectual debate has been the extent of the misunderstanding generated in the post-war era between British and German economists about each others' positions.

3.12 The evolution of British economic thought concerning structural policy can be briefly explained by a 'then and now' comparison between the position of the 'median' economist in the late 1940s and early 1950s and today. An influential and important writer in the immediate postwar period is James Meade, whose *Planning and the Price Mechanism* (1948) (later translated into German), can be taken as representing a median position along the 'interventionist' spectrum. Meade accepted the commonly supported objectives of full employment with a minimum of inflation and a limited amount of redistribution of income and capital. He totally rejected physical planning which perforce had dominated the war economy on the grounds of the inefficiency and corruption which it would generate, even as a temporary expedient in adjusting to a peacetime economy. He likewise rejected 'laisser-faire' primarily on the grounds of its poor performance in achieving an equitable distribution of income and wealth and not, interestingly enough, because of its failure to achieve an adequate rate of growth. His 'middle way' solution lay in combining the virtues of macro-economic controls over the level of aggregate demand and distribution of income and capital with a restoration in the use of the price mechanism as an efficient allocator of resources. Indeed, the restoration of the use of the price mechanism would entail vigorous anti-monopoly policy in respect of both commodity and labour markets and also support for the return as speedily as possible to free international trade.

3.13 There are several interesting features about this 'median' position of the time. The first is that economic growth as a policy target is never mentioned though the need to improve export performance is. Contemporary economic thinking subsumed that growth would follow from the promotion of economic stability. The second feature follows perhaps from the explanation of the first one. Selective intervention is regarded only as a necessary and very temporary evil associated with the adjustment of particular industries from a wartime closed economy to a peacetime open economy, and such intervention would be confined to import controls, within GATT rules, and would not require explicit subsidies. The third is that this 'median' position is quintessentially Keynesian and it is symptomatic of the degree of acceptance of this position at the time that Keynes is never mentioned in Meade's book! In contrast, the contemporary view by influential German writers of the 'Euckenkreis' is characterised by a sustained and bitter attack on all things Keynesian, is being argued that Keynesianism was synonymous with massive state intervention and support for inflationary policies[1]. As argued later, the reaction to Keynesianism had an important influence on the intellectual basis of German post-war economic policy.

3.14 The median position in the immediate post-war UK seems to have been influential for successive governments did, albeit somewhat reluctantly, give up physical controls, and concentrate on the use of fiscal policy. It is a debatable issue how far this Keynesian approach was responsible for the maintenance of high levels of output and employment, independently of other secular influences, but in general the reliance on 'fine tuning' is a clear recognition of the dominance of the median intellectual position.

3.15 The position is vastly different at the time of writing (1979). Curiously enough, a good case could be made for identifying the 'median interventionist position' in the mid 1970s with Meade 'up-dating' of his earlier book in his *'The Intelligent Radical's Guide to Economic Policy'* (1975). The aims of policy are broadly the same but the constraints on maximising them, particularly recurrent balance of payments crises and growing labour militancy in the late 1960s, colour the discussion of policy instruments. Even though it is clearly recognised that unemployment may be structural in nature and is not simply the result of a deficiency in demand, Meade sees the remedies in measures to promote labour mobility which eschew selective intervention. The only case of a structural policy requiring selective subsidies which Meade advocates concerns support for science and technology but the object here is to make their benefits available to small firms so that they can compete more effectively, and this is done by compensating firms for the state acquisition of patent rights. It may be claimed that Meade ignores one important characteristic of the 'median' position in the mid-1970s, namely the concern at the poor performance of the British economy, but even in this respect, a 'median position' could fairly be described as one in which fiscal policy would be used to promote a rise in the proportion of resources devoted to investment with possibly some discrimination in favour of investment in manufacturing in order to reap the benefits of economies of scale. The overriding factor which prevents Meade and others with similar views from supporting selective subsidisation of firms is derived from their concern to avoid measures which would prevent industrialised countries such as the UK and BRD from reaping the benefits of free trade. ' . . . it is not possible for the developed industrialised countries to bind themselves to a strict and effective free-trade code . . . and at the same time to intervene in their national economies (by taxes, subsidies or other means) to encourage or discourage any particular line of consumption or production on social grounds.' [Meade (1975), p.141]

3.16 As we shall record later, selective intervention grew apace in the UK economy, particularly from the late 1960s onwards until today it is a major facet of UK economic policy, though it may be argued that the Conservative Government (1970-74) adopted a policy of structural intervention with some reluctance, and are committed to dismantling the subsidy system developed by the Labour Government (1974-79). Why then had structural policy been so widely accepted by politicians and is so far out of line with 'median' thinking? One interpretation which will need further consideration in a later chapter, is that the 'welfare function' identified by the median economist is far removed from that of governments which will only follow his dictates if they conform to the political objective of keeping the government in power. Selective measures dramatise more effectively than general measures the action of individual Ministers responsible for their operation, thus improving their party's image and their individual chances of further promotion within the Cabinet. Indeed, such a reason may appeal to all politicians and not simply those who have an ideological commitment to selectivity. Another interpretation is that the 'median' economist view and the 'mode' (i.e. the most commonly held view among economists) are no longer close together. Looking along the interventionist spectrum, economists are no longer clustered in the middle but are polarised, so that the distribution of their views forms a bi-modal rather than uni-modal pattern. There is no longer consensus supporting planning through the price mechanism. Policy-minded economists are either arguing that capitalism has failed or that it is not being given the chance to operate properly. Such sharp divisions must reduce the influence of economists on policy. If, as in the case of structural policy in particular, the disagreements reflect a different technical view of the performance of private industry, actual or potential, then politicians can cheerfully disregard the scientific pretensions of economics. If the disagreements are in part ideological, then politicians will seek economists' advice only as apologists.

3.17 Keynes in his Preface to the German Edition of *The General Theory* already referred to placed his faith in German acceptance of his work not only on the experiences in planning then being undergone in the late 1930s but also on the lack of grip of the 'orthodox tradition' in Germany and rejection of formal theoretical analysis. He then wrote ' . . . can I hope to overcome Germany's economic agnosticism? Can I persuade German economists that methods of formal analysis have something to contribute to the interpretation of contemporary events and to the moulding of contemporary policy? After all, it is German to like a theory.' [Keynes (1973)] Apart from the fact that Keynes was not a particularly reliable historian of economic thought, it is ironical that the most influential body of economic doctrine in Germany for many years after the Second World War was derived from the 'orthodox tradition' which Keynes rejected and was markedly anti-Keynesian, reacting in a very different way than Keynes did against the planning experiences of the 1930s. On the other hand, as we shall discover, the inventors of the *Sozialmarktwirtschaft* have had not such a different view of the pretensions of structural policies as our 'median' economist in the UK as is frequently believed.

3.18 The influence of historical events on recent German economic thought is substantial and, at the cost of being superficial, some account of them must be given. Industrialisation in the late 19th century was achieved through extensive state control, state participation in industrial projects and investments and indeed with extensive state ownership of industry. Encouragement of industrial concentration and the creation of monopolies was provided by incentives to merge and the promotion of cartels whilst the economic climate was decidedly protectionist and blatantly opposed to doctrines of free trade. The adoption of multiple exchange rates in 1931, in the attempt to control the balance of trade, represented a fundamental step in the direction of a centrally planned economy, necessitating as it did a whole series of price controls, exchange controls, export licences and the like. Comprehensive price controls, adopted in 1936, were an attempt to control inflation whilst simultaneously pursuing expansionary (and remarkably Keynesian monetary and fiscal policies in the interest of employment creation. The result, predictably enough, was eventual recourse to rationing, shortages, blackmerkets and suppressed inflation. The resulting mis-allocation of resources hardened attitudes towards central government controls and intervention and also against Keynesian economic policy prescriptions. Moreover, in this latter regard and despite the severity of the depression years when unemployment topped 7 million, the dominant fear remained inflation arising from the experience of the 1919-23 period. Price stability financing was ruled out as an orthodox policy instrument. In short, interventionist policies became associated with both massive resource mis-allocation and also massive inefficiency. The experiences of the 1930s were confirmed by the attempts of the Allies in the early post-war period to 'suppress' inflation by price control coupled with rationing of both producer and consumer goods and which were, as Meade pointed out, manifestly unsuccessful.

3.19 The famous and familiar doctrine of the 'social market economy' is first and foremost not 'laisser-fairist'. While it is believed the decentralised decision making by many economic units is the economic system which best guarantees individual freedom, this 'economic order' (Wirtschaftsordnung) can only be achieved by state action [See Eucken (1955), Böhm (1971), and for a most useful short account in English, see Zweig (1976)]. Indeed, the 'economic order' requires constitutional guarantees which vouchsafe individual rights and which enable the state to enforce competition. Immediately two vivid contrasts with British thinking should be noticed. The first is that the idea of specifying a 'social welfare function' to be maximised by government is totally alien. The state does not lay down any specific economic goals translatable into economic magnitudes such as the growth rate, unemployment rate, etc, but only enforces the rules which must govern individuals' pursuit of their own interests. In consequence, in the earlier statement of the Euckenkreis, collection of economic data designed to identify movements in macro-variables were frowned upon[2] and today latter-day members of the Eucken or Ordokreis are extremely sceptical of even global economic forecasting [see, for example, Watrin (1978)]. The second is the attention paid to embodying constraints on the action of the legislature in respect of economic policies by the so-called Basic Law (Grundgesetz) which must be subject to interpretation by the BRD constitutional court. Despite the influence of the Ordokreis economists and lawyers on the formulation of the Grundgesetz it is regarded as an open question in the BRD whether in guaranteeing fundamental rights and freedoms of the individual the Grungesetz specifically demands the guarantee of a social market economy. [For summary of discussion, see Lampert (1976)]. The point remains that the evolution of the constitutional position with respect to economic matters is regarded as a matter of fundamental importance, and we shall illustrate this point later.

3.20 The need to promote competition (Wettbewerbsordnung) was recognised in the back-up given to the grundgesetz by an elaborate law against restriction of competition [Gesetz gegen Wettbewerbsbeschränkung (1958)] but again it is clear in its operation and in the writings of its inspires that it was not expect-ted to aim at anything more than 'workable' competition — the de-nationalisation of the Bundesbahn was never contemplated whereas the nationalisation of British railways in the same era was surrounded by considerable controversy! The law and its supporters could therefore countenance subsidies to particular industries when faced with 'unfair' competition from abroad. Shipbuilding, relatively efficient compared with foreign competitors, has been a case in point and is considered in detail in Chapter 5. Certain forms of assistance to small firms might be necessary to counterbalance market imperfections which might prevent their survival and growth. [For detailed study, see Bannock (1976)]. In short, there is some similarity between this position and the 'median' position of British economists in the immediate post-war position. Selective subsidy policies were designed not to promote macro-economic aims but to promote the aims of the competitive order, and were to be strictly limited in their scope.

3.21 The story of the *Wirtschaftswunder* of the post-war German era is well known and partly documented in the comparative indicators of economic performance in Chapter 2. However, it is not comparative performance but expectations based on past performance within an economy which will be a principal determinant of attitudes to government policy. The move towards a 'social welfare function' approach to economic policy in the BRD was the direct result of the fear of growing inflation imported from abroad, but this was 'solved' by undervaluation of the exchange rate and strict control of aggregate demand which resulted in a fall in the growth rate and a rise in unemployment in the early 1960s. The recession of 1967 served as a warning signal to governments seeking electoral support and the famous Stabilisation and Growth Law(Gesetz für Förderung der Stabilität und Wachstum der Wirtschaft) was passed in 1967. It is important for our discussion in five respects. Firstly, the Law explicitly recognises four major national objectives of economic policy — promotion of economic growth, a high and stable level of employment, price stability and balance of payments equilibrium. Secondly, it recognises that the achievement of these objectives would require an extension in the armoury of macro-economic policy weapons including the use of 'Keynesian' fine turing and demand management techniques — what was earlier described as 'Globalsteurerung der Wirtschaft' (see Chapter 1, paragraph 1). Thirdly, it explicitly defined a role for selective aids to industry, distinguishing between subsidies and financial aids (including tax concessions) to promote structural adaptation and aids to promote productivity. Fourthly, it consolidated the system of economic reporting begun in the early sixties, giving a major role to the Council of Economic Experts (Sachverständigenrat) and the Bi-annual Report on Subsidies. Fifthly, the Law provided for tri-partite discussions between economic experts, the trade unions and employers to discuss the global aims of policy — the so-called 'concerted action' clause.

3.22 Prominent successors to Eucken and Böhm among the Ordokreis, have maintained that the 1967 Stability and Growth Law spelt the end of the 'social market economy', and have been very critical of the technical basis of this move towards 'global' macro-economic policy. [A notable example is Hans Otto Lenel (1971).] Here attention is confined to the issue of structural policy, leaving until later speculation over the broader question. Interestingly enough, the period from the passing of the Stability and Growth Law and the present is characterised by strong resistance by successive governments to any attempt to extend subsidy policy to promote short-term employment ends and to buttress unprofitable enterprises. If anything, the reporting system on subsidies offered the opportunity for more systematic monitoring of selective aid to industry and, furthermore, the government were required to include in the bi-annual reports proposals to reduce and even to eliminate financial assistance. While it is true that the claims of *Strukturpolitik* have been advanced more persistently in the light of rising unemployment and slower growth in the late 1970s[3], the Council of Economic Experts, whose terms of reference were specifically extended to include study of structural changes in the economy, have adopted a critical stance towards the expansion of selective aids to industry even as short-term remedies for the employment problem.

3.23 Summing up, it has been observed that structural policy, in the narrow sense of selective aid measures, has had only limited support from economists in both the BRD and UK and has not been promoted as a major weapon of the policy armoury. In contrast, whereas the economists' position is much in line with actual government policy in the BRD, this is far from being the case in the UK where selective aid has been increasingly used. In seeking to throw light on the interplay between economic ideas and actual policies, the analysis has ignored some of the more radical aspects of the policy debate such as the growing demand in both countries for 'steering' of investment (Investitionslenkung) and the ways in which economic analysis has been used to analyse the actual results of applying structural intervention. These and related matters will be taken up in Chapter 8 when the longer run consequences of structural policies are considered.

D. The ranking of policy objectives

3.24 It would be remarkable if the differences in economic philosophy and economic experience outlined above did not give rise to differences with regard to policy objectives. In fact, although there is a superficial similarity with regard to macro-economic objectives stated in general terms, as for example a consensus on the need for economic growth, full employment, price stability and so forth, there remains considerable disagreement over how these goals should be defined and in particular over which goals should be accorded priority in the event of conflict. In the United Kingdom, for example, the current price stability objective is summarised in the attempt to reach 'single figure inflation'. In the BRD, adherence to such permissiveness would be tantamount to political suicide. In both countries, there has been a regrettable, if understandable, tendency to state policy objectives in vague terms and usually it is politically advantageous to ignore issues of conflict. Nonetheless, it is possible to identify three major macro-economic goals with reference to structural policy where there has been a broad measure of agreement.

3.25 *Employment.* The major objective of selective industrial support to UK industry has been to maintain employment by financial backing for otherwise failing firms. While such measures have become frequent only since 1971, structural policies aimed at the planned contraction of industries date back to the inter-war period. In similar vein, by far the most important form of selective structural aid in West Germany is that, which from the standpoint of the social market philosophy is the least desirable, which seeks to shore up an industry and artificially maintain it, at least in the short period, in the face of intense competition and a decline in world demand. Such aid, categorised as aid for *adjustment and maintenance*, seeks to minimise the social distress consequent upon closure; on a more ambitious level it has sought to keep an industry alive until world demand recovers. Both motives have played a role in the aid granted to the shipping industry, for example. The pressure for such assistance has been increasing, both from employer organisations and from trade unions and there appears little doubt that such forms of aid will become more important and more permanent in the future, despite the commitment to the market economy and the pledges contained in the official subsidy report to eliminate such assistance at the earliest possible date.

3.26 *Promotion of 'future-orientated' industries.* The encouragement of investment in fixed capital, research and development has been adopted in both countries to stimulate long term economic growth by supporting 'high technology' industries such as aerospace, computers and electronics. The justification for such support lies in the belief that these industries generate spin-offs which are essential for the overall rate of growth but which face extremely heavy research and development costs which may have no known or a highly uncertain financial return. Because such investment entails high risk for the individual investor and yet promises the prospect of substantial external benefits for society at large, it is considered that the private capital market would furnish insufficient funds in the absence of government intervention. Selective assistance to these industries possibly also stems from the awareness that the advanced economies possess a comparative advantage in these sectors faced with the growing industrial competition in the more traditional manufactures from the emerging nations.

3.27 *Encouragement of exports and import substitution.* In the UK, subsidies to companies making an important contribution to exports have been particularly important as found in the support given to the motor vehicle, shipbuilding and aluminium industries. In West Germany, support for import substituting industries has been strategic rather than balance of payments oriented, as in the case of support to the domestic coal and oil producing industries.

3.28 Of these three objectives, there is little doubt that the employment goal has become the dominant one and the balance of payments and growth objectives are regarded more properly as secondary means to meet this end. In the United Kingdom, for example, improvement in the balance of payments has been looked upon as a necessary pre-requisite to sustain full employment levels of imports and indeed, it is the employment goal which underlies the persistent advocacy for import controls. In the BRD, growth is looked upon as essential in the creation of additional employment opportunities particularly in view of the secular decline of more labour intensive industry and the continued growth of the labour force. It will be noted that a price stability objective does not enter into the goals of selective structural policy and indeed this is what one would expect. The decision to grant aid to a specific firm or industry *per se*, has little relevance for the general price level. What relevance there is lies in the manner in which selective structural aid is to be financed and, accordingly, the price stability objective emerges as one of the major constraints upon the extent to which such selective policies can be pursued. As we shall see, differences emerge between the two economies with respect to the importance of this constraint. It is perhaps of greater interest to enquire into the differences in policy objectives in the respective economies — differences which do much to explain the divergent attitudes to selective structural assistance.

3.29 *De-industrialisation.* In the United Kingdom the objectives enumerated above have coalesced into one — that of preventing de-industrialisation. Selective aid has been granted to maintain admittedly inefficient and overmanned industries in the belief that it is imperative to maintain the industrial base. It is the industrial sectors which produce marketable output and which have to generate a surplus to provide for the consumption and investestment of those sectors producing non-marketable output, (particularly the public sector) and also to finance the supply to net exports. It follows that if the industrial base experiences a relative decline in the wake of comparative growth of the non-industrial sectors, then either exports or investment in the productive manufacturing sectors must fall with deleterious consequences for future growth and employment rates. It is noteworthy that over the period 1961-73, the percentage growth rate of the non-industrial sector (excluding agriculture) in the United Kingdom was about 32 per cent — approximately double that experienced in Western Germany[4]. In part, de-industrialisation reflects the relative ease, and electoral appeal, of moving out of recession by stimulating central and local government employment even at the cost of creating structural imbalance. It is in order to arrest this movement that selective aid has been granted to maintain firms that otherwise would have been rendered bankrupt. Similar reasoning justifies interventionist policies to aid export sectors hit by world recession (shipbuilding) or industry confronted by excessively subsidised competition elsewhere (steel). De-industrialisation has not been of any particular concern to the West German Government and for the very sound reason that this economy has not yet experienced any such notable development (c.f. Chapter 2, Section D). A recent empirical study found no switch into the tertiary sectors in Germany and concluded 'that the "Three Sector Hypothesis" does not apply to the Bundesrepublik' [Oppenländer (1977)]. Other studies demonstrated a strong swing from the production of consumption goods into the production of capital goods. This wide disparity in the comparative growth rates of the non-industrial sector is probably the most important single factor accounting for a much greater commitment to selective intervention in the United Kingdom. In addition, measures proposed by the EEC in response to world wide recession have taken on an increasingly protectionist attitude, strongly opposed by Bonn, and yet implying selective assistance in certain cases. Not only does the Bonn government feel compelled to abide by the EEC decisions, but only by entering into such decisions does the government receive any benefit from the common budget to which the BRD is the major contributor.

3.30 This commitment to the goal of competition also reveals itself in the strong opposition expressed by the German authorities to so-called 'hidden' forms of aid which might arise for example in the provisions of government procurement policies. The ability to assist industries in this way is in any event limited, owing to the independence exercised by the Länder governments in their purchasing policies but, in addition, precise rules often govern the tendering and acceptance of contracts. In the case of the government purchase of computers, for example, the tender request will apply equally to *European* producers. If the tender is competitive then there is a strong 'recommendation' to accept regardless of origin. This stipulation does reflect in part, a desire to avoid US domination but nonetheless illustrates the spirit underlying government purchases. Hidden forms of aid, as for example losses incurred by a nationalised undertaking supplying intermediate inputs to a specific industry, are held to be in conflict with the German liberal attitude to free trade and in this respect German officials have shown themselves to be strongly critical of what they regard as the highly protectionist policies being pursued in France and in the UK.

3.31 There can be little doubt that the differing attitudes to the importance of maintaining competition explains a good deal of the discrepancy in attitudes to structural policy in Britain and West Germany. But equally, these attitudes are partly determined by the prior concern (or lack of it) with the process of de-industrialisation. In the UK, the creation of monopoly power has sometimes been seen as essential to the survival of the industry and maintenance of the industrial base is looked upon, rightly or wrongly, as the key to employment creation and balance of payments equilibria.

3.32 *The inflation constraint.* As previously indicated, both countries pursue price stability objectives independently of structural policy. Nonetheless, the interpretation accorded to the price objective carries implications for the scope of structural policy. For expositional purposes, this question can best be pursued with reference to the familiar Phillips Curve which postulates a trade-off between inflation and employment objectives[5]. The impact of world recession, reinforced in Germany's case by the gradual but persistent appreciation of the Deutschmark, renders full employment unattainable at levels of inflation judged acceptable. Hence the rationale for selective structural policy which conceptually may be regarded as an attempt to promote a favourable inward shift of the Phillips Curve. Given the objective of full employment, it follows that the commitment to (or need for) selective measures will be determined by the position of the Phillips Curve upon the one hand and the permissiveness of the authorities in delineating the inflation objective upon the other. Despite the assumed 'superior' Phillips relationship in the case of the German economy, the lower tolerance of inflation may make it at first sight more imperative to have recourse to selective interventionist measures. Diagrammatically, this situation is illustrated in Figure I where the assumed 'permissible' inflation rates (of 3 and 10 per cent respectively) render the German economy further away from the employment goal than her UK counterpart.

3.33 It is therefore understandable why members of the Ordokreis have argued against the exact specification of economic policy goals, particularly, economic growth. Too much attention to specific targets raises expectations and creates the impression that governments have more control over economic forces than they actually have. They emphasise the growth in output at the cost of consumer choice. Accordingly, in periods when world markets are no longer rapidly expanding and structural change cannot be promoted so readily by small adjustments in prices and wages, commitment to both high levels of employment and growth and a low inflation rate may tempt governments into the extension of selective aids. At the time of writing, it seems more than likely that structural policies, at least in this narrow sense, will become an increasing element in the BRD's general economic policy and that the answer to the question — is there still a Social Market Economy? — might in the not too distant future be — No. However, this is to anticipate later argument.

E.   Political and administrative background

3.34 Political and administrative influences on selective intervention differ considerably between the UK and BRD. In the United Kingdom, at least until the mid-1970s, successive governments of different political complexion enjoyed satisfactory working majorities. Accordingly, though attention would have to be paid in the run-up to elections to the influence of the floating voters, sufficient weight could be given in policy measures to political ideology in the evolution of economic policies, though this is not to say that in the case of structural policies there was not a considerable area of agreement. In contrast, the economic controversies which have divided the Social Democrats and the Free Democrats in the BRD dictated a degree of compromise in their policies so long as they operated as a coalition. Perhaps of more importance, in the highly centralised UK, the economic policies of the central government dominate government influence over the economy. While local government expenditure has formed as large a proportion of total public authorities' expenditure as in the BRD, the large proportion of this expenditure financed from the centre and controlled by central government regulatory legislation has effectively prevented local authorities from operating independent economic policies. Consequently, regional economic policy in the UK emanates from the centre.

3.35 In contrast, the federal structure of BRD grants considerable economic power to the state governments which may be used to counter and offset the impact of Federal policy. The disposition of the Federal

Figure One

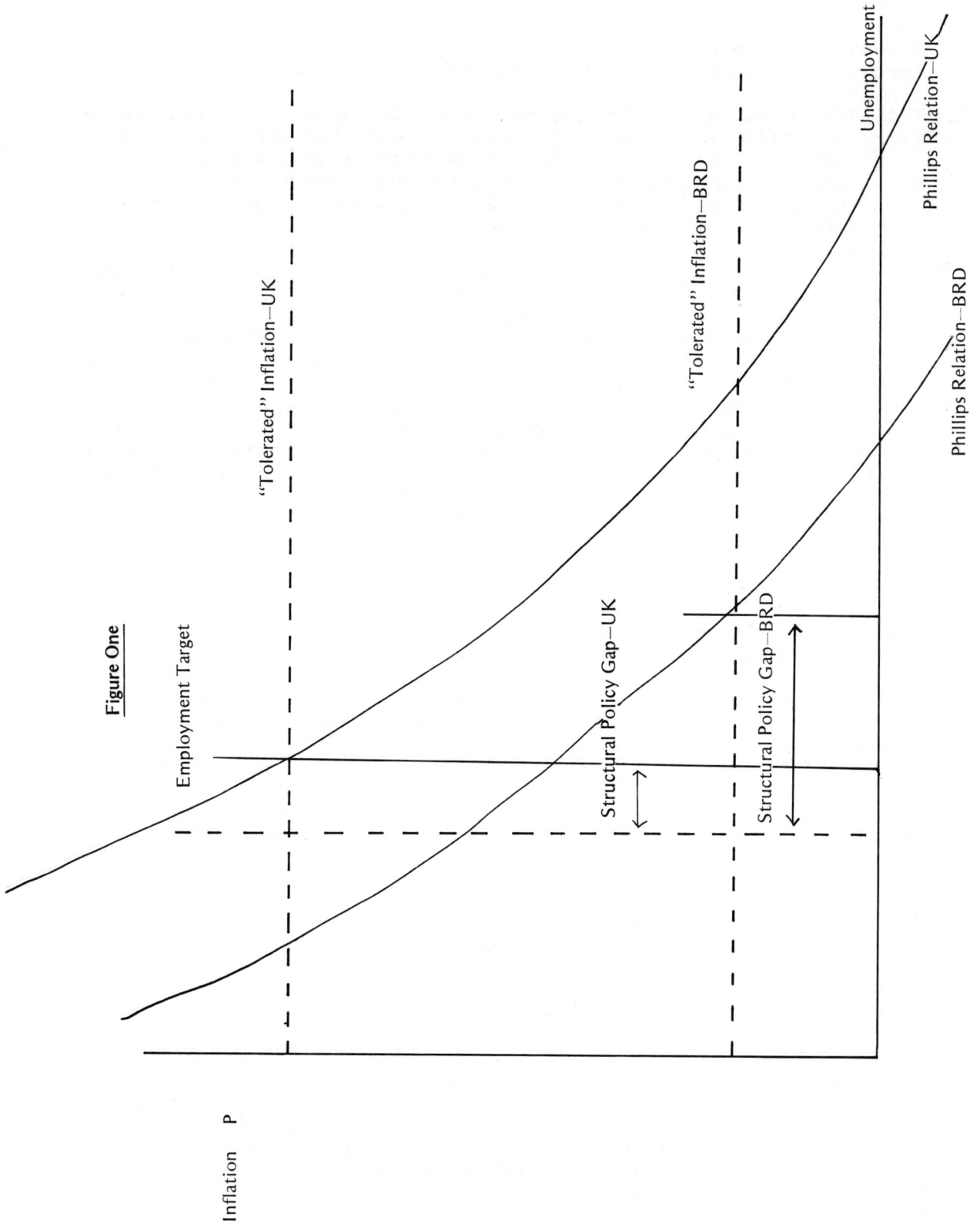

Inflation   P

Employment Target

"Tolerated" Inflation—UK

"Tolerated" Inflation—BRD

Unemployment

Phillips Relation—UK

Phillips Relation—BRD

Structural Policy Gap—UK

Structural Policy Gap—BRD

Government to exercise overall economic control has been accordingly weakened — as indeed in some cases so has the need.

3.36 Secondly, and in marked contrast with UK experience, selective intervention in Germany appears far less 'ad hoc'. In part, this is to be explained by the fact that those charged with the operation of structural policy in West Germany feel a strong obligation to conform with the decisions and grounds established by the relevant EEC Commissions and the directives emanating from OECD. The importance of OECD lies in the fact that it provides the forum for discussion with Japan whom the Germans regard as vital to the formulation of concerted policies for world trade and more specifically to any tangible agreement on world shipping policy. Government measures to aid selected industries have to have advance registration in Brussels and require formal approval before they can be put into effect. Such action is not looked upon as a pure formality and there is a strong commitment to adhere to the rules and to avoid seeking escape clauses which conflict with the spirit of the agreement. At the same time, it is probably the case that emphasising the omnipotence of Brussels carries certain political advantages when the government wishes to limit its intervention.

3.37 Confirmation of this view is found in regulation of aid with respect to time periods and formal guidelines. In the case of aid to shipyards, for example, the government favoured a block grant procedure, fixed in amount over a four year period, and allocated to shipyards on fulfilment of contract according to a predetermined formula. Ministerial discretion is thus curtailed imparting a certain inflexibility to the policy, but the compensatory advantage lies in the fact that the shipyards know precisely the form of assistance they can expect and can negotiate with potential purchasers accordingly. An element of continuity is thus introduced into the system of support and unlike British procedures is less likely to be jeopardised by a change of government.

F. Conclusion

3.38 This chapter has endeavoured to explain the developments in structural policies in both countries in terms of a general policy model. The differences in policy at different points of time within a country and differences between countries are derived from many influences — differences in policy aims and trade-offs between aims, differing political and economic constraints and differing technical judgments about the efficacy of the various forms of financial aid. Two points stand out in reviewing this survey of influences. The first is the substantial scepticism, until recently in the UK, on technical grounds expressed by economists in both countries about the value of selective aid as a means of achieving macro-economic objectives, though their value judgments differ considerably. The second is the much greater influence of such scepticism on actual policy in the BRD than in the UK, though, as indicated, this influence must be sensitive to the view taken by policymakers of future economic prospects and the effect these prospects will have on the choice of alternative policy instruments. These points will form one of the main themes of later discussion.

Notes to Chapter 3

1. Keynes did not make it easy for German liberals, some of whom suffered at the hands of the Nazis, to accept any part of *The General Theory*. The Preface to the German Edition contains the following passage: '...the theory of output as a whole, which is what the following book purports to provide, is much more easily adapted to the conditions of a totalitarian state, than is the theory of the production and distribution of a given output produced under conditions of free competition and a large measure of laissez-faire.' [Keynes (1973)]. On the other hand, 'Euckenkreis' economists took no account of developments in Keynes's own thinking after 1936 and his own 'generalisation' of *The General Theory* to cover the economics of inflation as well as deflation. For a typical outburst against Keynes, see Hahn (1949). As late as 1952 the editor of this study was still trying to dispel the 'myth of Keynesianism' in an article of that title [Peacock (1952)]. Finally, it is interesting to note that the harsh treatment meted out to Keynes contrasts with the very sympathetic review of the German edition of Meade's book in ORDO, the annual collection of articles produced by members of the Euckenkreis [Irmler (1951)]. This was possibly the result of Meade's own criticisms of the suppressed inflation policy followed by the Allied Military Governments in West Germany before the currency reform of 1949.

2. The editor of this volume attended a conference in 1958 at which Ludwig v. Mises, one of the inspirers of the Ordokreis, argued that those who employed the concept of the national income might be suspected of being national socialists.

3. In 1971 the BRD government established an important commission to study the possibility of promoting technical and social change 'within the framework of a market economy' which included representatives of trade unions, employers as well as technical experts. A majority were in favour of the extension of structural

policy particularly to promote technical change but provided the subsidised sectors were competitive in the longer run. A minority were strongly opposed to any extension of subsidy policy. See *Gutachten der Kommission für wirtschaftlichen und sozialen Wandel* (1976).

4. These estimates are taken from Bacon and Eltis (1976). The underlying argument, it may be noted, is not too dissimilar from the thesis previously argued by Kaldor (1966) that economic growth requires the transfer of labour from agriculture, characterised by diminishing returns into manufacturing activity where increasing returns to scale prevail.

5. The UK in 1978 experienced approximately 8 per cent inflation combined with 1.5 million unemployed; this compares with figures of approximately 4 per cent and 1 million in the BRD. Very crudely, this suggests an inferior Phillips relation for the UK.

References

Bacon, R. and Eltis, W. (1976), Op cit.

Bannock, Graham (1976), *The Smaller Business in Britain and Germany*, Wilton House Publications, London.

Boehm, Franz (1971), "Freiheit und Ordnung in der Marktwirtschaft", *Jahrbuch für die Ordnung von Wirtschaft und Gesellschaft* (ORDO) Volume 2, Helmut Küpper, Düsseldorf und München.

Eucken, Walter (1955), Op cit.

Hahn, Albert (1949), "Die Grundirrtümer in Lord Keynes 'General Theory', *Jahrbuch für die Ordnung von Wirtschaft und Gesellschaft* (ORDO) Volume 2, Helmut Küpper, Düsseldorf und Munchen.

Irmler, H. (1951), "Der Mittlere Weg", *Jahrbuch für die Ordnung von Wirtschaft und Gesellschaft* (ORDO) Volume 5, Helmut Küpper, Düsseldorf und München.

Kaldor, Nicholas (now Lord) (1966), *Causes of the Slow Rate of Economic Growth of the United Kingdom*, Cambridge University Press

Keynes, Lord (1973), *The Collected Writings of John Maynard Keynes: Volume VII – The General Theory of Employment, Interest and Money.* Preface to the German Edition, p.xxv. Macmillan for the Royal Economic Society.

Kommission für wirtschaftlichen und sozialen Wandel (1976), *Wirtschaftlichen und Sozialer Wandel in der Bundesrepublik Deutschland: Gutachten der Kommission* published by the Bundesregierung.

Lampert, Heinz (1976), *Die Wirtschafts = und Sozialordnung der Bundesrepublik Deutschland*, 5th Edition, Part III. Günter Olzog Verlag, München-Wien.

Lenel, Hans Otto (1971), "Haben wir noch eine soziale Marktwirtschaft?" ORDO, Volume 22

Meade, James (1948), *Planning and the Price Mechanism*, George Allen and Unwin, London

Meade, James (1975), *The Intelligent Radical's Guide to Economic Policy*, George Allen and Unwin, London

Oppenländer, J.H. (1977), Op. cit.

Peacock, Alan (1952), "Der Mythos des Keynesianismus" *Frankfuter Allgemeine Zeitung* 16 August.

Sachverständigenrat zur Begutachtung der Gesamtwirtschaftlichen Entwicklung (1976), *Zeit zum Investieren: Jahresgutachten 1976-77*, Verlag W. Kohlhammer Stuttgart und Mainz . . . .

Watrin, Christian (1978), "Grenzen der Staatstätigkeit: Das Beispiel der vorauschauenden und der lenkenden Strukturpolitik" in Besters, H. (Editor), *op. cit.*

Zweig, Konrad (1976), *Germany through Inflation and Recession*, The Centre for Policy Studies, London

CHAPTER 4

A SURVEY OF STRUCTURAL POLICIES AND THEIR EVOLUTION IN THE BRD AND UK

A. Introduction

4.1 Chapter 3 discussed some of the factors which account for the divergence in the development of structural policies between the UK and BRD. Among the more important were:

— the greater severity of economic problems in the UK, in particular balance of payments weakness and an insufficient rate of industrial expansion which has made it difficult to absorb the labour displaced by declining industries and increasing productivity, which has created a greater need for structural policies in the UK;
— the influence of a more market-orientated economic philosophy in the BRD as compared with the growing
— prominence of interventionist thinking in the UK;
— the different priorities accorded to the common policy objectives of employment, balance of trade and growth in the two countries;
— differences in political and administrative structure and constraints.

In this chapter it is shown how these factors have influenced the development and operation of structural policies in the BRD and UK by describing the main features of structural policies.

4.2 In common with elsewhere in the report, practical considerations necessitate concentration on particular areas of structural policy. As explained in paragraph 1.8, the main interest is in structural policies which aim at the achievement of macro-economic goals, and hence we exclude structural policies aimed primarily at influencing the allocation of resources to particular sectors such as housing policies, transport policies, health and social services. In both countries the most prominent field of structural policy since the mid-1960s has been selective industrial intervention, particularly financial assistance for individual firms and industries. It is this area of structural policy upon which attention is concentrated, an emphasis further justified by the fact that, in relation to regional development policies, agricultural policies and competition policies, selective industrial intervention is an area of structural policy which has, until recently, received scant attention from economists.

B. Structural policy in the BRD

4.3 *The principles of structural policy.* Before 1967 structural intervention by the BRD in industry was limited and consisted primarily of a collection of *ad hoc* measures designed to meet specific problems. In the immediate post-war period government intervention was necessitated by the problems of reconstruction followed by the need for regional assistance measures in the areas affected by partition. The problems of certain basic but unprofitable industries, notably coal mining and the railways influenced government provision of financial assistance, as did the need to develop certain technologically-based industries such as aircraft and atomic power. In general, however, structural interventions were restricted and structural policy was not viewed as a means for achieving such national economic objectives as growth and employment. The limited role of structural policies reflected an antipathy towards state intervention in the economy which is indicated by the avoidance of the term 'subsidy' in policy statements during this period.

4.4 The 1967 Stabilisation and Growth Law established the principles of state intervention for the achievement of macro-economic goals. The motivation for increased state intervention was the slow-down in the rate of growth of the German economy during the 1960s accompanied by stronger cyclical fluctuations and, in particular, the recession of 1967. As already pointed out, the Act set out the macro-economic objectives of policy as

— stability of the price level,

— a high level of employment,

— external balance, and

— a constant and acceptable rate of economic growth,

and established a policy framework in the form of Annual Economic Reports (Jahreswirtschaftsberichte). The Act in identifying the need for structural policies and the requirement that the Federal government should publish a separate Subsidies Report indicated the importance it attached to financial aids. The aims of structural financial aids were classified by the Act as:

i.   *structural maintenance* — the safeguarding of jobs and wages, the stabilisation and increase of producers' income and maintenance of production;

ii.   *structural adjustment* — the improvement of adjustment flexibility, the acceleration of adjustment procedures, reduction of excess capacity and avoidance of too precipitate adjustment; and

iii.   *productivity* — increasing sectoral growth potential and stimulating innovation.

4.5   Between 1968 and 1970 the framework and principles of structural intervention were established in four policy statements: *Principles of Regional and Sectoral Structural Policies* (Bundestagsdrucksache 1968), the *Principles of Structural Policy for Small and Middle-Sized Companies* (Bundestagsdrucksache 1970) and two *Structure Reports* (Bundestagsdrucksache 1969 and 1970).

4.6   Structural policies were designed to fulfil two objectives. First, promotion of growth, in which case the emphasis should be on 'future orientated' industries, the appropriate types of aid being productivity aid and adjustment aid to accelerate structural adjustments. Second, social objectives requiring the avoidance of unemployment and social tension and upheaval directed attention towards contracting industries by using maintenance aid to control structural adaptation and adjustment aid to alleviate the effects of structural adaptation. The emphasis of the policy outlines was heavily on adjustment and to a lesser extent on productivity aid, the role of maintenance aid being viewed as very limited. Selective policy measures (Marktsteuerung) should not supercede or prevent the operation of market forces, but should aim only to facilitate, accelerate or retard them, as was clearly established in the *Principles of Sectoral Structural Policy:*

—   'Primarily it is the managers of industry who are responsible for the necessary structural adaptation in the context of the freely competitive economy;

—   Special government aids and other interventions can only be used if the economic circumstances affecting individual sectors are undergoing excessively rapid and sharp changes, and if the process, left to itself, would result in undesirable economic and social consequences;

—   Government aids must take the form of help for self-help, and can be granted only if they will durably strengthen the competitive ability of the enterprises;

—   The aid must be of a temporary nature and digressive in character, and must not restrict the functional viability of free competition.' (OECD 1971, p.16)

4.7   Structural economic policies in the BRD have mainly involved the provision of financial incentives through grants, loans, interest remissions and tax concessions. These subsidies are provided primarily by the Federal government but also by the Länder and by local authorities. Administration of subsidies is undertaken by the following Federal ministries:

Federal Ministry for Economics (assistance to industry)
Federal Ministry for Transport (assistance to shipping, the railways and airlines)
Federal Ministry for Food, Agriculture and Forestry (agricultural support)
Federal Ministry for Town, Planning and Housing (assistance for housing and social infrastructure)

4.8   An additional source of financial assistance has been the European Recovery Programme established initially with US funds to administer reconstruction under the Marshall Plan. The ERP Special Fund now finances a number of different programmes, primarily those involving regional development, but also for environmental protection, labour market incentives and selective industrial schemes. Although financial incentives are the main tools of structural policies and indeed the only ones strictly compatible with the concept of the market economy, other forms of intervention are used the for the achievement of structural goals (e.g. the promotion of cartels, state guarantees for loans and the encouragement of industrial reorganisation).

4.9   Concentrating on government subsidies alone, the trend during the post-war period has been almost continuously upwards, reflecting a steady increase in government intervention in industry. For the period before 1966 estimates of financial assistance have been published by Zavlaris (1970). Although the coverage and classification of subsidies differs from that in the later Subsidy Reports, the figures reveal a remarkable growth in aid to industry and agriculture during the late 1950s and early 1960s (see Table 4.1). From 1966 official statistics of subsidies in the form of direct financial aid (grants and loans) and indirect financial aid (tax relief) are available in the bi-annual Subsidy Reports. The Reports cover the financial aids of the Federal Government and, since 1971, of the Länder and local authorities as well. The Reports exclude aid from the ERP and support for the railways and postal service. Included, however, are some financial aids to households in the form of housing subsidies and tax allowances. The subsidy payments are classified by:

i.   type of aid — maintenance, adjustment and productivity aid (see Table 4.2);

ii.   recipient sector — food agriculture and forestry, industry, transport and housing (see Table 4.3). Industrial aid is further broken down into particular programmes (see Table 4.4).

4.10   Table 4.2 shows an uninterrupted expansion of total subsidies between 1966 and 1978. The breakdown of total assistance between the various forms of aid — maintenance, adjustment and productivity — shows the importance of maintenance aid which accounted for about one half of direct subsidies and about 55 per cent of tax allowances up until 1974, after which the proportion of total aid devoted to maintenance fell. This predominance of maintenance support seems surprising in view of the statements of role and objectives of structural policy which have regarded the maintenance of particular industries as justifiable only in special circumstances. The breakdown of subsidies by sectors and programmes in Tables 4.3 and 4.4 sheds light upon the prominence of maintenance support: the major recipients of government aid have been agriculture, mining and industries located in less favoured regions. These subsidies have been devoted primarily to the maintenance of employment for social and strategic reasons.

4.11   As has been already noted, the main focus of our attention is on structural policy towards industry since industrial policy is the area of structural policy which is most closely related to the macro-economic goals of growth, employment and balance of payments. The breakdown of industrial support the Table 4.4 reveals the enormous growth in grants and loans to the mining and energy sectors between 1973 and 1975, the growth in assistance to aerospace and innovation and the regions and the recent growth in subsidies to manufacturing industry. Support for individual industries is discussed in some detail in the following sections.

4.12   *Regional structural policies.* Unlike the UK where regional problems have focused upon well-defined peripheral regions and declining industrial areas highly dependent upon coal mining and heavy industry, the regional problems of the BRD are more 'sub-regional', involving a number of different areas distributed across the whole country. During the 1950s the Federal Regional Promotion Programme (Regionales Förderungsprogramm) offered low interest loans to industry and local authorities in annually delineated 'emergency areas', while special assistance was provided to border areas under the Zonal Border Promotion Act of 1951. During the 1960s the emphasis of regional policy changed with the increasing problems which arose from the decline of the coal mining and iron and steel industries of the Ruhr, the criteria for regional assistance were changed and Federal policy placed more emphasis on infrastructure investment and less on assistance to industry.

4.13   The Programme for the Improvement of Regional Economic Structure (Gesetzüber die Gemeinschaftsaufgabe Verbesserung der regionalen Wirtschaftsstruktur) of October 1969 established a comprehensive approach to regional planning involving joint action by the Federal Government and the Länder in the identification and the assistance of less-developed regions through the establishment of joint planning committees. Regional policies have been formulated within a series of programmes. The current programme is the sixth plan covering 1977-80 [see Casper (1978)]. The principal incentives offered to industry are:

—   the investment allowance — a 7.5 per cent grant covering almost all investment projects in the assisted areas;
—   the investment grant — a discretionary investment grant of up to 25 per cent of project expenditure;
—   ERP 'soft loans' available to small and medium-sized firms for projects not eligible for investment allowances and grants; and
—   special depreciation allowances with an initial depreciation allowance of up to 50 per cent, these special allowances being available only in the Zonal Border Area.

4.14   In addition to financial support for private industry, regional policy measures include investment in infrastructure (notably roads and urban renewal), removal assistance for workers, retraining allowances and the freight transport subsidy for firms in the border area.

4.15   Of particular interest for the purpose of comparing UK and West German approaches to regional policy is the use of planning and quantitative criteria and measures in the regional policy of the BRD. Assisted areas are delineated periodically on the basis of a weighted combination of three indicators: shortage of employment opportunity, income per head and level of infrastructure. While legislation establishes the maximum rates of assistance, limitations and criteria for policy measures, implementation is undertaken under the annual framework plans (Rahmenplan) of each planning committee.

4.16   In addition to the basic framework of regional planning, special regional assistance is available under particular schemes, for example the particularly heavy support for West Berlin, the Tourist Promotion Areas and the 1975-77 employment creation scheme to counter the problems of redundancies at Volkswagen.

4.17   *Assistance to particular industries in the BRD.* Selective financial assistance has been offered to a relatively small number of extractive and manufacturing industries. The major recipients have been coal mining,

Table 4.1

GOVERNMENT ASSISTANCE TO INDUSTRY AND AGRICULTURE, 1951-65

		1951	1952	1953	1954	1955	1956	1957	1958	9 month year 1959	1960	1961	1962	1963	1964	DM millions 1965
I	Food, Agriculture P	274.7	440.6	416.8	552.7	676.3	1293.6	2011.2	2157.8	2360	2075	2870	3515	3830	3990	4610
	T									710	745	830	830	885	940	1240
										3070	2820	3700	4345	4715	4930	5850
II	Industrial Sector P	24	53	72	73	71	414	438	270	130	240	255	260	440	660	870
	T									2165	2530	3505	4030	5185	5530	5985
										2295	2770	3760	4290	5625	6170	6855
III	Transport* P	28.7	41.6	43.9	45.3	79.9	95.8	134.3	157.3	200	220	400	405	445	475	490
										650	560	570	500	600	670	855
										850	780	970	905	1045	1145	1345
IV	Housing P	50	56	62	72	64	78	131	129	140	145	295	335	385	465	525
	T									985	1155	1275	1415	1525	1655	1770
										1125	1300	1570	1750	1910	2120	2295

Notes: P — payments (grants and loans)
T — tax allowances
* — railways, airports, Lufthansa, shipping

Source: Zavlaris (1970)

Table 4.2

TOTAL FINANCING AID, 1966-78

	1966	1967	1968	1969	1970	1971	1972	1973	1974	1975	1976	1977	1978
Total Assistance (DM mn)	13,339	15,565	18,573	19,895	24,690	27,382	29,736	33,191	35,518	36,819	39,439	41,268	42,063
Total Grants & Loans (DM mn)	6,549	7,490	8,849	8,572	10,965	10,387	10587	12,325	13,212	13,700	15,278	16,833	16,554
Total Tax Allowances (Dm mn)	6,790	8,072	9,274	11,323	13,725	16,995	19,149	20,866	22,306	23,119	24,161	24,385	25,509
Maintenance (% of total)		55.2	61.2	49.1	55.4	51.1	50.1	50.7	51.1	35.2	33.8	35.2	34.5
Adjustment (% of total)		42.0	35.9	44.9	38.1	41.9	42.1	41.3	42.2	54.3	57.4	55.1	56.1
Productivity (% of total)		2.8	2.9	6.0	6.5	7.0	7.8	8.0	6.7	10.5	8.8	9.7	9.4

Note: In addition to assistance to companies, these figures include assistance to households, mainly in the form of subsidies for housing and saving.

Source: *Subsidy Reports*

50

Table 4.3

SUBSIDIES BY SECTOR, 1966-78

		1966	1967	1968	1969	1970	1971	1972	1973	1974	1975	1976	1977	1978
I Food, Agriculture and Forestry	P	2855	2678	2604	2158	2168	2687	2064	2850	3225	3218	3162	3136	3246
	T	873	881	1041	1186	1237	1483	1745	1917	1834	1995	1962	1998	2005
	Total	3828	3559	3645	3344	3405	4170	3809	4767	5059	5213	5124	5134	5251
II Industrial Sector (Without Transport)	P	692	1107	1230	867	1077	1024	1149	1605	2054	1935	1796	2272	2588
	T	2608	3799	3826	4800	5449	6686	7670	7926	8513	7613	7975	7784	8044
	Total	3300	4906	5056	5667	6526	7710	8819	9531	10567	9548	9771	10056	10632
II Transport (Without Rail)	P	111	103	158	261	275	302	458	568	601	672	871	912	1295
	T	484	491	680	807	833	846	847	967	1014	1061	1104	1146	1218
	Total	595	594	838	1068	1108	1148	1305	1535	1615	1733	1975	2058	2513

Notes: (1) Financial assistance by the EEC (mainly to agriculture) is excluded.
(2) Subsidy payments by the Federal government, Lander and local authorities are included. Since 1970 Federal tax allowances have amounted to a little under half of total allowances to the above sectors.

P = Direct payments (grants and loans)
T = Tax allowances

Source: *Seventh Subsidy Report*

Table 4.4

SUBSIDIES TO THE INDUSTRIAL SECTOR

DM millions

	1966	1967	1968	1969	1970	1971	1972	1973	1974	1975	1976	1977	1978
GRANTS AND LOANS													
— Mining	278	786	960	493	379	280	458	913	1215	889	770	991	1323
— Energy and raw materials	255	161	47	18	16	78	28	47	226	349	196	309	379
— Aerospace and innovation	26	48	84	122	186	248	256	269	294	289	297	354	321
— Special technological support	–	–	–	–	–	–	–	–	–	63	63	53	35
— Regional structural measures	43	55	78	136	240	190	215	167	146	159	244	228	193
— Other measures	90	57	61	98	256	228	192	209	173	186	226	337	337
TOTAL	692	1107	1230	867	1077	1024	1149	1605	2054	1935	1796	2272	2588
TAX ALLOWANCES													
— Mining	235	219	349	350	361	363	346	172	355	292	287	277	287
— of which Federal	88	79	120	125	153	148	139	77	58	130	127	123	125
— Regional structural measures	1135	2195	2305	3017	3470	4490	5343	5790	6255	5595	6183	5900	6175
— of which Federal	419	1323	1396	1624	1811	2306	2653	2916	3110	2795	3114	2990	3097
— Banking	569	680	433	454	492	570	598	535	64	643	358	414	444
— of which Federal	156	183	107	115	196	231	244	210	260	294	154	156	171
— General industry	669	705	739	979	1126	1263	1383	1429	1339	1083	1117	1193	1138
— of which Federal	264	246	261	286	465	524	577	561	536	410	416	447	498
TOTAL	2608	3799	3826	4800	5449	6686	7670	7926	8513	7613	7975	7784	8044
of which Federal	927	1831	1884	2150	2625	3209	3613	3746	4064	3629	3811	3716	3891

Source: *Seventh Subsidy Report*

mineral oil production, shipbuilding, nuclear energy, aerospace, computers and electronics. The objectives in supporting these industries have been to reduce dependence on overseas supplies of strategically important inputs (notably in the case of the energy industries), to prevent excessive increases in unemployment (in the case of coal mining and shipbuilding) and to encourage innovation through supporting R&D (aerospace, computers and electronics). Policies towards the shipbuilding (and shipping) industries and the computers industry are examined in the following two chapters, the main features of structural policies towards the other industries are described below.

4.18   *The coal mining industry* of the BRD is the sole German example of an industry in long-term decline which has received maintenance assistance from the Federal government on a large scale. Government intervention was prompted by the declining demand for coal which began with the world recession in 1958 and continued throughout the 1960s. The measures introduced were:

—   an import tariff on coal (1959 Coal Customs Duty);
—   a subsidy for the transportation of coal (1960);
—   taxes on heating oil (1960); and
—   restrictions on the use of heating oils including stock piling obligations and import duties.

In addition, measures were introduced to relieve the regional problems associated with the decline in the number of coal miners.

4.19   The Law on Adjustment and Restructuring of Coal Mining (1968) introduced a comprehensive framework of government intervention and state aid directed towards the structural reorganisation of the industry. A Federal Commissioner for Coal Mining was appointed with powers to allocate production between mines, guide investment and promote rationalisation and concentration. Under the influence of the Commissioner the greater part of the industry merged into three companies: Ruhrkohle AG, Eschweiler Bergwerksverein and Saarbergwerke AG (owned jointly by the Federal Government and Saarland). During the 1970s the principal direct financial support for coal mining has been in adjustment aid for investment, reorganisation and closures while the principal maintenance support has been in the form of taxes on competing sources of energy (notably the mineral oil tax and *Kohlepfennig* paid by electricity consumers) and voluntary and mandatory requirements for the electricity and steel industries to purchase domestic coal. The rapidly increasing price of crude oil since 1974 has reinforced the Government's efforts to maintain its coal industry. In recent years the coal industry has been hard hit, however, by the recession in the steel industry. Support for 1978 totalled about DM5,000 mn including the additional Federal and Länder support measures announced in April and May 1978 (German Tribune, 11 June 1978).

4.20   Government policy towards the coal industry is of considerable interest since not only does it contrast with the typical unwillingness of government to support declining industries, but the structural interventions by government are quite inconsistent with the principles of *Marktkonformes Mittel*. Industrial policy measures normally considered to be consistent with the competitive market mechanism are non-discriminatory financial incentives. However, in the coal industry not only has government been willing to intervene directly to force consuming industries to increase their use of domestic coal, but government has also severely restricted competition in the industry by reorganising it into fewer companies and imposing upon it a regulatory commission.

4.21   Federal support for the production of *civil aircraft* has many similarities to support for the computer industry. Both are examples of technologically based industries in which the high costs and uncertain returns from R&D make it unlikely that either industry could survive without at least some initial support from government. Both occupy a strategically important position, the computer industry because of the key role of electronic technology in the future development of the industrial sector, and aircraft industry because of its initial defence role. The enormous cost of civilian aircraft development, the need for international cooperation and the oligopolistic structure of the industry internationally has meant that the aircraft industry has been often regarded as one in which the principle of workable competition cannot be invoked and the industry has been subject to considerable government intervention. Government has encouraged mergers with the result that the industry is reorganised into two companies: VWF-Fokker and MBB. In common with the UK and France, the aircraft industry of the BRD has suffered from the inability to achieve sufficient sales of individual models to reap the benefits of scale economies. Also in common with the UK and France, government policies have been influenced by considerations of national prestige and over-optimistic projections of commercial success. Both the VFW 614 short haul aircraft and the Franco-German airbus have incurred substantial losses caused by high development costs and limited sales — the direct result of failure to break into the US market.

4.22   Considerations of economic and defensive strategy and self-sufficiency which have been identified as important motives in the financial support of the coal, computer and aircraft industries, are the dominant influence on Federal assistance for the *oil industry*. The dependence of the economy on imported crude oil and the absence of any German-based multinationals in the international petroleum industry has meant that disruption of oil supplies has been regarded as a major threat to the security of the BRD. Government promotion of mergers in the coal industry was paralleled by a similar policy in the oil industry from 1968 onwards. In the interests of security, it was considered that at least one quarter of the nation's supply of crude oil should come from German firms (Kruster, 1974, p.77). DEMINEX, a joint venture involving 7 oil companies, was established with government encouragement and government backing of DM575 mn over six years. The company was expected to engage in exploration for new sources of petroleum and to form joint ventures with other oil companies and the governments of producer countries for the ownership and operation of oil and gas fields.

4.23 The activities of the Federal Government in encouraging increasing concentration in the oil industry have been the subject of considerable controversy. In 1974 the government-backed merger between VEBA, the state-owned energy conglomerate, and a smaller oil company, Gelsenberg AG, was turned down by the Cartel Office. The decision was overruled by the Economics Minister only to be upheld by the Monopolies Commission.

4.24 It would seem that the government's strategy for the internal growth of the domestic oil industry has been a failure with no major discoveries of crude oil and few joint ventures with other companies. In 1978 a takeover of VEBA's petroleum interests by BP was turned down by the Cartel Office.

4.25 *Structural policy and firm size.* An industrial policy based on the maintenance of the market system for the allocation of resources might be expected to adopt a neutral position towards enterprises of different sizes allowing the competitive mechanism to promote the emergence of optimally-sized firms. In practice a range of measures has been introduced to assist investment by small and medium-sized business (SMBs). The justification for such measures is, first, that some measure of public support is needed to offset the handicaps which face SMBs in capital markets, in sponsoring R&D and in complying with legislation and government regulations; second, SMBs provide important sources of output and employment growth and an entree for new managerial talent and innovative ideas to the industrial sector. A further factor influencing the Government's attitude towards SMBs is that in Germany SMBs account for a smaller share of industrial employment (12 per cent) and industrial production (10 per cent) than in any other OECD country. The support measures include:

— low interest loans for capital investment by SMBs by the Reconstruction Loan Corporation (at 6½ per cent rate of interest) together with special assistance for SMBs in textiles and clothing and leather and footwear (1974);
— adjustment aid for SMBs from the ERP (1975);
— tax concessions to SMBs to enable them to carry forward losses (1976);
— a special programme for assisting the establishing of new firms (DM270 mn budgeted in 1977 with an additional DM600mn in 1978); and
— assistance for SMBs introducing new innovations (funds increased from DM10 mn in 1976 to DM15 mn in 1980).

4.26 During the early 1970s total financial assistance to SMBs was as follows [O.E.C.D. (1978)]

	1971	1973	1974	1975
DM millions	342	429	458	490

As indicated above, since 1975 the number of programmes assisting SMBs and the amount of expenditure has increased considerably.

4.27 In spite of the assistance by government to SMBs and the general support which government has expressed for the principles of the competitive market economy, in some industrial sectors government policy has fostered the growth of large-sized firms. Apparently influenced by the ideas contained in Galbraith's *New Industrial State* (1968) and Servan-Schreiber's *Le Défi Americain*, the Federal Government recognised a need for large companies capable of competing in international markets and keeping abreast of technological change. Herr Schiller in particular emphasised that competition was not to be regarded as a policy goal, but as one of a range of policy instruments [see Schiller (1955)]. In a comment upon the Cartel Office Report for 1967 the Federal Government stated: 'The Common Market and the trend to world-wide economic integration have created new premises for competition. Larger markets demand in many ways larger and more efficient company units ... The Federal Government is concerned to remove obstacles which stand in the way of concentration of enterprises now blocked by cartel law, so that the development of firms of optimum size will not be hindered.' (*Stellungnahme der Bundesregierung zum Tätigkeitsbericht des Bundeskartellamtes fur 1967*, pp.2-3, quoted in Kuster (1974). Concern over sub-optimal sizes of firms and plants may seem surprising in view of the large average size of large plants in the BRD (see paragraph 2.57 above) though, on average, industrial concentration is lower in the BRD than the UK (see paragraph 2.53). While the favourable attitude of the Federal Government towards increasing company sizes undoubtedly encouraged mergers between large manufacuring firms between the mid-1960s and early-1970s, with the exception of coal and oil industries (see above), the Federal Government does not appear to have taken a direct role in effecting industrial mergers.

4.28 *Structural policies towards the labour market.* Structural change in industry is dependent not only on the investment decisions of firms but also on the responses of workers to changing employment opportunities and incentives. The ability of an economy to take advantage of technological change and the changing structure of final demand partly depends upon the degree of occupational and geographical mobility of the labour force. In the BRD high labour mobility has been greatly facilitated by the presence of a large number of foreign workers. Until recently, the principal manpower problem has been the continuing demand of Germany's growing manufacturing industry for highly skilled personnel necessary for the maintenance of Germany's export strength based on high quality, technologically advanced manufactured products. To avoid serious manpower shortages in key skilled occupations, the Federal Government has placed considerable emphasis on vocational training and incentives to occupational and geographical mobility. Manpower and employment policy is carried out by the Federal Employment Bureau which implements the Vocational Training and Employment Promotion and the 1971 Act on Vocational Training. In 1975 there were 271,000 persons undergoing state-supported vocational training and retraining schemes and about another 200,000 who undertook other supported training (OECD, 1978, p.120). The types of training for which financial assistance is available are:

— *conversion* courses for workers faced with redundancy;
— *adaptation* courses for entrants to new jobs;
— *occupational advancement* courses for workers seeking to improve their skills and qualifications within a particular occupation;
— *refresher* courses for workers seeking to maintain their level of skill; and
— *Pre-training* and *preparatory* courses for young people between 16 and 18 before taking up employment.

Table 4.5 shows expenditure by the Federal Employment Bureau (note that this includes expenditure on unemployment benefits as well).

Table 4.5

EXPENDITURE BY THE FEDERAL EMPLOYMENT BUREAU

	DM million
Personnel training assistance	2,802
of which: initial training	277
further training	374
retraining training	159
subsistence allowances during training	1,991
Assistance to training institutions	64
Assisting entry into employment	186
Rehabilitation of handicapped persons	434
Short-time working allowances	2,207
Bad weather pay	396
Aid to productivity in building industry in winter	50
Other aid to building firms and workers	17
Employment creation measures	127
Unemployment benefits	7,766
Supplementary unemployment benefits	776
TOTAL PAYMENTS	15,743

Source: OECD, 1978, p.114

4.29 Until the mid-1970s government policies towards the labour market were concerned chiefly with encouraging skill acquisition and greater efficiency in the allocation of manpower resources. With the emergence of structural problems of industry and higher rates of unemployment after 1974 the Federal Government has become increasingly involved in the maintenance of employment on social grounds. In 1975 the first programme of wage subsidies was introduced for firms offering non-temporary employment to unemployed persons. The scheme operated for six months with an expenditure of DM600 million. Further programmes for increased support were introduced in 1976 and 1977. In May 1977 the budget for employment creation measures was increased from DM650 million to DM1150 million with particular emphasis on work creation for the long term unemployed and training courses for school leavers. Considerable use has been made too of short term working and various work-sharing arrangements.

C. Structural policy in the UK

4.30 *Structural intervention in theory and practice.* In contrast to the BRD, structural policies in the UK have not been formulated within such a coherent set of principles as those of the *social market economy.* As has been noted in Chapter 3, the much heavier emphasis on structural economic policies in the UK as compared with the BRD primarily reflects the view that UK's greater need for structural intervention follows from its less satisfactory economic performance. The increasing resort by UK governments to industrial intervention would seem to have been encouraged by the failure of more traditional tools of macro-economic policy to achieve the elusive goals of stability and growth. While UK structural policy has been moulded more by pragmatism and political opportunism than by philosophical considerations, it is possible to identify certain directions of economic thought which have been influential. The post-war German faith in the political virtues and economic efficiency of the competitive market system found little echo in the UK debate over economic policy, and even under Conservative governments it is difficult to identify the introduction of any significant constraints on government intervention in industry arising from a belief in the efficiency of the free market system. Even in competition policy where controls over cartels, monopolies and mergers in the UK have pre-dated those of the BRD, the UK approach has been marked by extreme pragmatism with a lack of whole-hearted commitment to the principle of competition. In fact, the most influential direction of economic thought on the UK policy formulation has been a belief in the efficacy of government sponsored economic planning as a means of stimulating increased investment and economic growth. This belief that economic planning could remedy the poor performance of the UK with regard to growth, inflation and international trade, was greatly strengthened by comparisons with policy and performance in some other European countries. The indicative planning practices of France, the active role of the state-owned conglomerates in Italian industry and the wage bargaining system of Sweden were all held up during the early 1960s as models for the UK to imitate.

4.31 Government attempts at a comprehensive structural policy within a medium-term planning framework have been associated with the role of the National Economic Development Council (NEDC). The establishment of NEDC in 1962 was stimulated by the success of French indicative planning and represented a remarkable conversion in the attitude of the Conservative party towards intervention in the economy. The NEDC provided a forum of representatives, from government, business and the unions, backed by a planning office (NEDO) and a number of Economic Development Committees for individual industries. The work of NEDC was embodied in five year plans which represented a consensus view of economic growth and development and a commitment by government to orientate its policy towards the achievement of the growth targets.

4.32 While the Conservative party's commitment to indicative planning during the 1960s was somewhat half-hearted, to the Labour government of 1964 national economic planning backed by extensive micro-economic intervention was the basis of its economic strategy. After 'the thirteen wasted years' of Conservative rule, the party's election manifesto promised 'a deliberate and massive effort to modernise the economy; to change its structure and to develop with all possible speed the advanced technology and the new science-based industries with which our future lies'. In addition to new ministerial powers and new agencies for government intervention in industry, the Labour government's policy was notable for its commitment to overall economic planning at the national level. Economic planning involved the creation of new planning institutions. The industry-based Economic Development Committees were supplemented by geographically defined Economic Planning Councils. The Department of Economic Affairs was established for the construction of national plans which were to be implemented through the machinery of NEDO, the EDCs and the Regional Economic Planning Councils. This bold attempt at indicative planning crumbled almost as soon as the *National Plan* of 1965 had been published. The introductions by government of deflationary measures in order to meet the balance of payments in 1966 made the growth targets of the Plan unattainable.

4.33 The failure of the National Plan and the subsequent demise of the Department of Economic Affairs resulted in the discrediting of 'national planning'. In particular it was noted that it was easy to establish performance targets for the economy, but impossible to ensure they would be fulfilled without sufficient tools of of government policy to influence the economy at macro and micro level. While the failure of planning in the 1960s may have encouraged the Conservative party to move towards a more market-orientated economic philosophy, no such tendency can be observed in the Labour party's approach to economic policy. Although the 1974-79 Labour Government made no attempt to revive medium-term planning of the national planning, its belief that government leadership and extensive industrial intervention in industry were necessary to overcome the fundamental problems of the UK economy was the basis of the Industrial Strategy launched in 1975. Unlike the National Plan, the Industrial Strategy involved no national targets for growth and employment and little coordinated planning at a national level. The approach was to use the organisation of the NEDC to identify structural and performance problems in individual sectors of UK industry, and then to formulate government policies to remedy these defects. Statements of the content of the Industrial Strategy were deliberately vague. In *An Approach to Industrial Strategy* (HMSO, 1975) the Government emphasised the need for economic policies to take a longer term perspective aiming in particular to remove the obstacles to long term economic growth rather than to concentrate on short term policies directed at the immediate problems of unemployment, inflation and balance of payments deficit. The only formal planning which the Strategy envisaged was at company level through *Planning Agreements* between government and individual companies. This area of the Industrial Strategy was a conspicuous failure. In practice, the major thrust of the Industrial Strategy was to identify sectors of industry where economic growth and increasing productivity were supposedly hindered by inadequate investment and to introduce sectoral assistance schemes aimed at increasing and accelerating capital investment.

4.34 At an ideological level, therefore, the history of economic policy since 1964 has consisted to two periods, 1964-70 and 1974-79 when government was committed to extensive structural intervention in the economy, and two periods, 1970-74 and June 1979 onwards when government declared its support for market-orientated economic policies. Yet neither under Conservative nor Labour government have the actual structural policies which have been introduced corresponded to any marked degree to the philosophical inclinations or election statements of the parties. In the case of Labour governments one would have expected structural policies to have taken the form of comprehensive programmes aimed at long-term goals of output and productivity growth and greater equality in income distribution. While Labour governments have been associated with increased structural intervention, the policies have comprised a variety of different schemes administered by different departments and agencies with little overall planning and directed more towards short- than long-term goals. Under the 1970-74 Conservative government the gap between principle and actual policies was even more evident. Apart from the abolition of a few interventionist agencies, there is no evidence of a shift towards laissez-faire policies and it was this government which established the framework for selective industrial intervention that was to be subsequently expanded between 1974 and 1979.

4.35 The contrast between ideology and practice is one which characterises UK economic policy in general, but is particularly evident in the case of structural policy towards industry. Despite differences in the economic philosophy of the Labour and Conservative parties, intervention in the economy increased over the period 1964-1979 with only minor interruptions. Despite the emphasis of policy statements on the longer term problems of lack of investment and low growth industrial intervention has tended to be orientated more to short term employment maintenance than to long term growth. Again, despite the emphasis of the Labour party on coordination of economic policies with a framework of medium term planning, industrial interventions have been haphazard and *ad hoc*. This course of structural economic policies and the apparently limited influence of economic philosophy reflects the dominance of circumstances over ideas. The tendency for UK governments of quite different political complexions to adopt similar economic policies reflects not so much the pragmatism of policy makers as the severity of the short-term economic problems and political pressures that constrain the choice of policy instruments and goals. We proceed by identifying some of the trends in UK structural policy and examining some major areas of structural policy towards industry.

4.36 *Instruments of structural intervention and trends in structural policy.* In the UK as in the BRD structural economic policies have operated primarily through the provision of financial incentives to industry. Financial incentives have mainly been subsidies for capital investment: investment grants, tax allowances, low interest loans and interest relief grants. The forms of financial incentive and assistance offered by UK governments have been more varied than in the BRD. In particular, subsidies for the employment of labour have been important in the UK, notably the Regional Employment Premium and the Temporary Employment Subsidy. Also UK governments, particularly during the period 1974-79, have provided long-term finance to private industry in the form of equity capital.

4.37 Unlike the BRD Subsidy Reports, the UK Government does not provide a comprehensive account of financial assistance to the private sector. Financial assistance to industry which takes the form of government expenditure (i.e. grants, loans and equity purchases) is classified in the annual White Papers on Public Expenditure. Table 4.6 shows expenditure by central government on industry and employment between

1969/70 and 1977/78. The figures are misleading as an indication of subsidies to industry. First, the figures aggregate loans and grants, and, second, no account is taken of tax allowances. Calculation of the subsidy element in loans is difficult since it depends upon the rate of interest charged compared with that which would have been charged on an identical loan by a financial institution and also upon whether or not the loan is repaid (many of the loans made to unprofitable firms ultimately become grants). In recent years interest relief grants have become a particularly important method by which government provides selective assistance to industry. The Department of Industry has noted that this form of aid is advantageous from the Government's point of view since it involves less public expenditure than the provision of loans and the Department is relieved of the responsibility of evaluating the commercial viability of the project and administering the payment and repayment of the loan (see *House of Commons*, 1978, pp.15-17).

4.38 Structural policies have not relied exclusively on financial incentives to encourage industrial adjustment and growth, and numerous instruments of direct intervention into the industrial sector have been employed by British governments. Regional development policies have traditionally involved governments in a range of direct intervention, notably direct control of industrial location and the provision of social and industrial infrastructure. Since 1964 governments have become involved on a wider scale in direct intervention in industry to change industrial structure, to exploit new investment opportunities and to improve industrial performance. The work of the Industrial Reorganisation Corporation in effecting mergers in several manufacturing industries and the promotion of new enterprises by the Department of Industry and agencies such as the National Enterprise Board and Scottish and Welsh Development Agencies are notable in this respect. The more flexible approach to public ownership than that represented by traditional nationalisation has been a significant feature of the past two Labour administrations: 1964-70 and 1974-79. The use of part-public ownership to support financially particular companies and to encourage structural changes in industry was inaugurated by the Government's purchase of shares in the Fairfield shipbuilding company in 1964. By the beginning of 1979 the shareholdings of the National Enterprise Board covered a large number of companies in a wide range of industries.

4.39 As we have noted, Table 4.6 is rather misleading as a guide to trends in financial assistance to UK industry. The Table shows that total expenditure on industry and the labour market was, in real terms, much the same in 1969/70 as in 1978/79, a peak being reached in 1974/75. The figures are distorted by the replacement in 1970 of investment grants by investment allowances, investment allowances not being included in the Table. If payments of investment grants are excluded from the totals, then the Table shows that finance for industry and the labour market increased by 86 per cent in real terms over the period, with a remarkable increase of 171 per cent over the five year period 1969/70 to 1974/75. The decline in expenditure between 1974/75 and 1978/79 is interesting, but closer inspection reveals that this is due not to a contraction of government industrial policy but to a change in the system of financing export credits and the abandonment of the severe restraint on nationalised industry price increases.

4.40 Probably the principal change in industrial policy over the period has been the relative decline in the importance of regional assistance but it is not easily identified in Table 4.6 because the principal regional aid during the early 1970's 'higher investment grants in the development areas, is not included under 'regional support and regeneration'. The growing importance of selective assistance to particular firms and industries is clearly indicated in the Table. Other trends which are worthy of note are the fall in expenditure on aircraft development and production (notably the Concorde and RB211 projects); second, the increase in government expenditure on the labour market. Some of these policy programmes are now discussed in more detail.

4.41 *Regional policy.* In the UK, as in the BRD, regional policies have provided the foundation for the development of wider structural policies towards industry. A large part of the growth of industrial intervention in the UK during the 1970s has involved an extension of financial aids originally intended for regional development to companies and industries outside the development regions. The origins of UK regional policy lie in the inter-war years, the 1934 Special Areas Act representing the first measures aimed at encouraging industry to site in particularly depressed areas. During the post-war period the regional problem is reflected in above average rates of unemployment in the well-defined regions of Scotland, North West and North East England, Wales and Northern Ireland with particularly serious problems affecting certain conurbations within these regions — notably Clydeside, Tyneside, Merseyside, and Belfast. The principal form of aid has been inducements to invest in the development areas in the form of investment grants, initial allowances and accelerated depreciation provisions. Higher rates of investment incentives were made available for the specially depressed 'Special Development Areas' (established in 1967) and lower rates were introduced in 1970 for 'Intermediate Areas', The most active phase of regional policy was the period 1966 to 1970. The 1966 Industrial Development Act introduced investment grants in Development Areas at the rate of 40 per cent of the cost of plant and machinery and 25 per cent of the cost of buildings. In 1967 the Regional Employment Premium introduced a cash subsidy of £1.50 per week for each full-time worker employed in the Development Areas. In addition, industry was directed towards the Development Areas by means of the discriminatory issue of Industrial Development Certificates and by inducements in the form of advance factories and new towns.

4.42 After 1970 the emphasis of regional policy changed. Investment grants were replaced by investment allowances in 1970 (although regional development grants were reintroduced in 1972) and the Regional Employment Premium was withdrawn in 1973. The primary emphasis of regional policy after 1972 was towards a more selective approach. Under Section 7 of the 1972 Industry Act, the Department of Industry was empowered to offer selective industrial assistance to individual companies and projects which would have the effect of creating employment in the Development Areas. The shift from generally available regional incentives towards selective incentives produced a basic change in regional policy. Although selective assistance under Section 7 of the Industry Act is available only in the 'assisted areas', these areas include all of UK with the exception of the Midlands and the South East and the flexibility of the criteria. Moreover the growth in selective assistance to industries and firms outside the development regions has had the effect of further weakening the importance of regional incentives. This weaker emphasis on regional problems *per se* has partly reflected a change in the nature of industrial problems. During the 1970s unemployment has increasingly become a national problem and the growing severity of the problems of industrial decline, import competition and structural change have resulted in the emergence of localised economic problems outside the traditional development regions. Notable examples have been the rising unemployment in the West Midlands — traditionally a high income, high employment area — during the recession in the engineering industries in the mid-1970s and the growing problems of inner city areas. Its unemployment and industrial decline have become associated more with particular industries than with particular areas.

4.43 *Selective assistance to industries and companies.* While structural intervention by government in UK industry through the provision of financial assistance to selected industries and companies has become a dominant feature of UK industrial policy only since 1972, it is important to note that selective intervention by government in private industry is over forty years old. During the inter-war period in particular the pressures on government posed by balance of payments difficulties and unemployment with its attendant social problems placed pressures on government which were similar to those posed by the problems of the post-war recessions. Structural intervention by government was primarily at an informal level using government influence on firms and industry, the encouragement of cartels and the introduction of protective tariffs rather than financial subsidies. Government policy towards the cotton industry through the 1936 Cotton Spinning Act and 1959 Cotton Industry Act was the first example of the formal approach to structural policy (Miles, 1968).

4.44 Selective financial assistance to industry since 1966 has taken two main forms. First, assistance directed primarily towards the maintenance of employment in industry, and secondly, assistance aimed primarily at the promotion of growth through support for capital investment and research and development in newer and technologically-based industries. Both these objectives have been influenced by balance of payments considerations, and in almost all cases of support for declining industries and unprofitable firms, the industry or firm has been a significant exporter. Prior to 1972 selective assistance to industry was limited. The severe adjustment problems of particular industries — notably shipbuilding and cotton textiles — resulted in legislation making available financial assistance for these industries. In addition, government provided substantial assistance to the aircraft industry partly because of the need to maintain the capacity to build military aircraft and partly through a belief in the importance of R&D spin-off from aerospace. Assistance took the form of grants for research and development costs and the requirement that the nationalised airlines purchase domestically built planes. Legislation empowering ministers to offer discretionary assistance to particular firms across industry as a whole was introduced by the 1964-70 Labour administration as part of its policy to stimulate innovation and the development of science-based industries. The 1965 Science and Technology Act and Development of Inventions Act increased government support for research and development, while the 1968 Industrial Expansion Act empowered the Minister concerned to give financial support in almost any form to projects designed to 'promote efficiency; to support technological advance; or to create, expand or sustain productive capacity' (HMSO 1968). The main beneficiaries of the Industrial Expansion Act were International Computers Ltd (see Chapter 5), the aluminium smelting industry which was established in the UK with generous subsidies under the Act and the aircraft industry.

4.45 The enormous growth in the amount of selective financial assistance to industry shown in Table 4.6 followed the passing of the Industry Act in 1972. The purposes of selective financial assistance have been described by the government as follows:

— to promote the development or modernisation of industry;
— to promote the efficiency of an industry;

- to create, expand or sustain productive capacity in an industry, or in undertakings in an industry;
- to promote the reconstruction, reorganisation of conversions of an industry or of undertakings in an industry;
- to encourage the growth of, or the proper distribution of undertakings in an industry; and
- to encourage arrangements for ensuring that any contraction of an industry proceeds in an orderly way (Trade and Industry, 19 January 1979).

Selective assistance can be offered under Section 7 and 8 of the Act. Section 7 assistance is designed to provide and maintain employment in the assisted areas, Section 8 assistance is available for the support of projects anywhere in the country so long as it benefits the economy and serves the national interest. In the case of selective assistance to individual companies under both Sections 7 and 8 of the Act, it would appear that the maintenance of employment in relatively unprofitable companies has been a dominant criterion in the allocation of aid. Table 4.7 below shows the most important allocations of financial aid to individual companies, in the great majority of cases aid has been to companies in serious financial difficulties and has been in order to maintain employment.

4.46 In addition to selective assistance for individual companies and projects, a number of financial assistance schemes have been established under Section 8 of the Act to support investment in selected industries. These schemes have been closely linked to the Industrial Strategy of 1975-79, a principal feature of which was the establishment under the NEDC of sector working parties to identify areas where increased capital investment was necessary to relieve production bottlenecks and increase productivity. Table 4.8 shows the schemes introduced under the Act. They include a wide variety of industries, some such as the electronic and instrumentation schemes are in areas of high technology, most of the others are in more traditional areas where productivity and capacity growth has been hindered by inadequate investment. In all cases, however, the basic reasoning has been the belief that unsatisfactory growth performance of British industry has been due in part to a lack of capital investment and the presence of capacity bottlenecks in certain areas of industry which have inhibited attempts by government to attain non-inflationary growth.

4.47 *The sectoral distribution of financial support.* The use of selective financial assistance to maintain employment in declining industries and to rescue unprofitable manufacturing companies from bankruptcy raises the issue of whether government subsidies to British industry have the effect of inhibiting rather than promoting the structural adjustment of the economy. Some indication of whether industrial subsidies have had the effect of supporting low growth sectors of the economy is provided by the industrial distribution of financial assistance under the 1972 Industry Act in Table 4.9. Ranked by the amount of financial assistance per employee in each SIC order, no clear pattern emerges. Heaviest support would appear to be for basic manufacturing industries (notably coal and petroleum products, chemicals, metal manufacture) and shipbuilding. In general, support would appear to be concentrated on low rather than high growth sectors of industry. The average level of assistance per employee in the six slowest growing orders was £568, in the six fastest growing orders it was £220.

4.48 *Industrial restructuring and the promotion of new enterprises.* Financial incentives to industry are generally regarded as market-orientated policy measures where the adjustment of market prices and rates of return by means of subsidies influences decision making by firms. Such a view is largely correct in the case of non-discretionary assistance (e.g. Regional Development Grants) but in the case of selective assistance, the award of finance is a matter for discussion and bargaining between government and the company, such that government is able to use the offer of financial assistance to influence a company's decisions in a number of respects. For example, the aid given to Chrysler UK involved the company agreeing to maintaining its Scottish plant (Linwood), producing certain models in the UK and signing a 'planning agreement' with government which gave government the right of consultation over the company's planning. In a number of areas government has sought to invervene directly in industrial structure both to reorganise industries through the promotion of industrial mergers and to encourage the establishment of new business ventures. Such direct structural intervention has been associated with particular government agencies. For example, the National Research and Development Corporation has been responsible for promoting the exploitation of British inventions, the Industrial Reorganisation Corporation was closely associated with the encouragement of mergers, the National Enterprise Board has been responsible for encouraging the establishment of new enterprises aimed in particular at exploiting growth areas in industry. In all cases intervention has been accompanied by the provision of finance to the enterprises concerned, generally in the form of equity purchases.

4.49 The work of the Industrial Reorganisation Corporation during its existence from 1967 to 1971 is of particular interest on account of the large-scale structural reorganisations which it promoted in a number of manufacturing industries. The objective of the Corporation was to promote the industrial efficiency and international competitiveness of British industry in areas where market forces were not resulting in efficient performance, particularly where firm size was considered too small to maximise the benefits from scale

Table 4.6

GOVERNMENT ASSISTANCE TO UK INDUSTRY

	Year ending March					£mn at 1978 prices				
	1970	1971	1972	1973	1974	1975	1976	1977	1978	1979
Regional support and regeneration										
— Regional development grants	—	—	—	19	223	358	428	452	385	430
— Provision of land and buildings	40	38	29	30	12	22	30	18	19	30
— Selective assistance to industry in assisted areas	—	—	—	1	50	58	74	35	34	92
— Other regional support	14	13	16	15	15	16	16	15	23	30
— Regional employment premium	359	333	302	253	227	277	303	269	3	—
— Residual expenditure under repealed sections of the Local Employment Act, 1972	70	87	73	106	56	—	-4	-15	-10	-8
— Scottish and Welsh Development Agencies	—	—	—	—	—	—	7	28	64	112
TOTAL	484	471	420	425	584	730	853	803	518	686
Industrial innovation										
— General industrial R & D	61	56	46	45	50	51	51	44	41	51
— Department of Energy non-nuclear R & D	—	—	—	—	2	3	9	13	18	24
— Aircraft & aeroengine general R & D programme	21	26	28	33	38	33	26	23	20	17
— Concorde — development	177	181	164	122	81	73	58	32	25	21
— production	17	21	39	64	71	60	52	28	24	19
— RB 211	88	36	179	121	43	88	-3	12	-6	29
— Other aircraft and aeroengine projects and assistance	33	104	66	6	31	29	93	—	5	45
— Space	31	21	21	19	24	30	34	40	35	33
— Nuclear	99	136	121	124	126	115	139	157	114	120
TOTAL	527	581	665	535	465	482	459	348	275	358
General support for industry										
— National Enterprise Board	—	—	—	—	—	—	12	158	368	70
— Selective assistance to individual industries, firms and undertakings	—	—	—	19	32	35	423	105	59	225
— Promotion of tourism	16	18	31	43	63	30	22	20	20	23
— Refinancing of home shipbuilding lending	—	—	—	108	207	174	152	88	-98	10
— Interest support costs of home shipbuilding lending	—	—	—	—	47	57	43	54	28	33
— Assistance to the shipbuilding industry	24	1	16	40	28	63	36	15	35	30
— Other support services	76	73	-59	-57	-31	-13	1	—	8	2
— Investment grants	1571	1428	1121	683	416	173	82	26	6	2
TOTAL	1687	1520	1109	835	762	520	771	466	427	396
Support for nationalised industries (other than transport industries)										
— Compensation for price restraint	—	146	107	128	748	1096	92	—	—	—
— Assistance to the coal industry										
— Coal Industry Acts	74	70	282	268	624	114	60	82	91	136
— Pneumoconiosis scheme	—	—	—	—	—	60	40	—	—	—
— Other compensation	2	2	2	45	9	14	17	78	24	21
TOTAL	76	217	391	441	1381	1285	209	160	115	157
International trade										
— Export promotion and trade co-operation	22	22	19	17	18	18	18	17	17	19
— Refinancing of fixed rate export credits	—	—	—	759	813	796	751	616	-287	193
— Interest support costs	—	—	—	—	212	245	204	244	127	202
— Cost escalation guarantees	—	—	—	—	—	—	—	-1	1	1
— Regulation of domestic trade and industry & consumer protection	13	3	1	2	26	35	34	28	32	40
TOTAL	35	25	20	778	1069	1093	1007	905	-110	454
Functioning of the labour market										
— Employment services and employment rehabilitation	70	78	81	99	92	86	118	150	162	167
— Industrial training	79	109	91	128	116	138	232	280	311	374
— Redundancy & maternity fund payments	119	132	176	119	62	76	135	114	112	110
— Industrial relations & other labour market services	13	13	12	81	-2	10	25	154	291	324
TOTAL	282	330	359	428	269	310	510	697	876	974
Health and safety at work	—	—	—	—	18	16	32	42	42	44
Central & miscellaneous services										
— Employment	74	73	71	70	85	56	43	53	54	54
— Other	147	89	68	67	58	76	74	71	90	110
Transactions in British Petroleum Company shares	—	—	65	65	—	318	—	—	-590	—
GRAND TOTAL	3312	3307	3168	3644	4692	4886	3958	3545	1698	3232

Table 4.7

MAJOR OFFERS OF SELECTIVE ASSISTANCE TO INDIVIDUAL COMPANIES UNDER SECTIONS
7 & 8 OF THE INDUSTRY ACT 1972

Year	Company	Amount of offer	Section of the Act
1972/3	Mersey Docks & Harbour	3.50	7
	Govan Shipbuilders Ltd	35.0	7
	Camell Laird	20.0	7
	Kearney, Trecker and Marwin	1.25	8
	Norton Villiers Triumph	4.8	8
1973/4	Harland and Wolff	—a	7
1974/5	Ferranti	6.0*	7
	Fodens	2.0*	7
	Kirkby Manufacturing & Engineering	3.9	7
	Scottish Daily News	1.2	7
	Austin & Pickersgill	9.0	7
	Sunderland Shipbuilders	25.0b	7
	Alfred Herbert Ltd	3.0*	8
	British Leyland	50.0*	8
	Kearney, Trecker and Marwin Ltd	3.5	8
	Norton Villiers Triumph	8.0*	8
	Synova Motors Ltd (Meriden motorcycles)	4.95	8
1975/76	Ferranti Ltd	15.0	7
	Triang Pedigree Ltd	3.5	7
	Sunderland Shipbuildings Ltd	6.0	7
	Alfred Herbert Ltd	26.18	8
	British Leyland	265.0c	—
	Cambridge Instrument Co Ltd	4.5	8
	Chrysler UK Ltd	162.5	8
1976/7	British Leyland	30.0	8
	Kearney, Trecker and Marwin Ltd	1.9	8
1977/8	Ford Motor Company	75.0	7
	British Leyland	150.0	8

Notes:
* Loan guarantee only
a Financed jointly by Department of Industry and Northern Ireland government
b Including a payment of £16m to Court Line for its shipbuilding assets and a loan of £9m to Sunderland Shipbuilders.
c This sum was for equity finance and was provided under the British Leyland Act 1975.

Source: *Industry Act 1972. Annual reports.*

Table 4.8

SECTORAL SCHEMES OF ASSISTANCE UNDER SECTION 8 OF THE INDUSTRY ACT 1972

Scheme	Date of introduction	Closing date	Assistance offered to 31 March 1978 £m
Wool textile			
— Stage 1	19/ 7/73	31/12/75	16.7
— Stage 2	29/11/76	31/12/77	1.2
Ferrous foundry	5/ 8/75	31/12/76	78.4
Machine tool	5/ 8/75	31/12/77	14.4
Clothing	15/10/75	31/12/77	5.7
Paper and board	15/ 6/76	30/ 6/78	11.5
Non-ferrous foundry	24/ 1/77	31/ 7/78	4.6
Electronic components	24/ 1/77	31/ 7/78	4.0
Instrumentation and automation	1/11/77	31/12/78	1.5
Drop Forging	8/11/77	31/12/78	nil
Printing machinery	13/ 8/76	31/12/77	3.5
Textile machinery	13/ 8/76	31/ 3/77	2.0
Poultrymeat processing	4/ 8/76	31/ 3/77	4.9
Redmeat slaughterhouse	9/11/76	30/11/78	3.3

Source: *Industry Act 1972. Annual reports.*

Table 4.9

FINANCIAL ASSISTANCE UNDER THE 1972 INDUSTRY ACT 1972/3-1977/8 BY SIC ORDER

SIC ORDERS		Regional development grants	Selective regional assistance (Section 7)	Selective* investment scheme grants	Sectoral* assistance schemes under Section 8	Total	Total financial assistance per employee £	Growth of production 1972/3 to 1977/8 %
II	Mining and quarrying	80.0	1.4	—	—	82.2	236	59.4
III	Food, drink & tobacco	132.9	9.6	1.1	8.2	151.8	208	10.0
IV	Coal & petroleum products	75.5	0.2	—	—	75.7	1992	-6.3
V	Chemicals	271.6	19.1	5.0	—	295.7	698	32.8
VI	Metal manufacture	283.9	11.2	0.1	83.0	378.2	788	-18.5
VII	Mechanical engineering	-80.4	32.1	1.3	19.9	133.7	142	-2.1
VIII	Instrument engineering	10.1	2.6	—	1.5	14.2	92	23.3
IX	Electrical engineering	51.3	32.9	0.4	4.0	88.6	114	23.2
X	Shipbuilding & marine engineering	36.7	6.2	—	—	42.9	232	-10.3
XI	Vehicles	41.1	16.3	2.3	—	59.7	78	-1.1
XII	Metal goods nes	38.1	7.6	0.6	—	46.3	86	-3.0
XII	Textiles	50.5	18.7	0.2	17.8	87.2	165	-7.4
XIV	Leather, leather goods & fur	2.8	3.0	—	—	5.8	139	-8.6
XV	Clothing & footwear	14.5	2.9	—	5.7	13.1	33	16.9
XVI	Bricks, pottery, cement, glass	50.6	4.4	0.8	—	55.8	200	11.0
XVII	Timber, furniture, etc	24.0	5.2	—	—	29.2	109	8.6
XVIII	Paper printing & publishing	51.7	7.6	10.5	11.5	81.3	146	3.6
XIX	Other manufacturing industries	34.5	13.8	1.3	—	49.6	146	22.4
XX	Construction	105.6	1.9	—	—	107.5	83	-12.6
	Other	17.3	6.9	—	—	24.2	—	—
	TOTAL	1454.0	203.7	23.7	151.6	1833.0	194	6.0

*Offers of assistance

Source: *Industry Act 1972. Annual reports, Annual Abstract of Statistics*

economies, innovation and export marketing. In a number of industries IRC promoted mergers resulted in the amalgamation of all the domestically owned producers into a single company, notably in car assembly (BMC and Leyland Motors), heavy electrical goods (GEC, AEI and English Electric), and ball bearings (Hoffman, Ransome and Marles, and Pollard). Table 4.10 shows the distribution of IRC finance between different industries.

4.50 The National Enterprise Board established by the 1975 Industry Act has been less ambitious than the IRC in intervening to restructure private industry. It was designed to encourage investment into growing and profitable areas of UK industry. In addition to acting as a management and holding company for state shareholdings in companies such as British Leyland, Alfred Herbert, Brown Boveri Kent Ltd, Cambridge Instruments and other companies involved in government rescues and restructuring, the NEB has taken an active role in promoting new enterprises in areas of rapid technological change — notably micro-electronics (see paragraph 5). It might be argued that the existence of agencies such as the NEB and IRC to undertake selective financial assistance for individual companies is to be preferred to the direct provision of aid by government departments as semi-independent agencies are able to adopt a more commercial strategy and may be subjected to less political pressures.

4.51 *Structural policies towards the labour market.* Although this chapter has concentrated on structural policies towards industry, note must be taken of policies towards the labour market since these may be regarded as complementary and, to some extent, alternatives to industrial policy. The process of structural change in industry in recent years has been characterised by the relative immobility of labour with the result that increasing rates of structural unemployment coexist with large numbers of unfilled vacancies. The increasing expenditure by government on the labour market during the 1970s (see Table 4.7) reflects government's determination to encourage greater efficiency in the labour market both to stimulate economic growth and to avoid the social problems which accompany industrial change.

Table 4.10

INDUSTRIAL REORGANISATION CORPORATION FINANCE BY INDUSTRY, 1967-71

	£m
Automobiles	34.0
Computers	18.0
Aircraft	10.0
Instrument engineering	9.5
Ball bearings	9.4
Heavy engineering	7.0
Textiles	4.6
Paper	4.0
Shipbuilding	3.8
Machine tools	2.9
Nuclear energy	1.1
Mechanical engineering	0.7
TOTAL	105.9

4.52 The principal problem of the UK labour market has been seen to be an insufficient supply of trained manpower, particularly skilled manual workers. The first comprehensive attempt at encouraging an expansion in industrial training was the 1964 Industrial Training Act which established a system of grants to encourage training administered by Industrial Training Boards. The establishment of the Manpower Services Commission by the Employment and Training Act 1973 was aimed at a more integrated approach to labour market policies by bringing together employment information and exchange facilities and government training schemes under a single body. During the 1970s expenditure on industrial training and re-training has increased greatly, although this greater expenditure seems to have had little success in solving the problems of labour immobility and the shortage of certain categories of skilled labour. To a great extent, however, policies to encourage greater geographical and occupational mobility have been offset by other government policies. Incomes policies between 1972 and 1979 have had the effect of suppressing wage differentials and preventing the normal operation of the forces of supply and demand in the labour market, while the Employment Protection Act of 1975 has made it more difficult for firms facing declining demand to shed excess labour. Measures directed at the short term maintenance of employment have directly operated against policies which have sought to achieve a more efficient allocation of labour. Selective support of unproductive and unprofitable companies has been discussed above, in addition the temporary employment subsidy has directly encouraged the retention of labour in unproductive employment. The temporary employment subsidy may be regarded as a disguised subsidy to industry, the benefits of which have accrued to declining industries. Table 4.11 shows the distribution of the temporary employment subsidy by industry.

Table 4.11

PAYMENTS OF TEMPORARY EMPLOYMENT SUBSIDIES BY INDUSTRY,
18 AUGUST 1975 TO 31 MARCH 1977

	Workers covered	% of industry labour force
Clothing & footwear	64,038	17
Textiles	52,864	11
Leather	3,473	8
Timber, furniture	7,164	3
Shipbuilding	4,064	2
Other manufacturing	74,055	1
Non-manufacturing industries	23,589	—
TOTAL	229,247	

Source: *Financial Times*, 30 January 1978, p.21

D. Conclusions

4.53 A detailed comparison of structural economic policies in the UK and BRD is complicated by the difficulties of obtaining comparable statistics on the amounts of financial aid and its distribution and the problems of distinguishing the practical operation of structural policies from official statement of policy aims and effects. Nevertheless, from the foregoing description of some of the principal features of structural policies in the two countries, some generalisations may be proposed.

4.54 The most obvious difference between the countries in the use of structural policy is the much heavier emphasis placed by UK governments on the instruments of structural intervention in attaining macro-economic goals. This is evident in the greater expenditure in the UK on industrial subsidies (see Tables 4.4 and 4.7). Comparisons of tax allowances involve numerous problems, but a simple comparison of direct aid to industry (grants and loans) shows that in 1977 and 1978 UK industrial aid (excluding support for national-ised industries) totalled £2,837 million (approx DM11 billion) while that for the BRD was DM4.9 billion. This difference almost entirely reflects the more widespread use of subsidies in the UK. Comparing individual programmes shows that in the BRD grants and loans for aerospace and innovation and mining and energy exceeded those in the UK, while expenditure on regional support was broadly similar (though with a greater emphasis on tax allowances in the BRD). But, while in the UK almost all manufacturing in-dustries receive some degree of selective subsidisation, financial aid to German manufacturing industry is restricted to very few industries, notably shipbuilding.

4.55 The instruments of financial aid are broadly similar in the two countries — investment grants, grants to-wards R&D, tax allowances for investment expenditure, low interest loans, loan guarantees and interest relief grants. The main differences lie in their application. In general, subsidies have been used far more selectively in the UK than in the BRD. In the BRD industrial support other than regional policy has been in the form of sectoral schemes together with more general schemes for innovation and small and medium-sized businesses. The UK government, on the other hand, has acquired powers to offer financial support in virtually any form to almost any company, so long as the support is regarded as in the national interest.

4.56 Such highly selective and discretionary powers for offering financial aid confers upon government the ability to make highly specific structural interventions in industry. The offer of aid to individual com-panies has sometimes been conditional upon the detailed involvement of government in the companies' decisions. The wide powers of various government agencies to make loans and purchase equity has allowed these agencies, notably the IRC and the NEB to intervene directly in industry to effect structural change. The over-ruling of the market mechanism by direct structural intervention by government, extensions of public ownership and attempts at government to establish formal planning arrangements with individual companies would clearly be contrary to the prevailing economic philosophy in the BRD as well as to its *Principles of Structural Policy.*

4.57 Nevertheless, too great an emphasis on the formal aspects of structural policy may result in underestimating the powers of government to intervene in industry at the micro level. Even in Germany where a strong and stable consensus view has been taken of the limits of government intervention in the economy, it would seem that, in the search for solutions to economic problems, policy principles do not impose binding constraints. Both in the UK and the BRD an important area of industrial policy is at the informal level through persuasion and pressure on private sector organisations and companies. Galbraith has noted that, in the modern industrial state, government and industry are forced into close cooperation through mutual dependence. The increasing complexity of society results in expanding contacts between government and the private sector for the purpose of economic, social and environmental policies. Within such a frame-work, informal persuasion may be considered to be a more efficient and effective means of structural intervention than legislative controls and financial incentives through taxes and subsidies. Prior to 1945 it was in West Germany rather that the UK where cooperation between business and government was a primary feature of economic policy and economic development. It is possible that the more selective interventionist approach of the British government to structural policy may reflect not only the commitment of the Federal government to the principles of the market economy but also the greater ability of the Federal government to command the voluntary adherence of German industry to national economic policies without the need for formal powers of intervention. This thesis is supported by the comparative success of the West German Government in its voluntary wage and price policies through the programme of Concerted Action, as compared with British governments' reliance on statutory powers over wages and prices. The ability of the Federal government to intervene informally in industry in the BRD is further assisted by the influential position of the banks in German industry and the close links between government and the banking sector.

4.58 In both countries governments have stressed the need for structural intervention to be directed towards the promotion of industrial growth and technological advance. In both countries, however, financial aids have been used primarily for the maintenance of the output and employment in relatively unprofitable industries rather than towards the encouragement of growth industry. Yet comparing the two countries, it is quite clear that the maintenance of declining industries and unprofitable firms has been accorded a far greater priority in the UK than in the BRD. Maintenance aid in the BRD has been allocated mainly to mining the energy industries and transportation; with the exception of shipbuilding little aid has been given to declining manufacturing industries and virtually none to particular enterprises in financial difficulties. The contrast between the policies of the two governments towards their domestic motor car industries is particularly revealing. In both countries the car industry experienced a severe recession in 1974/75 with the major manufacturer facing financial difficulties. The response of the UK government was to acquire the equity of British Leyland and to offer it heavy financial support in order to maintain output and employment. In the BRD, the Federal government was faced with similar social problems and political pressures arising from the financial difficulties of Volkswagen. Its response, however, was not to interfere in the plant closures and redundancies by the company, but to offer financial incentives to the expansion of industry and employment in the areas affected by Volkswagen's contraction.

4.59 It has been argued by Peters (1971) that the 'sectoral economic policy in the Federal Republic of Germany has greatly undermined general economic policy'. The purpose of structural policy has been to lend assistance to the ailing rather than the growing branches of industry, reflecting according to Kuster (1974, pp.84-86), the political pressures exerted by the owners, managers and workers in declining industries on government. Yet, despite the growth in Federal government assistance to declining industries since 1975, in comparison with the UK, structural policy would appear to provide only limited interference with the process of structural adjustment through the market mechanism. Heavy subsidisation has been restricted to industries considered to be strategically vital (e.g. energy), where external benefits are considered important (e.g. transport), or which are technologically based, such as computers and aerospace. While maintenance and adjustment aid must inevitably retard the transfer of resources from declining to expanding sectors of the economy, these rigidities in the market mechanism may partly be overcome by encouraging mobility in the labour market. It is notable that during the period 1974-75 while government vocational training and retraining schemes covered about 114,000 persons in the UK, in the BRD the figure was 893,000 persons (OECD, 1978, pp.119-120). In the case of geographical mobility in the UK in 1974/75 and 1975/76 31,263 workers were assisted in employment transfer schemes, compared with 697,253 under similar schemes in the BRD (OECD, 1978, pp.126-127).

REFERENCES

Bundestagsdrucksache V/2469 (1968), *Grundsätze der Regionalen und Sektoralen Strukturpolitik* (Principles of Regional and Sectoral Policy). January.

Bundestagsdrucksache VI/1666 (1969), *Grundsätze einer Strukturpolitik fur Kleine und Mittlere Unternehmen* (Principle of Structural Policy for Small and Middle-sized Companies).

Casper, U. (1978), *Background Notes to Regional Incentives in the FDR.* International Institute of Management.

Galbraith, J.K. (1968), *The New Industrial State.*

House of Commons, 60011, 281 (i) and (ii) (1978), Report from the Expenditure Committee. Regional and Selective Assistance to Industry.

HMSO (1975), *An Approach to Industrial Strategy,* Cmnd 6315.

HMSO (1968), *Industrial Expansion,* Cmnd 3509.

Kuster, G.H. (1974), *Germany* in R. Vernon (ed) *Big Business and the State Changing Relations in Western Europe,* Macmillan.

Miles, C. (1968), *Lancashire Textiles: a Case Study of Industrial Change,* Cambridge University Press.

OECD (1971), *The Industrial Policies of 14 Member Countries,* Paris.

OECD (1978), *Selected Industrial Policy Instruments. Objectives and Scope,* Paris.

Peters, H.R. (1971), Strukturanpassungsgesetz gegen wuchernden Branchenprotektionismus, *Wirtschaftsdienst,* Vol.51, No.12.

Schiller, Karl (1955), *Socialismus und Wettbewerb,* Verlagsgenossenschaft deutscher Konsumgenossenschaften.

Zavlaris, D. (1970), Die Subventionen in der BRD seit 1951. *Deutsches Institut für Wirtschaftforschung: Beiträge zur Strukturforschung,* Heft 14.

CHAPTER 5

STRUCTURAL POLICIES IN THE UK AND BRD TOWARDS THE COMPUTER INDUSTRY

A. Introduction

5.1   The differences in industrial policies that have been observed in the previous chapter reflect a number of factors including the different political and economic philosophies that have been influential in the post-war period, the poorer overall performance of the British economy, differences in economic structure and structural change and differences in the political and economic constraints within which policies have been formulated. In the case of the computer industries of the two countries and the policies towards them, it is the similarities rather than the differences which are most apparent. The structure of the industry and its importance to the economy has been similar in both countries, the problems of the industry in the two countries have been virtually identical and the objectives of government policy towards the industry have been much the same. The computer industry therefore provides a particularly interesting study in the policy approaches of the two governments to a technologically-based growth industry.

B. Motives for government support of the computer industry

5.2   Government support for the computer industry in the BRD and the UK has taken place because of the importance of computers to industry and government in the modern economy and the contribution of computers to technological advance and economic growth. The OECD has compared the political and economic significance of the computer in the advanced economy with that of steel in industrialising economies [OECD (1969)]. Steel was regarded as a foundation for almost all other manufacturing industries and was of major importance in defence in the construction of ships and armaments. The computer's significance to industry, defence and public administration is the enormous expansion it makes possible in the processing of information. The UK Ministry of Technology noted in 1970 that 'now we have reached the stage where (the computer) is accepted as an integral part of the activities of government, banking, insurance, industrial management, transport control, retailing, production, engineering design, and scientific research and development' (Select Committee on Science and Technology, 1970, Vol.1). In industry, as in government, information is the basic input required for management and the introduction of computers has improved the quality of management decision making, increased the efficiency of production and distribution processes, and has revolutionised the operation of the financial sector. In defence, computers are vital for strategic and tactical planning and control, and for specific applications such as the flight control of ballistic missiles. The changes which computer technology has brought to industry have been referred to as the 'second industrial revolution'. Indeed, it may be that the computer revolution is only the first stage of a wider electonic revolution. The importance of the electronic technology to the future development of Europe has been recognised by the Commission of the European Communities: 'A strong capability in these related industries is essential to Europe's future' because:

i.   The character of our society will depend on our skill in using these new technologies, with their almost limitless possibilities.

ii.   Most industries and many services will become dependent on these technologies.

iii. The remarkable growth rate of the market for these industries means that by 1980 they will be responsible, together, for over 6 per cent of Europe's gross national expenditure. [Commission of the European Communities (1976) Vol.1 p.1].

5.3   It is this rapid rate of growth of the computer and electronic industries as compared with the relatively sluggish growth of manufacturing industry as a whole in West Germany and UK during the 1970s which identifies this sector as a major source of employment and economic growth for the next decade. The rate of growth of the computer industry has been such as to develop from infancy in the early 1950s to being the world's third largest industry (after petroleum and automobiles) in 1977. The growth of output of computers and associated equipment in the UK and the BRD is shown in Table 5.1. The growth of the computer industry has provided an important stimulus to growth and technological advance in related industries — components, telecommunications, consumer electronics and medical equipment. The increase in computing power and fall in computing cost made possible by the micro-processor suggests that the potential spinoff from electronic technology to the economy as a whole has yet to be fully realised.

5.4   Governments' concern to encourage and protect their domestic computer industries is heightened by the key strategic role of computers and computer technology. This was explained by a British government minister: 'What is certain, is that the role of the computer and its ancillaries will continue to expand and to penetrate both wide and deep into the nation's activities . . . it is not surprising therefore that the computer and the national capacity to move forward into this "computer age" should be a matter of deep pre-occupation not only to the British Government, but to all the Governments of Western Europe and to Japan. There is also evidence of the same pre-occupation in Russia and the countries of Eastern Europe and it is safe to assume the same will apply either now or in the near future in most other countries of the world.' [Select Committee on Science and Technology 1970, Vol.1, (S.C.S.T.)] .

5.5   Concern by the two governments over the development of their domestic computer industries also reflects the domination of the world computer industry by American companies. In the late 1960's OECD estimated that US-owned companies accounted for about 90 per cent of computer installations in the western world, with one company, IBM, possessing about three-quarters of the world market by value (c.f. Table 5.2). IBM was the fourth largest US corporation in terms of capital employed and the IBM subsidiaries in France, Germany, UK and Italy form by far the largest European manufacturer of computers. In no other European industry is the dominant position of US multinationals more apparent or has given rise to more national concern than computers. At the same time, however, both governments have been wary at putting at risk their access to American computer technology. The British government explained the problem as follows: 'We are confronted with a powerful and pervasive technology which will rapidly become decisive in most of the nation's activity — but with the danger of its being entirely under the control of American owned companies. Should one therefore adopt a chauvinistic attitude to repel the invader and seek to create an entirely indigenous industry? But to do this would not only undermine longstanding and important trading relationships with the USA. It would also deny the UK the very kind of technological input it needs. Yet to fail to produce an indigenous industry would expose the country to the possibilities that industrial, commercial, strategic or political decisions made in America would heavily influence our ability to manufacture, to trade, to govern or to defend'. [S.C.S.T. (1970)] .

C.   The computer manufacturing industries of the UK and the BRD

5.6   The size and growth of the computer industries of the two countries are compared in Table 5.1. By the mid-1970s the electronic data processing (EDP) industries were of approximately the same size. Up to 1975 the UK computer industry achieved a higher rate of sales growth than the German industry, but since 1975 the German industry has grown substantially faster.

5.7   Foreign trade in computers in relation to the size of the domestic market and the output of the domestic computer industry is important in both countries. Table 5.3 shows imports and exports of computers. The figures must be treated with caution. The trade classification differs between the two countries, and the classifications have been revised over the period. Although the UK industry has exported a higher proportion of its output, the German computer industry appears to have been more successful in competing with imports — the market share of imports is much larger in the UK than BRD. Moreover, while BRD has had a strongly favourable trade balance in computers since 1974, that of the UK has been adverse.

5.8   The structure of the computer industry in both countries reflects a single dominating factor — the enormous research and development expenditure required for any company to keep abreast of technological change in the industry. As a result, in both the UK and the BRD, the domestically-owned sector of the industry has developed by merger and rationalisation culminating in the formation of a single manufacturer of large and medium-sized mainframe computers. In the BRD Siemens acquisition of the computer interests of Telefunken-AEG made it the sole German-owned manufacturer of a range of computer systems. In the UK, the formation of ICL in 1968 was the climax of a long series of mergers and acquisitions among domestic manufacturers.

5.9   In meeting the 'American challenge' in the market for medium and large computers, the UK has been in a far stronger position than Germany. As was noted by the UK Select Committee on Science and Technology [1970, Vol.1] : 'The UK is the only country outside America which has a significant indigenous computer industry capable of development into a world class international enterprise.' But while ICL held almost half the UK market in 1969, its market share has fallen compared with Siemens growth of its share of the German market (See Table 5.4). The problems facing the European computer manufacturer when competing against the US-owned multinationals is illustrated by Table 5.5. As a percentage of sales revenue, ICL's R and D expenditure exceeds that of the major manufacturers yet IBM's R and D budget was twice the size of ICL's total sales revenue.

5.10   ICL has developed and marketed its computers independently of other companies. Siemens on the other hand has developed its computers primarily in association with other companies. These associations have been unsuccessful and under these difficult circumstances Siemens' ability to expand its share of the West German computer market has been remarkable. Between 1963 and 1971 Siemens manufactured the RCA

Table 5.1

COMPUTER PRODUCTION AND EMPLOYMENT, BRD AND UK

		1971	1972	1973	1974	1975	1976	1977
BRD								
Computers	DMm	—	1691	1515	1277	935	1085	2045
	£m	—	210	233	212	172	240	505
Peripherals	DMm	—	1722	1310	1659	1439	1572	1820
	£m	—	213	202	275	265	347	450
Total computer sales	DMm	2419	3412	2825	2936	2374	2657	3865
	£m	285	423	435	487	437	587	955
Employment (thousands)		33	34	39	41	40	36	38
UK								
Computers	DMm	—	1048	864	729	690	724	765
	£m	—	130	133	121	127	160	189
Peripherals	DMm	—	1177	1195	1434	1543	1805	1862
	£m	—	146	184	238	284	399	460
Total Computer sales	DMm	1576	2306	2292	2450	2652	2674	2697
(MLH 366)	£m	186	286	353	416	489	591	675
Employment (thousands)		58	50	51	45	43	44	45

Note: The exchange rates used were as follows: 1971   DM1 = £0.118   1972   DM1 = £0.124
       1973   DM1 = £0.154   1974   DM1 = £0.166
       1975   DM1 = £0.184   1976   DM1 = £0.221
       1977   DM1 = £0.247   1978   DM1 = £0.262

Source: UK *Business Monitor; UK Census of Production*, 1972; *Production Produzierender Gewerbe*

Table 5.2

THE WORLD COMPUTER MARKET: SHARES OF INSTALLED GENERAL PURPOSE COMPUTERS BY MANUFACTURER (BY VALUE) AT 1.1.75

	World	Western Europe	USA	West Germany	UK	France	Japan
IBM	56.60	54.40	68.76	61.56	39.72	58.46	35.50
Honeywell	8.19	10.22	8.96	7.00	9.58	15.04	1.02
Univac	6.52	5.68	7.61	5.29	4.80	3.97	7.50
Comecon manufacturers	5.17	—	—	—	—	—	—
Japanese producers	4.69	—	—	—	—	—	50.23
Burroughs	4.64	3.28	5.74	1.09	5.26	3.77	3.22
ICL	3.14	8.3	—	—	31.14	2.97	—
Unidata[1]	2.68	8.82	—	17.56	—	9.91	—
NCR	2.41	2.03	2.87	0.98	2.89	1.29	1.83
Others	5.96	7.26	6.06	5.45	6.61	8.19	0.70

Note: 1 = Includes Siemens

Source: Third data processing programme of the Federal Government, 1976-1979

Table 5.3

IMPORTS AND EXPORTS OF COMPUTERS

£m

		1974	1975	1976	1977	1978
Analogue and hybrid	IMPORTS	5.0	1.9	2.6	3.5	3.3
machines	EXPORTS	1.6	1.3	0.5	2.6	5.2
Computer systems	IMPORTS	11.7	16.2	25.0	28.6	39.5
	EXPORTS	47.7	43.6	72.0	95.0	108.3
Central processing units	IMPORTS	66.3	69.7	113.3	135.3	170.7
	EXPORTS	42.8	42.5	64.8	126.8	112.2
Central memory units	IMPORTS	19.8	30.6	36.3	42.5	53.5
	EXPORTS	32.1	33.2	41.7	49.3	34.5
Punches, verifiers and	IMPORTS	5.7	5.1	5.3	4.7	4.6
calculators	EXPORTS	2.0	2.6	3.8	4.0	9.2
Other independent units for computing and data	IMPORTS	11.7	9.8	—	22.2	25.5
storage	EXPORTS	3.7	4.4	—	7.2	8.0
TOTAL IMPORTS		164.9	177.7	240.5	309.9	394.0
TOTAL EXPORTS		206.4	193.6	312.2	408.2	411.2
UK						
Automatic data processing	IMPORTS	41.0	49.3	89.0	91.6	94.6
machines	EXPORTS	46.2	54.8	69.9	70.8	141.7
Central processing units	IMPORTS	12.6	18.4	17.3	33.1	69.3
	EXPORTS	4.3	5.0	10.7	6.7	34.8
Peripheral and other	IMPORTS	115.4	134.8	227.6	337.5	378.3
units	EXPORTS	114.9	152.9	191.8	263.3	273.5
Parts	IMPORTS	177.8	180.8	218.5	229.8	297.2
	EXPORTS	104.1	119.3	134.7	168.3	192.9
TOTAL IMPORTS		345.8	383.3	552.4	679.4	879.4
TOTAL EXPORTS		269.5	332.0	407.1	509.1	642.9
Business monitor figures of computer exports		208.0	242.2	317.3	337.6	

Note: Deutsche marks have been converted to £ sterling at the rates shown in Table 5.2

Sources: *Aussenhandel, nach Waren und Ländern* (Spezial handel); *UK Overseas Trade Statistics; Business Monitor*

Table 5.4

MARKET SHARES BY VALUE IN UK AND WEST GERMANY, 1969 and 1976

	UK		West Germany	
	1969	1976	1969	1976
IBM	28	46	46	
Honeywell	8	8	2	7
ICL	49	26	1	1
Siemens	—	—	13	19
Univac	—	5	7	5

Sources: Stoneman (1975) p.21, Soris Report (Turin June 1970), *Financial Times,* 19 February 1979 p.17.

Table 5.5

SALES, PROFITS AND R AND D FOR SOME MAJOR COMPUTER MANUFACTURERS, 1976

	Sales ($m)	Pretax Profits ($m)	Profit/Sales Ratio	R & D ($m)
IBM	16,304	4,519	28	1,012
NCR	2,313	173	7	94
Burroughs	1,902	315	17	108
Sperry Univac	1,438	96	7	159
Honeywell	1,428	117	8	126
Control Data	1,358	92	7	59
Digital Equipment	736	119	16	58
ICL	502	40	8	50

Note: * = Group totals

Source: *Economist*, 13.8.77, p.64

Specta 90 series under licence. In 1971 RCA abandoned its computer interests and, together with Philips and CII, Siemens formed Unidata. In 1974 Unidata folded following CII's decision to merge with Honeywell-Bull. Since 1974 Siemens has concentrated on the independent development of a range of computers plug-compatible with IBM. In March 1978 Siemens entered the small office computer market and later in 1978 agreed with Fujitsu, Japan's leading computer manufacturer, to market Fujitsu computers in Europe.

5.11 In the manufacture of small computers the UK's superiority in large computers is reversed; German manufacturers have been far more commercially successful. Table 5.6 shows the two countries' production and trade in this sector of the market.

Table 5.6

THE MARKETS FOR AND PRODUCTION OF MINI COMPUTERS AND SMALL BUSINESS SYSTEMS IN 1974

	Market £m	Production £m	Exports £m	Imports £m
WEST GERMANY				
Mini Computers[1]	9.7	5.4	1.8	5.7
Small business systems	72.0	87.0	34.0	19.0
UK				
Mini Computers[2]	9.3	4.4	0.6	5.5
Small business systems	35.0	25.0	7.5	11.0

Note: 1. General purpose mini computers costing up to $40,000
2. e.g. Systems sold by Mixdorf, Philips, NCR, Olivetti

Source: Commission of the European Communities 1976, Vol.III, p.91.

The comparative success of the German manufacturers may, in part, reflect the larger size of this sector of the market in the BRD. In 1973 the numbers of installed computers were estimated as follows:

	Very Small	Small	Medium	Large	Total
West Germany	3,584	8,196	2,233	417	14,330
UK	1,978	4,461	1,244	310	7,993

Source: Commission of the European Communities, 1976, p.67

5.12 Despite the entry of large computer manufacturers (including IBM, ICL and Siemens) into the small computer market, this market is supplied primarily by specialist companies, notably the US-based Digital Equipment Corporation. The principal German manufacturers are Nixdorf (with about 35 per cent of this market), Kienzle, Triumph-Adler (owned by Litton) and Dietz. In the UK specialist domestic manufacturers of small computers such as Computer Technology Ltd, have not obtained a large market share, as shown in Table 5.7.

Table 5.7

NUMBERS OF MINI COMPUTERS INSTALLED IN THE UK AT THE BEGINNING OF 1977

Digital Equipment Corp. (US)	4,337
Data General (US)	2,250
OAL (US)	1,800
GEC (US)	1,688
Ferranti (UK)	791
Computer Technology (UK)	445

Source: *Financial Times*

5.13 One of the most significant features of the computer market in the two countries has been the growing importance of peripheral equipment — terminals, printers and magnetic memory units. Tables 5.2 and 5.8 show that in both UK and BRD the output of peripherals now exceeds in value the output of central processing units and complete systems. In both countries the market for peripherals is dominated by US suppliers and their subsidiaries; Table 5.8 shows the share of the market supplied by imports was 82 per cent in the BRD and 77 per cent in the UK.

Table 5.8

THE MARKETS FOR AND PRODUCTION OF COMPUTER PERIPHERALS IN 1974

	Market £m	Production £m	Exports £m	Imports £m
WEST GERMANY				
Local computer[1] peripherals	560	104	19	475
General purpose[2] terminals	96	56	20	60
UK				
Local computer[1] peripherals	260	60	5	205
General purpose[2] terminals	100	44	14	70

Note: 1. Discs, drums magnetic tapes, fast printers etc.
2. Visual display, teleprinters, heavy terminals.

Source: Commission of the European Communities, 1976, Vol.III, p.89.

C. Other sectors of the computer industry: Computer services and integrated circuits

5.14 While the computer industry is normally identified with the manufacture of EDP hardware, there are two related sectors which from their importance to the national economies and public policy cannot be ignored. The first is computer services (the supply of software, data processing services and consultancy) the second is electonic components, notably integrated circuits.

5.15 As the price of computer hardware has continued to fall in real terms so the relative importance of the labour intensive computer service industry, as measured by value of output, has grown. Table 5.9 shows the growth in total revenue of the UK computer services industry. Official statistics on the output of computer services tend to be under-estimates. It is generally agreed, however, that software accounts for over half the total costs of bringing a computer system into operation, adding the value of other computer services would imply that the output of services exceeds the value of the output of hardware.

Table 5.9

SALES BY THE UK COMPUTER SERVICE INDUSTRY

Tot		1971	1972	1973	1974	1975	1976	1977
Total billings of which:	£m	69.2	79.7	104.0	128.6	164.3	220.7	265.4
UK public service clients	£m	7.7	11.1	13.8	15.2	18.4	30.3	33.1
Foreign clients	£m	2.5	3.9	4.8	5.7	7.6	10.6	13.6

Source: Business Monitor SDQ9

5.16 The importance of integrated circuits derives less from the value of their output (see Table 5.10) as from their role as the principal component for computers and the primary vehicle for the transfer of electronic technology to other sectors of the economy. American companies dominate a world market characterised by fierce competition in technology and price. Of a total world market for integrated circuits estimated at $3,150 million in 1976, US companies were estimated to have 62 per cent (Commission of the European Communities, 1976, Vol.III, p.95). The largest manufacturers are Texas Instruments, Motorola, Fairchild and RCA. IBM is also a large manufacturer but only for its own use. In Germany the manufacture of integrated circuits is led by Siemens and AEG-Telefunken. Siemens sales of integrated circuits amounted to about $75 million in 1978. In Britain the manufacture of integrated circuits is a relatively under-developed area of electronic component manufacture. UK companies with interests in integrated circuits are Plessey, Ferranti and GEC. The UK accounts for 18.2 per cent of the Western European integrated circuit market as compared with 37.2 per cent for the BRD. Both West Germany and the UK have large negative balances in the trade of integrated circuits (Table 5.10).

Table 5.10

PRODUCTION, EXPORTS AND IMPORTS OF INTEGRATED CIRCUITS AND OTHER MICRO-CIRCUITS

			1973	1974	1975	1976	1977
Manufacturers'							
sales	BRD	DMm	276	308	282	336	444
	UK	£m	30.4	40.8	37.4	49.0	73.6
UK Exports		£m	7.2	15.0	14.3	21.1	41.2
UK Imports		£m	27.1	43.0	46.6	70.5	99.2

Source: Business Monitor PQ 36.

D. Policies of the BRD and UK governments towards computer technology and the computer industry: an overview

5.17 BRD policies towards the computer industry have been in the form of three electronic data processing programmes between 1967 and 1979 which have covered financial support to the industry for R and D, research programmes undertaken by universities and institutes and the training of manpower for the effective use of computer technology. The programmes have been implemented by the Federal Ministries for Economics and Finance and the Federal Ministry for Education and Science. UK policies towards the computer industry and EDP technology have comprised a number of policy measures including some schemes offering financial assistance to individual manufacturers and for the development .of particular types of products, preference in public procurement, the finance of research by universities and other public sector organisations. Unlike West Germany, British policy has shown little evidence of overall co-ordination. While support programmes for the industry are administered by the Department of Industry (between 1964 and 1972 by the Ministry of Technology) which also acts as the sponsoring department for the industry, central government procurement and policy on the use in government of computers is controlled by the Civil Service Department, computer education and training is the responsibility of the Depart-of Education and the National Enterprise Board (NEB) has also been involved in providing finance to the industry.

5.18 Probably the most noticeable single difference between the UK and West German policies towards their domestic computer industries is the much greater amount of financial assistance by the Federal government to the computer industry. Table 5.11 shows government expenditure on policies to develop EDP in West Germany, UK, France and Belgium. Comparing support for the computer industry and government expenditure on research, expenditure by the UK government between 1971 and 1975 was far below that of the West German and the French governments.

Table 5.11

STATE AID FOR ELECTRONIC DATE PROCESSING, 1971-1975

	Assistance to hardware industries	Application and research	Education
W. Germany	DM705.4 million (£112.9m)	DM784.6 million (£125.5m)	DM919.9 million (£147.2m)
UK	£37.1 million	£18.44 million	N.A.
France	FF870 million	FF616 million	FF420 million
Belgium	BF1950 million	BF186.6 million	N.A.

Source: Commission of the European Communities, 1976.

Table 5.12

THE DISTRIBUTION OF GOVERNMENT EXPENDITURE ON ELECTRONIC DATA PROCESSING IN WEST GERMANY

1st programme 1967-1970		2nd programme 1970-1975	3rd programme 1976-1979	
R & D SUPPORT TO HARDWARE MANUFACTURERS			R & D SUPPORT TO HARDWARE MANUFACTURERS	DM 554.3m
Min. of Economics & Finance	DM112.4m	DM 188.0m	System architecture and programme languages	DM 73.0m
Min. of Education & Science	DM128.2m	DM 514.7m	Data processing technology	DM 76.3m
			Remote peripherals	DM 62.0m
DATA PROCESSING APPLICATIONS			Small Systems	DM 149.0m
			Medium and large systems	DM 194.0m
Min. of Economics & Finance for software packages	DM 57.0m	DM 79.0m		
Min. of Education & Science for systems and development			APPLICATIONS	DM 561.6m
			Information systems	DM 165.0m
		DM 479.0m	Medical information	DM 141.3m
			Teaching	DM 15.5m
BASIC RESEARCH & SPECIAL PROGRAMMES			Computer aided design	DM 66.0m
		DM 226.6m	Process control	DM 94.8m
	DM 42.0m		Tele-processing	DM 31.5m
			Aid to users	DM 42.0m
DATA PROCESSING EDUCATION			Shape recognition	DM 5.5m
Higher education	DM 43.0m	DM 757.9m	TRAINING	DM 264.2m
Professional training centres	DM 4.0m	DM 162.0m	Supra regional research programmes	DM 86.5m
			Scientific data exchange	DM 6.0m
			Regional computing centre	DM 168.0m
			Professional training centres	DM 3.7m
			Gesellschaft für Mathematik = und Datenverbreitung	DM 194.8m
TOTAL	DM386.6m	DM2409.9m	TOTAL	DM1574.9m
R & D SUPPORT FOR ELECTRONIC COMPONENTS				
1971-1975	DM 2.2m	1969-1970 DM 189.8m	1976-1978	DM 184.0m
			1979	DM 200.0m

5.19 In view of the similar objectives of the two governments in relation to their EDP industries and the similar problems faced by both industries, close parallels in the EDP policies of the two countries might be expected. In both countries governments have sought to accelerate the technological development of their indigenous computer industries by means of subsidy. The primary means of achieving this have been R and D subsidies to the manufacturers of computer hardware and the financing of research by public sector bodies (universities and special research centres such as the Gesellschaft für Mathematik und Datenverarbeitung and the National Computing Centre). However, UK policies differ from those of the BRD in being more selective and more interventionist than those of the BRD. Thus in providing support for R and D most UK expenditure has been made available exclusively to ICL, whereas BRD support has been made available to a range of firms. Also, UK policy has extended beyond the offer of grants and loans to private firms to direct intervention in private industry (e.g. government was responsible for the merger which created ICL) and to the launching of new firms (the NEB has been responsible for launching new micro-electronics and software firms). Unlike West Germany, the UK has pursued a particularly active policy of directing public purchases of computers towards domestically owned companies.

5.20 Differences between the policies of the two countries are also apparent in the distribution of government aid between the different sectors of the industry. In the UK, support has been concentrated on mainframe computers (i.e. the basic product range of ICL). In West Germany, on the other hand, assistance has been distributed more widely to cover small as well as large computers, peripherals and, most notably, software and elecctronic components. It would seem, therefore, that while the UK government policy between 1968 and 1975 was concerned chiefly with the survival of ICL, the approach of the German government has been to encourage the development of the EDP industry as a whole.

Table 5.13

UK GOVERNMENT FINANCIAL AID FOR THE COMPUTER INDUSTRY

	1969/70 £m	1970/71 £m	1971/72 £m	1972/73 £m	1973/74 £m	1974/75 £m	1975/76 £m	1976/77 £m	1977/78 £m
International Computer (Holdings) Ltd	4.0	3.3	2.3	12.0	9.5	10.2	8.3	3.3	–
Advanced Computer Technology Project and other shared-cost computer projects	0.7	1.0	0.7	0.8	2.3	1.0	0.7	0.9	0.6
Software products scheme and systems and software development	–	–	–	1.5	0.8	0.4	0.4	0.3	0.5
Micro-electronics applications and production schemes	–	–	0.3	0.9	1.3	1.2	1.7	2.1	2.4
Electronic component sectoral scheme	–	–	–	–	–	–	–	–	4.0
TOTAL	4.7	4.3	3.3	15.2	13.9	12.8	11.1	6.6	7.5
Also, government support for: Computer Aided Design Centre	0.5	0.5	0.4	0.7	1.0	1.3	1.0	1.1	1.1
National Computing Centre	0.6	0.6	0.6	0.8	1.1	1.2	1.2	1.2	1.2

Sources: Research and Development Requirements Boards Reports, Trade and Industry 27 May 1977; Commission of the European Communities (1977)

E. Government financial aid to the manufacturers of computer hardware

The UK

5.21 British government financial support for the computer manufacturing industry has until recently consisted primarily of assistance to ICL, the part-publicly owned UK computer firm establish in 1968 from a government-sponsored merger of the major UK computer manufacturers, ICT and English Electric Computers. The resulting company, International Computer (Holdings) Limited (ICL) was owned 53.5 per cent by ICT shareholders, 18 per cent by English Electric, 18 per cent by Plessey and 10.5 per cent by the government. Government was to appoint one director to the Board of ICL but was not to interfere in the day-to-day management of the company.

5.22 Total finance provided by government amounted to £17m over 5 years. This included:

(a) £3½m for ordinary shares of £1 each in ICL, 2 shillings payable on issue and the balance in 1972;

(b)   £13½m from the Ministry of Technology over 5½ years as a grant towards R & D expenditure.

This sum was agreed on the basis of ICL's estimates of its required expenditure on R and D in order to maintain technological competitiveness with US manufacturers, and the funds which it was able to provide from its own resources. The intention was that by 1971 ICL should have developed its technology and its sales to the point where support for ICL's research and development, over and above allocations of funds for the development of specific projects, would be necessary.

5.23 During 1971 it became evident that ICL could not be expected to maintain technological competitiveness with American companies without considerable support from government in the development of a new range of computers. On 3 July 1972 the Government agreed to provide ICL with £14.2 million over the period to September 1973 to assist ICL with the launch of its new series. The amount of this support took account of ICL's need to converge to two product lines originating from ICT and English Electric, and the financial pressures on ICL due to rising costs and the world wide recession in computer orders. On 4 July 1973 it was announced that the government would provide a further £25.8m to support R and D over the period October 1973 to September 1976. These sums of financial support were in principle re-payable by a levy on sales. Again the government re-affirmed its intention that R and D support was temporary and noted that if the support was successful 'then in the company year 1976-77 ICL expects to have reached a level of size and profitability adequate to make further R and D support unnecessary' (S.C.S.T. 1973, Minutes of Evidence, p.28).

5.24 This support programme for the period 1972-76 was based on an appraisal of ICL's requirements and resources undertaken by officials advised by management consultants and merchant bankers. The sum of £40m in aid was based upon ICL's R and D expenditure on its 2,900 series of computers and the company's forecasts of its sales and cash flow over the period. The amount was to be recovered by a levy on ICL's pre-tax profits during the 7 year period in excess of 7.5 per cent of turnover up to a maximum of 25 per cent of pretax profit and subject to an overall maximum of £40m (discounted at 10 per cent per annum). Moni-toring was by the Department of Industry CSE division with the assistance of a firm of management con-sultants. Payments of instalments of aid were conditional upon 'the Department being satisfied that the progress of the R and D programme and the financial and general state of the company are reasonably con-sistent with the expectation of commercial success; that the company is providing a reasonable contribution to the R and D programme from its own resources, and that it does not without the consent of the Secre-tary of State pay more than a minimum dividend' [G.M. Field and P.V. Hills (1976)]. Since direct support ended in September 1977, ICL has not received finance from government specifically to support its R and D programme, though ICL does benefit from schemes which are available to the industry as a whole.

5.25 Government finance for more general programmes of R and D in the computer industry has been com-paratively meagre. The principal scheme, the Advanced Computer Technology Project set up in 1963 to en-courage co-operation between computer companies and government research laboratories in basic research, was aimed at developing new components and techniques in the computer field. The project was initially aimed towards pre-prototypes of new computer systems for future commercial production. In 1965 the scope of the scheme was widened to include all aspects of computer systems including peripherals and software. Selection of projects is undertaken with assistance from the ACTP Advisory Committee which includes representatives from the computer industry, the Department of Industry, government research establishments and the National Computing Centre. Government involvement is on a 50-50 cost sharing basis. All contracts contain a clause for the repayment of government assistance by way of a levy on sales or royalties arising from the projects. Expenditure on computer R and D through ACTP and other shared cost R and D schemes has been noticeably low as indicated in Table 5.13.

5.26 UK suppliers of computers have also benefited indirectly from the subsidies which have been provided to purchases of computers. The 1966 Industrial Development Act introduced investment grants to all firms purchasing computers whether or not these firms were engaged in manufacturing. In 1970 these grants were replaced by investment allowances. The purpose of these incentives was to encourage the adoption by industry of EDP technology rather than to support the national computer industry — the incentives were paid whether or not the computers were purchased from UK or foreign-owned suppliers.

THE BRD

5.27 Direct Federal government support for hardware manufacturers has been exclusively in the form of grants and loans for R and D by manufacturers. The Federal Ministry for Education and Science supports basic research into EDP technology of a long run nature, the Federal Ministries for Economics and Finance con-centrate on financing the applications of innovations and technological knowledge to the development and production of marketable products. Table 5.12 shows the budgets of the three programmes. Under the first programme, assistance was initially in the form of 20 year loans at 3 per cent, these loans then became

Table 5.14

PUBLIC SECTOR COMPUTER INSTALLATIONS IN NUMBER AND VALUE: BROKEN DOWN BY MANUFACTURERS IN THE UNITED KINGDOM

Manufacturers	Central Administrations			Local Administrations			Public Corporations			Total	
	number	value £ million	% by value	number	value £ million	% by value	number	value £ million	% by value	number	£ million
National											
ICL	247	94.1	50.0	235	44.0	54.2	176	57.1	37.4	658	195.2
GEC	268	11.2	6.0	18	1.0	1.2	105	6.3	4.1	391	18.6
Ferranti	125	7.3	3.9	3	0.3	0.4	113	7.8	5.1	241	15.4
Computer Technology	115	2.3	1.2	2	0.1	0.1	43	0.9	0.6	160	3.3
Plessey	3	0.5	0.3	3	0.8	1.0	1	0.1	0.1	7	1.4
Digico	41	0.2	0.1	10	0.1	0.1	30	0.2	0.1	81	0.4
Others	22	1.1	0.6	3	0.1	0.1	15	0.5	0.4	40	1.7
TOTAL	821	116.7	62.1	274	46.7	57.1	483	72.9	47.7	1578	236.6
Foreign											
IBM	86	31.3	16.6	85	18.2	22.4	118	50.5	33.0	289	100.0
Honeywell	83	3.9	2.1	43	6.2	7.6	81	8.1	5.3	207	18.2
Univac	14	6.0	3.2	12	2.3	2.9	24	6.6	4.3	50	14.9
CDC	15	13.8	7.3	—	—	—	3	0.2	0.1	16	14.0
Burroughs	76	6.1	3.2	32	1.6	1.9	7	0.7	0.5	115	8.4
DEC	264	4.3	2.3	147	1.9	2.3	147	1.9	1.3	556	8.1
NCR	10	0.4	0.2	63	3.1	3.9	23	1.1	0.7	96	4.6
Xerox Data	12	2.0	1.0	—	—	—	5	1.3	0.9	17	3.3
Philips	20	0.2	0.1	29	0.3	0.3	12	0.1	0.1	61	0.6
Others	186	3.6	1.9	52	1.1	1.4	580	9.0	5.8	818	13.7
TOTAL	766	71.6	38.0	463	34.7	42.4	1000	79.5	52.0	2229	185.8
TOTAL GENERAL	1587	188.3	100.0	737	81.0	100.0	1483	152.4	100.0	3807	421.8

Source: Commission of the European Communities, 1976, Vol.III, p.119

interest-free covering 25 per cent of project costs and repayable only in the event of commercial success of the project. The major recipients of support under the first programme were the two domestically owned manufacturers of medium and large computers: Siemens and Telefunken-AEG. In the second and third programme not only were the budgets for R and D support greatly increased but the percentage of project costs covered by government finance more frequently exceeded the basic 25 per cent level. Under the third programme assistance may be 25 per cent, 33 per cent or 50 per cent of production and development costs dependent upon the degree of risk of the project. The highest rates relate to basic research and grants were repayable if the project was commercially successful. Since 1973 repayment conditions have no longer been maintained. Following the first EDP programme support for computer hardware manufacturers has been increasingly directed away from the large computer manufacturers and towards small computers. Under the second programme over DM400 million was intended for Siemens, but this fell to around DM280 million in the third programme. In the third programme R and D support for medium and large systems was budgeted at DM194 million as compared with DM149 for small systems. The policy of assisting R and D into the small computer sector sharply contrasts with UK policy where government has provided only the most meagre support to specialist manufacturers of small systems. The German government's emphasis on the small computer sector is particularly significant in view of the precarious position of the German large computer sector following Siemen's disastrous associations with other companies and the large R and D requirement of Siemens following its decision to follow a 'go it alone' policy of developing IBM compatible equipment. German R and D support also contrasts with that of the UK in the support it has offered for the development of peripherals. In the third programme a budget was specifically allocated to the development of peripherals. As Table 5.1 shows, in both the UK and West Germany, the rate of growth output of peripherals has far outstripped that of computer systems and central processing units.

F.   Computer research by public sector bodies

5.28   In both the BRD and the UK the development of EDP technology has been regarded as too important to be left entirely to the private sector and in both countries major contributions to basic research have taken place both in universities and research institutes. Publicly financed EDP research in the BRD has been mainly at the Gesellschaft für Mathematik-und Datenverarbeitung (Institute for Mathematical and Data Processing) (GMD), Bonn. Under the third EDP programme the budget for the GMD totalled DM194.8 million. UK government expenditure on EDP research in public sector institutions has been a fraction of that in the BRD. Expenditure by the Science Research Council on computer-related research in the universities has averaged about £1 million annually during the 1970s. R and D expenditure by the Computers, Systems and Electronics Requirements Board in government research organisations increased from £2.4m to £4.4m between 1974/5 and 1977/8. The principal government financed organisations engaged in research on computer applications are the Computer Aided Design Centre, the National Physical Laboratory and the National Computer Centre.

G.   Support to the computer industry through public procurement policy.

5.29   Government policy regarding the purchase and use of computers in the public sector is of great importance to the computer industries of both countries since government is the most important single customer for computers and its level of purchases is the most important factor affecting the prosperity of the industry as a whole. In the UK the public sector market for computers was valued in 1974 at £421.8 million (35.1 per cent) out of a total UK computer market of £1,199 million. In the BRD public sector demand accounted for about 12.5 per cent of a total market worth about £11,850 million at the beginning of 1975. The public sector is of particular importance to manufacturers because of its demand for very large systems and its willingness to lead the private sector in installing advanced technology and new computer systems. Clearly a discriminatory public sector procurement policy offers a particularly potent means of support for indigenous computer manufacturers and European governments have justified such preference on the grounds that the US government has traditionally pursued a 'buy American' policy on computers. In fact, US procurement policy has followed a somewhat more complex strategy, for, not only has preference been given to domestic manufacturers, but, in addition, the Federal government has sought to counteract the dominance of IBM by offering the bulk of its business to smaller manufacturers.

5.30   Central government policy in the UK has, since 1965 been to purchase computers from British firms where reasonably possible and to encourage other public sector bodies to do likewise. Until 1968 the government sought competitive tenders from a number of different manufacturers, then in 1968 the purchasing procedure was modified so that for each order detailed negotiations were held with only three suppliers. Following the computer merger a single tender policy was introduced. Government procurement policy was explained by the Civil Service Department as follows (S.C.S.T. 1970, Vol.1, p.445):

'(1)   To acquire large computers by single tender action from ICL, subject to satisfactory price, performance and delivery dates.

Table 5.15

DP SYSTEMS INSTALLED IN THE PUBLIC SECTOR IN THE BRD AT 1.11.1975 (SMALL SYSTEMS EXCLUDED)

	Number (total)	Number of rent installations	Number of purchased installations	Monthly rental	Expenses for purchasing
		(1)	(2)	(3)	DM millions (4)
1. IBM	87	80	7	13.5	37.8
2. CDC	4	—	4	0.1	3.6
3. UNIVAC	1	—	1	0.1	0.0
4. Honeywell-Bull	1	—	1	0.0(5)	0.0
5. DEC	3	—	3	0.0(5)	6.7
6. CII	1	—	1	0.0(5)	0.0
7. Telfunken	15	4	11	1.1	15.0
8. Siemens	60	48	12	5.9	35.7
TOTAL	172	132	40	20.7	98.8

Note: (1) Data-processing systems the elements of which are principally leased.
(2) Data-processing systems the elements of which are principally purchased.
(3) Expenses for leasing and services.
(4) Expenses for purchased installations since 1971 and in operation.
(5) Rounded

Source: Commission of the European Communities 1976, Vol.III, p.116

(2)   To acquire smaller computers by single tender action (normally from ICL) when they are intended to lead-in·to the use of a large computer of the same family or where there are other reasons for seeking a compatibility or flexibility . . .

(3)   In all other cases to seek competitive tenders from not less than three firms including at least one offering a system of British manufacture: to evaluate the tenders objectively — and to award the contract on the merits of the evaluation, allowing preference in favour of any British machine provided that there is no undue price differential as compared with overseas suppliers, that the British machine is technically suitable and that no undue delay is involved.'

Table 5.14 shows that national manufacturers have gained a far larger share of the public sector market than of the private sector market. At the end of 1974 ICL accounted for about 46 per cent of the value of public sector computers.

5.31   In contrast to the UK, the BRD government has been scrupulously careful to avoid special preference to individual manufacturers, or even to national manufacturers as a group, in its purchasing policy. The computer purchases by the Federal government and Länder are subject to strict rules which require all purchases to be put out to tender. Tenders are assessed in terms of price and performance and only discrimination in favour of European suppliers is permitted. As a result European manufacturers at the end of 1975 had a larger share of the German public sector market (44 per cent) than of the total market (20 per cent). IBM was the largest supplier of computers to the German public sector with Siemens as a close second. How far the policy of European preference extends to giving preference to non-German European manufacturers is difficult to assess, but it is noticeable that Siemens and Telefunken are the only European manufacturers with a significant share of the German public sector market. Table 5.15 shows the breakdown of the German public sector market between suppliers. The European Commission has ruled that discriminatory purchasing of computers by governments must end by 1980.

H.   Government support for software

5.32   Financial support by the UK government is relatively recent and the sums involved have been small. Despite the large value of software business in the two countries and its rapid growth in relation to the hardware industry, it has received much less attention from government than the manufacturing sectors of the EDP industry. This is particularly true in the UK where government support has traditionally been biased towards manufacturing industry and has tended to favour large rather than small firms. In 1965 the Advanced Computer Technology Project was extended to software, but little finance was provided for software projects. While ICL was able to benefit from general government support to develop its software services, specialist software firms received little or no government support. In 1973 the government established a software development scheme on a 50-50 shared cost basis. Between 1974/75 and 1977/78, however, total expenditure under the scheme amounted to only £1 million. More recently direct intervetion by government into the software industry has taken place with the establishment of Insac Data Systems Ltd., a wholly owned subsidiary of the National Enterprise Board, which provides overseas marketing for UK software. An investment of £20 million over five years is envisaged.

5.33 In the BRD financial support for the development of software has been an integral part of government policy towards the EDP industry since the first EDP programme (1967-71), support for software development has been provided by the Ministries of Economics and Finance on the same basis as support for hardware development. The first payments for software development were made in 1970. Under the first programme software support by the Economics Ministry was as follows: 1970 DM3m (hardware DM30m), 1971 DM14m (hardware DM48m), (Select Committee 1971, Vol.III, p.32). Under the second EDP programme 1971-75 Economics Ministry support for software was budgeted at DM100m, compared with DM170m for hardware. The third EDP programme provides an even larger budget for computer applications.

I. Financial support for integrated circuits

5.34 Although the manufacture of integrated circuits is only a part of the electronic components industry with a modest production value, in both countries governments have introduced special schemes to encourage R and D into manufacture of and application of integrated circuits. This reflects the growth potential of this sector of the electronics industry and the importance of these components in transmitting electronic technology to other parts of the economy.

5.35 In the BRD support for R and D into electronic components has been the subject of four special programmes commencing in 1969 (see Table 5.11). Under the second, third and fourth programmes, the budgets for financial support have been almost identical — approaching DM200m. The major part of this budget has been for R and D into integrated circuits and in the current programme support is concentrated on the very large integrated circuits. In all of the four programmes the major part of the budget has gone to Siemens with AEG-Telefunken taking a significant share of the remainder.

5.36 In the UK, after virtually ignoring the electronic components industry, government departments and agencies now appear to be falling over one another to establish schemes to encourage the development and application of micro-electronic technology. As one industry expert has noted: 'never have so many politicians jumped on so small a thing as a micro-chip so late in the game' (Financial Times, 19 February, 1979, p.18). The principal schemes have been:

i. R and D Requirements Board for Computers and Systems and Electronics: — £7.4 million was made available in 25 per cent grants and 50 per cent shared most agreements between 1974/5 and 1977/8.

ii. The Electronic Components Scheme was launched by the Department of Industry under section 8 of the 1972 Industry Act. A £20 million budget was fully committed by the end of 1977.

iii. The micro-electronics Industry Scheme was established in July 1978 with a five year budget of £70 million for 25 per cent grants and 50 per cent shared-cost projects for the development of micro-electronic products and processes.

5.37 The two principal government-backed new ventures in integrated circuits have been support for two projects aimed at the establishment of plants to build very large scale integrated circuits. One, Inmost, is an entirely new venture backed by £50 million from the NEB. The other is a joint venture by GEC and Fairchild (a major US producer) backed by the Department of Industry.

J. Examination of the differences in the policies towards computers and the computer industry

5.38 Our overview of UK and West German policies towards the computer industry identifies three major differences between the policies of the the two governments: the amount of financial support, the choice of policy instruments and the distribution of support between the different sectors of the industry. In this section we examine these differences and attempt to explain them in terms of the different approaches in industrial policy in the two countries.

(i) The level of financial support

5.39 As tables 5.12 and 5.13 show, Federal government expenditure on the computer industry in the BRD has far exceeded that of the British government. During the period 1971-75 West German state expenditure on support for the computer manufacturing industry and computer applications and research was at least four times greater than British government expenditure although the German computer industry was not much bigger than that of the UK. British support for its computer industry has also been small in comparison with that of the French and Japanese governments. The lower level of government support to the computer industry in the UK might imply that the development of the computer industry in the UK has taken a lower priority in the UK than in West Germany. However, ministerial statements and the active intervention by government into the industry clearly indicate that this is not the case.

5.40 The level of UK support for the domestic computer industry compared to that in West Germany is brought into sharper contrast when compared with the far larger total budget for selective industrial support in the UK than in the BRD. Thus in the UK subsidies to the computer and electronics industry have been far less than the subsidies to shipbuilding, aircraft and motor vehicles. What emerges is that while German selective assistance for industry has been concentrated upon high technology growth industries and industries deemed strategically essential, UK subsidies have been primarily to financially weak industries and enterprises for the purpose of maintaining employment. This difference in the distribution of support between UK and West German industries reflects the greater weight accorded by the British government to the reduction of unemployment than to the stimulation of economic growth and priority of short-term over long-term objectives which has characterised post-war economic policy in the UK.

5.41 It could be argued that because the UK computer industry possessed for most of the 1960s a more secure basis of independent technology than that of Germany, the needs of the UK for government support of EDP research and development were smaller. Certainly in the manufacture of large computers, ICL has benefited from the technological expertise which has been built up over a number of years through the pursuit of an independent development strategy. Siemens, on the other hand, was forced to develop its own computer technology at a late stage after the failure of its associations with foreign manufacturers. If such an argument influenced the British government in determining its level of assistance to the computer industry, then it would have been based on a narrow perception of the computer industry which ignored the importance in the industry of small computers, micro-processes, peripherals and computer services — for in these sectors UK performance, as we shall see, has been unimpressive.

(ii) The choice of policy instruments

5.42 Two principal differences are apparent in the choice of policies which the two governments have used to encourage the development of their domestic computer industries. First, the range of policies introduced by the UK government has been wider than that of the Federal government and has involved greater direct intervention in the industry. In the BRD support for the computer industry has been entirely in the form of grants and loans towards research and development. In the UK, although most financial assistance has been in the form of R and D support, measures to support the domestic industry have included discriminatory procurement policies (almost exclusively to the benefit of ICL) and the provision of long-term finance (notably equity participation in ICL and the NEB in Inmos and Insac). The interventionism of the UK government is apparent in its promotion of the 1968 computer merger and its leading role in the establishment of the two micro-processor ventures, Inmos and GEC-Fairchild.

5.43 Second, UK support has been more selective than that of the BRD. The bulk of assistance for the computer industry prior to 1976 was to ICL. In the case of integrated circuits, assistance has been concentrated upon two new ventures with more limited support for the established manufacturers. Programmes which have been available to the industry as a whole, such as the Advanced Computer Technology Scheme, have been awarded only very limited funds. The EDP programmes of the Federal government have been selective in the sense that R and D support funds and officials retain some discretion in applying the criterion set out in programmes concerning the eligibility of applying firms for support and in determining the amount of support. In particular it has been argued that Siemens received a disproportional share of the total budgets. However, the German programmes have not been selective between individual firms in the sense that support has been available to the industry as a whole.

5.44 The more generalist, market-orientated support policies of the BRD government, as compared with the more selective interventionist policies of the British government, reflect major differences in the approach to industrial policy already referred to. As shown in Chapter III, the post-war economic policies of German governments have been based on economic liberalism with the competitive market rather than government as the principal regulator of economic activity. To the extent that selective subsidies represent government interference with the market economy, the Federal government's EDP programmes indicates a willingness to modify the principle of a market economy but with a minimum of government intervention and with the express purpose of establishing a self-sufficient EDP industry. Moreover, the Federal Government has argued that the goals of its EDP programme and the methods of achieving them have not been in conflict with the principles of workable competition. For instance, the fostering of German computer manufacturers has helped to create a more competitive market for computer equipment in Germany by reducing the dominance of IBM.

5.45 Competition has also been encouraged by making financial assistance available to all qualifying firms in the industry rather than by concentrating support on particular firms, or, as has occurred in the UK, on a single firm. By assisting competing firms and avoiding concentration on a few particular sectors of the EDP industry, it is likely that the government's programmes have avoided the distortions in resource allocation which would have resulted from a more selective policy.

5.46 It may also be argued that the limiting of subsidisation to R and D is a further manifestation of the Federal Government's adherence to the principles of the market economy. The finance of R and D can be justified as a means for promoting workable competition. Not only is R and D a particularly risky investment where returns are long term and uncertain and the capital market is unwilling to supply finance on a large scale, but in addition there are important economies (of scale and of risk-spreading) available to large multinational firms which justifies initial assistance to smaller companies. Support for R and D might also be justified as a means of promoting the external benefits of advances in EDP technology for other industries such as communications and engineering.

5.47 British government policies towards private industry have not been affected by the same philosophic constraints as has German industry policy. While British policies have also concentrated on supporting R and D and have been regarded as temporary supports to enable the industry to 'stand on its own feet', UK governments have been willing to achieve their objectives by public ownership and by discriminatory procurement policies. However, in comparison with other industries which have received government support over a long period (aircraft, shipbuilding, motor cars, textiles) in the computer industry there has been a more limited willingness on the part of government to set aside the market and to involve itself directly in company decision making over such matters as investment programmes, employment policy and locational decisions. Although the governemnt appoints two directors to the ICL board, there is no evidence of government using its power to influence decision making in the company.

(iii) The distribution of financial assistance

5.48 Probably the most significant difference between the policies of the two countries in terms of the influence on the development and performance of their computer industries is that while the BRD policies have been support programmes for the development of EDP industry as a whole, British policy was, until recently, essentially one of backing ICL. This strategy of merging the industry into a single firm and then supporting it is one which has been a feature of UK government intervention in a number of industries including motor car manufacture, heavy electrical goods, ball bearings and sugar refining. Taken to its logical conclusion it means nationalisation, as has occurred in the steel, shipbuilding and aircraft industries. In the case of the computer industry the practical result has been the concentration of support on those products which have been manufactured by ICL: principally medium and large sized computer systems. Those products in which ICL has not specialised — small computers, peripherals and integrated circuits — have received limited amounts of support in comparison with the support given to large computers and also relative to BRD aid for these sectors of the industry. The UK software industry has similarly been almost completely neglected by government until quite recently. While programmes have been introduced in recent years for the support of software (1972) electronic components (1973) and micro-processors (1977/78) these measures lagged considerably behind BRD assistance for these sectors of the industry.

5.49 The concentration by the UK government on the large computer industry and ICL in particular and the late extension of government support to other sectors of the EDP industry reflects a number of factors. In the first place, government seems to have identified the EDP industry with the manufacture of large computer systems. While the increasing emphasis on small systems, minis and micro-processors could not have been easily forecast at the beginning of the 1970s, it is certainly true that even in the late 1960s government had not fully recognised the importance of even peripheral equipment manufacture and software. Indeed, even after the Select Committee on Science and Technology drew attention to the importance of these sectors (see Moorman 1971 and Report to the Select Committee 1971), the UK government was slow to formulate policies towards these sectors of the industry. The failure to recognise the significance of the manufacture of computer equipment other than large computer systems and the importance of the services sector was probably exacerbated by the tendency for government industrial policy to be concentrated upon large manufacturing companies. The large-firm bias of the British government was paralleled by a relative neglect of small and medium-sized firms. This contrasts sharply with West Germany which has operated an active policy of assisting small and medium-sized firms.

5.50 Since 1976 it is clear that a strong shift in the emphasis of British policy towards the EDP industry has taken place. The clearest evidence of this is the heavy assistance being given to the manufacture and application of micro-processors. In a speech to Eurocamp '78, Martin Lam of CSE Division, Department of Industry noted: 'The maintenance of an independent capability was the main objective when ICL was set up but more emphasis is now being placed on improving the balance of payments in the computer field and in making sure that the benefits of present and future developments in the computing techniques, particularly micro-processors; are properly transferred to British industry generally, including sectors which have hitherto not been regarded as included in the computer industry'.

K. The effectiveness of policy towards the computer industry

5.51 The principal problem encountered in measuring the effects of government policy on the computer industry in each country is to estimate how the industry would have performed in the absence of government policy. The approach followed here is a modest one which compares the performance of the computer industry in the two countries in terms of growth, trade balance and technical progress and attempts to relate performance differences to differences in government policy in the two countries.

5.52 Tables 5.1 and 5.3 detail the output and imports and exports for the computer industry as a whole in the two countries. Although the UK industry has consistently failed to achieve a positive balance of trade in computer equipment, the rate of growth of output of the industry during the 1970s has compared favourably with that of the BRD. Thus, although the level of government financial support has been much lower in the UK than in the BRD, this has not had the effect of retarding the relative growth of the UK computer industry. The ability of the UK computer industry to export about half of its output between 1974 and 1977 similarly indicates that a relatively meagre subsidisation of R and D has not resulted in the UK computer industry falling behind its competitors in the technological race.

5.53 In the individual sectors of the industry, however, the comparative performance of the UK and BRD shows considerable variation. Probably the most interesting contrast is between performance in the manufacture of large computer systems and performance in other sectors of the industry. As we have noted, BRD support has been for the development of the EDP industry as a whole, whereas UK policy was concentrated on the manufacture of medium and large computers by ICL. These policies are clearly reflected in the performance of the two countries' industries. The most impressive performance by the UK computer industry has been the ability of ICL to withstand competition from IBM and the other US multinationals in the main computer market. In other sectors of the market, however, notably in small computer systems, peripherals and components (notably integrated circuits), UK performance has been poor. In contrast, the performance of the BRD computer industry has been more even: in medium and large sized computers Siemens failed to establish itself as a major international supplier but has succeeded in increasing its share of the domestic market. In small computers, office computer systems and process control computers, the German industry has been very successful with firms such as Nixdorf and Kienzle keeping the share of the market held by American and Japanese firms to the lowest for any European country. In integrated circuits Siemens and AEG are among the largest European manufacturers (after Philips).

5.54 Any assessment of UK computer policy must begin with an examination of the success of government policy towards ICL. By comparing the post-1968 performance of ICL with the performance of the constituent companies prior to 1968, Stoneman (1975) has attempted to measure the effects of the 1968 merger and the subsequent government support. Measuring the performance of British Computers in terms of their competitiveness with IBM computers, Stoneman found:

(a) ICL's relationship between price and size of computer differs from that for IBM, but generally ICL computers have been sold at higher prices than those of IBM once quality is standardised;

(b) There is no significant evidence of any change in the competitiveness of British computers relative to IBM's over the period 1960-1975 and no evidence that the 1968 merger affected the competitive position of the British industry.

ICL's maintenance of competitiveness wth IBM was during a period when the rate of technological advance was accelerating and the requirements for R and D expenditure to maintain technological competitiveness were continually increasing. 'The cost of developing a range of fourth generation machines (e.g. the ICL 2,900 series) to replace those of the third (e.g. ICL 1,900 series) is much greater than that required to replace second generation machines'. [Stoneman (1975), p.15]. The development costs of the ICL 2,900 series were estimated at £160m. Given ICL's sales revenue and pre-tax profits since its formation, it is implausible to conclude that sufficient finance for the development of the 2,900 series could have been generated internally by ICL and doubtful whether the funds could have been obtained on the capital market.

5.55 ICL has also been fairly successful in maintaining its share of the UK market. Although between 1969 and 1973 its market share fell, it has since then succeeded in maintaining its share of the market against its three major US competitors — IBM, Honeywell and Burroughs. Stoneman's conclusion is that 'the UK computer industry has been able to hold its own against the US companies . . . this performance has been achieved in a situation where IBM spends more on R and D than ICL's total turnover. The efficiency of their R and D process is therefore of commendable quality' [Stoneman (1975), pp.21-27].

5.56 Despite the success of ICL in the market for medium and large computers, the relatively poor performance of the UK in other sectors of the computer market raises doubts as to the wisdom of the selective approach of the UK government. This is particularly so in view of the trends in the industry away from large computer systems and towards smaller machines. At the same time the market for central processing units has become increasingly competitive in price and technology with growing competition to IBM from smaller American manufacturers such as Amdahl and Intel and from Japanese companies such as Fujitsu and Hitachi. In the rapidly growing market for small systems, the costs of the central processor represents something between 5 and 10 per cent of total system cost. The rest is peripherals, communications equipment and so on. It is in the peripherals field that the UK is particularly weak. It has been estimated (Financial Times, 21 February 1978, p.26) that the UK peripherals market is expanding at the rate of about 30-40 per cent a year of which a large proportion of the product is imported. While most of the major computer manufacturers have increasingly entered the peripherals field. (ICL which has been forced to concentrate its R and D and investment has concentrated on central processors through jointly NCR and CDC, and ICL has established CPI to develop peripherals. The other specialist UK manufacturer of peripherals is Crico, now owned by the NEB.)

5.57 BRD performance in peripherals has been far more impressive and, despite strong US competition, BRD manufacturers have achieved a consistently favourable trade balance. The extent to which the peripherals industry has benefited from government support for R and D is impossible to assess, but it is clear that in some areas it is West Germany's leadership in certain areas of technology, apart from any marketing skills, which has been the key to success. Thus BASF's hold on magnetic media technology has been a vital part of the company's success in international markets. The situation in integrated circuits is similar. Heavy support by the German government for the development of micro-electronic technology seems to have been an important factor in establishing West German companies in the forefront of the electronic component market — though almost certainly lagging behind the USA and Japan. In the UK separate attempts by the Department of Industry and the NEB to establish companies to manufacture micro-electronic circuits seem to be a classic case of 'too little, too late'.

5.58 It has been claimed that the widespread provision of public R and D support throughout the EDP industry, often for competing developments by competing companies, wastes public money. Indeed, the funds supplied to AEG-Telefunken for the development of large computers were certainly wasted when the company gave up its interest in this field. However, to be selective in the allocation of government support requires that the government is able to forecast, with some accuracy, future developments in the data processing market. In fact, the pace of technological advance is so rapid that such forecasting can be little more than guesswork. In this event, the prudent policy may be to provide government support to all research which looks promising. While the failure rate is likely to be high, such a policy can be justified in terms of the vital importance of EDP technology for technological progressiveness not only in the computer industry, but in communications, engineering, consumer electronics and, ultimately, industry as a whole.

5.59 It is apparent that exercises in industrial planning, involving the selective subsidisation of particular firms and projects requires government to forecast, with some degree of accuracy, user demand and technological change over the medium term. Two issues arise here. First, how does the performance of government in forecasting the technologically and commercially successful projects of the future compare with that of the private sector? Second, is there a danger that the selective application of subsidies may involve high risks in industries where the rate of technological advance is rapid? Thus, might not a more prudent policy be to provide more general R and D subsidies which do not distort competition within the industry?

5.60 The UK policy of concentrating assistance on ICL may not only have meant a lack of government support for the other sectors of the computer industry, but may have positively hindered the development of other firms. Smaller firms both in the hardware and software sectors have been particularly critical of the British government's policy of buying large computers exclusively from ICL. While ICL and the government have regarded the single tender policy as necessary to provide ICL with a secure home market base for its international operations, it may be that the benefits to ICL from the policy have been outweighed by the costs to other firms in the industry. ICL preference in larger computers has often meant that ICL is called on to provide complete systems, and software as well. Thus specialist suppliers of peripherals and software have felt that they have been excluded from the public sector market. Software suppliers have been particularly critical of the British government's reliance on its own resources for programme development and where external contracts have been offered they have often been allocated in a single package with the order for the computer system. The Select Committee noted: 'To many software houses the symbol of Government neglect. was the London Airport Cargo EDP scheme where, in circumstances strongly suggesting government intervention, ICL having secured the contract for the project subcontracted the software implementation to an American-owned software house.' (1971, Vol 1, paragraph 171)

5.61 Given a commitment to selective aid policies, the comparative neglect of the software industry by the UK government in comparison with the generous support offered by the BRD government would seem to have been a major omission. British software expertise has been generally regarded as second only to that of the Americans, and it is a sector where the Japanese and, to a lesser extent, the Germans have invested extremely heavily in order to develop their own software services industry. The growing cost of software in relation to hardware has provided considerable opportunities for the UK software houses, but the potential to increase overseas earnings, so it is claimed, has been limited by the fragmented nature of the industry.

L. Conclusions

5.62 In the UK and BRD the objectives of government policy towards the computer industry and computer technology have been similar: to support the industry because it is a growth industry, to encourage the development of computer technology under domestic ownership and control because of the economic and strategic importance of this branch of technology, to encourage exports and limit imports of computer equipment, to encourage the assimilation of EDP technology by other industries.

5.63 Nevertheless, the policies of the two countries show some differences. While both governments have been concerned chiefly with supporting R and D into computer technology, in the BRD such support has been provided to the EDP industry as a whole, in the UK the policy has focused on support for ICL. Not only has UK policy been more selective, it has also been more interventionist; UK policy measures have included public ownership, industrial restructuring and discriminatory public purchase policy; West German policies have been concerned exclusively with financing R and D. West German policy has taken the form of three medium term programmes for the data processing industry. UK policy has not been provided as and when needed by the company and the recent shift of emphasis towards micro-processors, small systems and peripherals has been in response to recognition of deficiencies in the UK's EDP performance.

5.64 Again, these contrasts in policy reflect general differences between the conduct of industrial policy in the two countries: UK industrial policy tending to be more selective, more interventionist, more concentrated upon large firms, and heavily influenced by short-term factors. German industrial policy has been less *dirigiste* and has sought to be compatible with the competitive market economy by avoiding direct structural intervention and discrimination between individual enterprises.

5.65 West German expenditure on support for its computer industry has greatly exceeded that of the UK despite the fact that public subsidies to private industry are, in aggregate, far greater in the UK. This limited support for the computer industry in the UK reflects the greater priority given to the maintenance of employment than to the encouragement of growth and technological change.

5.66 In both countries the computer industry has achieved a rapid growth of output and exports and at the same time there has been heavy import penetration, notably from the USA. In the manufacture of medium and large computers, Britain has built on its early development of computer technology to develop a profitable, growing and internationally competitive indigenous manufacturer. Following a more hazard-strewn path, Siemens has achieved a similar position. With regard to small computers, microprocessors, peripherals and software, the performance of the West German industry has been superior to that of the UK, despite an early lead by the UK in many aspects of electronic technology.

5.67 The differences in performance of the different sectors of the EDP industry in the two countries partly reflect public policy. The 'success' of ICL must, in part, be a result of government policy, first in creating the company and second in supporting it by finance and preference in government contracts. The weak performance of the other, and more important, sectors of the industry must also reflect, in part, the comparative lack of government support in these sectors. In West Germany the major strengths of the EDP industry has been in those sectors which are weakest in the UK — small systems, peripherals and integrated circuits — and it is notable that these sectors have been heavily supported under the Federal government's programmes.

5.68 The low level of public support for the UK computer industry in relation to that of the German computer industry and in relation to other UK industries raises questions about the appropriateness of the priorities of UK industrial policy. The more general EDP support measures of the BRD as compared with the ad hoc selective support measures in the UK raises the question of whether the quality of government forecasting and project selection in industries subject to rapid technological change is sufficient to justify the greater risks of selective policies. From the evidence received in this Chapter, it would appear that the neglect of government of some of the most important sectors of the UK computer industry — notably small systems, peripherals, computer services and electronic components — provides an argument for more general industry support on the German model. The deficiencies of UK policy in relation to that of the BRD may also reflect the better information and more balanced forecasting which is encouraged by policy decision-making which is firmly based on medium-term programmes for the industry as a whole.

REFERENCES

Der Bundesminister für Forschung und Technologie (1976), *Drittes DV — Programm 1976-1979*, Bonn.

Commission of the European Communities (1976) *A Four Year Programme for the Development of Information in the Community*. COM (76) 524, Vols. I-III, Brussels.

G.M. Field and P.V. Hills 'The Administration of Industrial Subsidies' in A. Whiting (ed.) (1976), *The Economics of Industrial Subsidies*, H.M.S.O., London.

German Chamber of Industry and Commerce (1978). *The German Computer Industry — A Review*. London.

E. Moonman (ed.) (1971) *British Computers and Industrial Innovation. The Influence of the Parliamentary Select Committee*. George Allen & Unwin, London.

O.E.C.D. (1969) *Gaps in Technology: Volume 1 Electronic Computers*. Paris.

Select Committee on Science and Technology (1970). *The UK Computer Industry*. Session 1969-70. Vols.I & II. (1971) *The Prospects for the UK Computer Industry in the 1970's*. Vols I, II & III, H.M.S.O. (1973) *Second Report on the UK Computer Industry* (First Part). Session 1972-73, H.M.S.O.

P.S. Stoneman (1975) *Merger and Technological Programmes: the case of the British Computer Industry*. Warwick Economic Research Papers No.79.

CHAPTER 6

STRUCTURAL POLICIES TOWARDS THE SHIPBUILDING
AND SHIPPING INDUSTRIES OF THE BRD AND THE UK

A. The relationship between the shipping and shipbuilding industries

6.1 Although shipbuilding and shipping are quite distinct industries, their problems have been similar and policies towards one industry have an important influence on the other. Therefore policies towards the two industries are considered together. There are close parallels in the competitive factors which influence the two industries. Both industries have to compete in an international market in which Japan is the largest supplier and in which fierce price competition is provided by developing, also by Comecon countries. In shipbuilding Japan has accounted for almost one half of world output during most of the 1970s (see Table 6.1); in shipping Japan has the largest merchant fleet including the flag of convenience countries. Brazil and South Korea in shipbuilding and Liberia and Panama in shipping are important sources of low-cost competition. In both industries Comecon countries represent a growing source of competition. The economic fortunes of the two industries tend to be closely correlated. Fluctuations in the demand for shipping caused by cycles in world trade obviously create fluctuations in shipbuilding demand. Fixed costs represent, for both industries, a high proportion of total costs, so excess capacity (such as exists at present) encourages vigorous price competition. The close vertical relationship between the two industries also means that policies affecting one industry have important indirect effects on the other. Thus an important form of assistance given to the shipbuilding industries of UK and BRD has been subsidies paid to customers. The spillover effects of support policies are not always beneficial. Assistance to the world shipbuilding industry aimed at maintaining output and employment in each country has greatly exacerbated the problem of excess capacity in the world shipping industry.

6.2 Although the two industries are closely related and face common economic problems, structural policies towards them differ because of their different positions within the national economic structure. The shipbuilding industry is an important employer both in UK and BRD and its employment is geographically concentrated. Shipbuilding is also an important customer of other industries, notably steel. The shipping industries of BRD and UK are less integrated into the national economic structure. A high proportion of employees are non-national and in consequence fluctuations in the level of business do not have such important consequences for the national employment situation. The shipping companies purchase ships and other inputs freely between countries according to relative prices, so that the fortunes of the supplying industries of the two countries are not entirely dependent upon the domestic shipping industries. As a result, the maritime policies of the two countries have been concerned more with shipbuilding than with shipping. This is particularly true in the UK where the level of financial assistance to shipbuilding and the extent of structural intervention has been greater than for almost any other manufacturing industry, while policy towards shipping has comprised limited general support measures. This contrast of policies is less evident in the BRD. First, the Federal Government has not been willing to adopt such interventionist industrial policies as the UK Government. Second, German shipping policy has the important strategic objective of maintaining and expanding its merchant fleet. This is a reflection of the small size of Germany's fleet (less than one third of UK tonnage), particularly in relation to Germany's very large overseas trade, (see Table 6.3).

B. The structure of shipping and shipbuilding in the UK and West Germany

6.3 Although in both countries the maritime sector is of great importance to the national economy, the relative importance and performance of shipbuilding and shipping varies between the two countries. In the UK, shipping is the more important industry in terms of its earnings, assets, employment and contribution to the balance of payments. Indeed, following the fall in the international position of the UK shipbuilding industry from 2nd to 7th place during the past 20 years (see Table 6.1), Britain's claim to be one of the world's leading maritime nations is based on the importance of the UK merchant fleet which, excluding the flags of convenience, is the largest after that of Japan (see Table 6.2).

6.4 In the BRD the relative roles of shipping and shipbuilding are reversed. Shipbuilding is more important than shipping in terms of earnings, employment and balance of payments contribution. Germany has the 4th largest shipbuilding industry in the world in terms of 1977 output, but only the 11th largest merchant fleet (see Tables 6.1 and 6.2).

6.5 The small size of the German shipping fleet is surprising in view of the position of Germany as the world's largest trading nation after Japan. The reasons are largely historical — the loss of most of Germany's merchant fleet during the Second World War and the subsequent partition of Germany and Europe which

Table 6.1

THE SHARES OF WORLD SHIPBUILDING COMPLETIONS

	1956	1968	1969	1970	1971	1972	1973	1974	1975	1976	1977
World Total (million GRT)	6.29	16.84	18.74	20.98	24.39	26.75	30.41	33.54	34.20	33.92	27.53
of which: %											
Japan	24.04	49.06	48.09	48.00	45.07	48.01	48.05	50.04	49.08	46.08	52.05
West Germany	17.03	7.02	9.05	6.03	8.01	5.02	6.03	6.04	7.03	5.05	5.08
Sweden	7.07	6.05	6.07	7.03	7.06	7.06	7.05	6.05	6.04	7.04	8.04
Netherlands	6.03	1.06	2.06	3.01	2.03	2.08	2.08	2.08	3.00	1.09	0.09
France	4.04	3.07	3.07	4.01	4.05	3.08	3.09	3.01	3.04	4.09	4.00
Italy	4.03	3.00	1.09	2.06	3.06	3.04	2.08	2.08	2.03	2.01	2.08
Norway	3.00	3.06	3.03	3.04	3.06	3.01	3.02	2.09	3.01	2.02	2.01
Denmark	2.02	3.01	3.02	2.05	3.00	3.06	3.03	3.02	2.08	3.01	2.06
USA	2.00	2.02	2.05	1.08	2.00	1.08	3.02	2.02	1.04	2.04	3.07
Spain	1.02	2.07	3.04	3.01	3.04	4.00	4.03	4.07	4.07	3.09	6.06
Comecon countries	*	*	*	5.07	5.06	5.01	4.09	4.02	5.00	5.06	5.08

Table 6.4

UK SHIPBUILDING: OUTPUT AND EMPLOYMENT

	1968	1969	1970	1971	1972	1973	1974	1975	1976	1977
Completions of merchant ships number	152	138	144	134	139	137	134	144	140	104
GRT ('000)	1046	814	1297	1259	1208	1069	1189	1203	1460	1008
Estimated value (£m)	116	137	180	180	220	230	228	270	375	262.2
For overseas registration (£m)	51	38	34	51	59	61	62	98	144	133.2
Total sales of shipbuilding and marine engineering—MLH 370 (£m)				551.8	648.3	749.9	810.0	946.4	1279.5	1365.0
Employment ('000)			182.7	177.3	179.9	181.6				

Source: Business Monitor. Employment data from Census of Production

Table 6.2

THE MAJOR SHIPPING NATIONS OF THE WORLD, 1977

	GRT (million)	DWT (million)	Per cent (World GRT)
Liberia	80.0	156.0	20.3
Japan	40.0	65.9	10.2
UK	31.6	51.7	8.0
Greece	29.5	49.3	7.5
Norway	27.8	49.2	7.1
Soviet Union	21.4	23.0	5.4
Panama	19.5	31.6	4.9
USA	15.3	22.1	3.9
France	11.6	20.1	3.0
Italy	11.1	17.7	2.8
West Germany	9.6	15.6	2.4

Source: Verband Deutscher Reeder, Seeschiffahrt 1977.

Table 6.3

IMPORTANCE OF SHIPPING TO THE NATIONAL ECONOMIES

		1970	1971	1972	1973	1974	1975
Share of national trade carried by home fleet (%)							
UK							
Imports		31	32	31	30	29	31
Exports		47	44	40	43	44	46
WEST GERMANY							
Imports		25	23	21	17	15	18
Exports		39	37	34	28	25	27
Employment[1] (millions)	UK	—	—	—	—	83	89
	West Germany	491	46	39	35	32	32
Revenue (US$millions)	UK	—	3299	3199	4044	4955	—
	West Germany	2038	2160	1906	2007	2659	2778

Note: [1] Including nations and non-nationals.
Source: US Department of Commerce Report 1977, pp.III.27 and VI.23-24

affected Germany's traditional Baltic trade.

6.6   The result of the different sizes of shipping fleets is that a much larger proportion of the UK's foreign trade is carried by the national fleet, and that the UK fleet must rely much more upon international cross-trading than the German fleet (see Table 6.3). As regards the shipbuilding industries, the UK purchases a much larger proportion of its ships abroad than do the Germans, and the German shipbuilding industry must look much more to export sales than the UK shipbuilding industry.

6.7   Although shipbuilding was one of the most rapidly growing sectors of world manufacturing industry between 1960 and 1975, shipbuilding in the UK has been a declining industry. Despite some short-lived booms during the 1960s and 1970s the trend in tonnage output has been downward, (see Table 6.4). The performance of the UK industry in respect of price, quality and the meeting of delivery dates has been poor in relation both to low-cost competitors (Far East, Brazil, Spain) and to high-cost competitors (Scandinavia, Germany, France and USA). The factors which characterise declining industries in Britain:— weak management, poor industrial relations, a concentration on short-term problems to the neglect of longer-term planning and budgeting, and a failure to respond to the changing requirements of the market have all been evident in UK shipbuilding.

Table 6.5

WEST GERMAN SHIPBUILDING: OUTPUT AND EMPLOYMENT

	1968	1969	1970	1971	1972	1973	1974	1975	1976	1977
Completions of merchant ships number	239	296	279	263	267	233	196	215	195	187
of which inland	37	87	84	85	105	93	58	42	32	18
GRT ('000)	1323	1779	1539	1990	1541	2053	2238	2386	2154	1618
of which inland ('000)	41	87	116	137	172	140	73	46	48	27
Value of new ships produced (DM millions)	2070	2547	2467	3072	3282	4190	3988	4575	5097	5454
of which inland (%)	1.4	2.6	3.5	3.5	4.9	3.9	2.4	1.7	1.6	1.1
Turnover of shipbuilding industry (excluding non-ship building activities) (DM millions)	2645	3178	3220	4018	4027	4891	5743	6293	6621	6545
Export turnover of industry (DM millions)	1336	1663	1305	1859	2182	3001	2793	4255	4188	3885
as % of turnover	45.2	47.7	36.2	41.5	48.2	55.6	44.7	60.5	56.6	53.0
Export tonnage ('000)	843	1413	750	1086	880	1357	869	1747	1479	1180
Employment annual average ('000)	80	81	80	80	78	74	75	78	74	70

Source: Verband der Deutscher Schiffbauindustrie.

Table 6.6

LABOUR COSTS IN SHIPBUILDING 1977 (DM PER HOUR)

West Germany	18.92
USA	17.76 ($ = DM 2.32)
France	12.23 (100F = DM 47.26)
Italy	11.83 (L1000 = DM 2.632)
Japan	10.57 (100 Yen = DM 0.867)
UK	8.09 (£1 = DM 4.051)

Source: Verband der Deutschen Schiffbau industrie

The competitive position of the shipbuilding companies of the BRD has also been handicapped by the rising international value of the mark and the lack of a large maritime fleet. The ability of the German shipbuilding industry to expand despite the difficulties it has faced reflects primarily the ability of the industry to use its commercial and technological expertise to build sophisticated and technologically advanced ships for specialised use, such as container ships, roll-on-roll-off ships, gas carriers, ferries, refrigerated ships and factory ships. The German yards have been in the forefront of technological advance in production methods and have maintained a high rate of investment which has allowed the introduction of more productive working methods (such as the series production of larger ships). Innovation, investment and diversification of the German shipbuilding industry has been assisted by the fact that the shipbuilding companies tend to have extensive interests outside the shipbuilding industry. Of the six largest shipbuilders, four are general engineering companies. Yet, despite the successful development of the shipbuilding industry over the post-war period, Germany is one of the countries most heavily hit by the current world shipbuilding crisis. Table 6.7 shows the principal shipbuilders of the BRD.

Table 6.7

MAJOR GERMAN SHIPBUILDING COMPANIES

	Employment 1976	Location of yards
Howaldtswerke-Deutsche Werft	14,700	Kiel and Hamburg
AG Weser	8,290	Bremen and Bremerhaven
Blohm and Voss AG	6,700	Hamburg
Bremer Vulkan Schiffbau und Maschinenfabrik	5,606	Bremen
Thyssen Nordseewerke GmbH	4,750	Emden
Flender Werft Atkiengesellschaft	1,988	Lübeck
Flensburger Schiffbau — Gesellschaft	1,807	Flensburg
JJ Sietas Schiffswerft	1,568	Hamburg
Schiffbau Unterweser AG	1,544	Bremerhaven

Source: *German Shipyards for Ocean Going Vessels* — Verband der Deutschen Schiffbauindustrie

6.9   In shipping the relative superiority of German over British industrial performance that characterises ship-building (and many other manufacturing industries) is not apparent. Britain, despite its falling share of world trade, has rapidly expanded its merchant fleet and has remained the world's second largest ship-owning nation. Indeed, during the 1970s the growth of the UK fleet did not lag far behind that of the Japanese fleet, even without the enormous partially-captive cargo market available to Japanese operators. Between 1970 and 1975 the West German shipping fleet expanded at only one third of the rate of the British fleet. Tables 6.8 and 6.9 show the two countries' share of the world fleet and their tonnage growth. Nevertheless, the replacement rate of the merchant fleet of the BRD has been extremely high with the result that the German fleet is among the youngest of the world. A concentration on modern, labour-saving ships offering a highly efficient service has been the principal strategy of German shipowners to overcome their cost disadvantages vis-a-vis other shipping nations.

C.   The shipping and shipbuilding industries in crisis

6.10 The most important factor influencing the development of maritime policies of the British and West German governments since 1975 has been the slump in world demand for shipping and ships combined with rapid growth in world shipping and shipbuilding capacity. In Germany the threat to the existence of its shipping and shipbuilding posed by the 1970s crisis has resulted in the introduction of support measures the justification of which stretch the philosophy of the non-interventionist social market economy to the limit. In Britain the crisis precipitated the nationalisation of the shipbuilding industry. To understand the current support policies of the two countries requires a brief analysis of the major factors responsible for this situation.

Table 6.8

UK AND BRD SHARES OF WORLD MERCHANT FLEET (DEADWEIGHT TONNAGE) AND AVERAGE AGE OF FLEET

		1966	1968	1970	1972	1974	1975
National deadweight registration as per cent of world fleet							
Total	UK	11.5	11.0	11.3	10.9	10.5	9.9
	W. Germany	3.3	3.4	3.6	2.9	2.7	2.4
Tankers	UK	12.0	12.4	13.6	12.7	12.0	10.9
	W. Germany	1.7	1.9	1.9	1.7	1.7	1.9
Bulk carriers	UK	9.9	8.9	8.6	9.9	9.9	9.7
	W. Germany	3.9	3.5	3.7	3.0	2.8	2.7
Freighters	UK	11.2	10.2	9,7	8.4	7.6	7.2
	W. Germany	5.0	5.4	6.3	5.4	4.2	3.8
Average age of fleet (years)							
	UK	12	11	11	10	10	10
	W. Germany	11	10	9	6	7	7
	World	17	13	13	12	12	12

Source: US Department of Commerce Report, 1977.

Table 6.9

GROWTH OF NATIONAL FLAG FLEETS

		1970	1971	1972	1973	1974	1975	1978
Total ships (no.)	UK	1772	1713	1627	1596	1609	1576	—
	West Germany	993	958	797	702	668	611	—
DWT (million)	UK	37.1	40.7	43.5	47.8	53.0	54.9	—
	West Germany	11.7	12.5	11.5	11.4	13.6	13.5	9.7
GRT (million)	UK	24.1	25.8	27.2	29.4	32.2	33.2	30.9
	West Germany	77.8	8.2	7.6	7.5	8.5	8.3	9.7

DELIVERIES TO THE FLEET (GRT)

		1970	1971	1972	1973	1974	1975	1978
Total	UK	2.8	2.9	3.3	3.7	3.7	3.0	1.6
	West Germany	1.2	1.1	0.8	0.7	1.3	0.4	0.02
Tankers	UK	1.9	1.7	0.7	1.8	2.7	2.3	—
	West Germany	0.4	0.1	0.05	0.1	1.1	0.3	—
Bulk carriers	UK	0.6	0.8	1.8	1.4	0.8	0.6	—
	West Germany	0.2	0.4	0.2	0.4	0.1	0.1	—
Freighters	UK	0.4	0.4	0.8	0.5	0.1	0.1	—
	West Germany	0.6	0.6	0.6	0.2	0.1	0.03	—

Source: US Department of Commerce Report, 1977.

6.11 *Demand Factors:* Three influences have combined to promote a substantial and prolonged fall in the demand for freight carrying services. First, 50 per cent of all bulk freight is in the transportation of iron ore and coal for the steel industry. Hence any decline in the demand for steel, as witnessed during the world depression commencing in 1974, exerts an immediate impact upon freight rates. Second, in the dry bulk freight trade, much depends upon Soviet grain harvests. A shortfall in agricultural output and the necessity for substantial wheat imports has given a considerable fillip to transportation rates in the past but over the recent years of depression such a stimulus has not been forthcoming. The most significant demand factor, however, has been the OPEC-induced rise in the price of oil which has drastically curtailed the demand for oil tanker services. More and more countries have attempted to economise on oil imports by turning to alternative sources of fuel or by exploiting domestic energy sources. The impact upon freight rates was not just confined to oil as ship owners reacted by using tankers to carry alternative cargoes. To these influences on the demand for freight transport one has to add the decline in passenger transportation services which have not helped the shipowners' plight. The rapid technological and cost-reducing innovations in air-passenger services have virtually eliminated demand for sea travel whilst at the same time improving air freight services. Significantly, Hapag-Lloyd one of Germany's leading shipping lines, found it necessary to diversify into plane chartering activities in the attempt to 'reclaim back passenger traffic'.

6.12 *Supply Factors:* Independently of demand conditions, supply influences conspired during the mid-1970s to promote a world-wide fall in freight shipping rates, to such an extent that it became uneconomic to put newly-built ships on ocean-going voyages. One factor has been the tendency for the industry to over-react to favourable demand conditions and buoyant prices. This arises from the inelastic nature of short-term supply conditions for obviously tonnage cannot be increased substantially overnight. Consequently, any increase in demand tends to have a disproportionate impact upon freight prices causing freight profits to spiral. Excess profits promote new entry and new orders for ships which ultimately depress freight rates, but the countervailing adjustment does not come into play until considerable excess capacity has been generated owing to the time lag in the supply response. This is precisely the situation which prevailed in the creation of the surplus in tankers. The 1960s witnessed a steady growth in the consumption of oil and oil-related products. There was consequently a steady rise in the demand for shipping to transport oil and by 1973 tanker freight charges had risen to 420 (1947=100). The closure of the Suez Canal in 1973 encouraged shippers to order tankers of a size which took full advantage of scale economies in tanker transport. Tankers of 250,000 dwt, were ordered and built. During 1973-74 the world tanker tonnage more than doubled. Such were the economies of scale and so buoyant were oil freight charges that it was possible to recoup the outlay of a super tanker in a comparatively few voyages.

6.13 Such conditions would inevitably have produced an eventual surplus of tankers even without the OPEC-induced fall in demand for oil. The resulting drastic fall in oil freight rates has led to tankers being completed and laid up without ever seeing service. For example, in 1975 six tankers were completed in West German yards at a total cost of DM600 million to be immediately laid up, the reason given being that it would be more expensive to put them out to sea. Since 1975 such lay-ups have become common in UK and West Germany. In addition, other freight rates have been adversely affected as disillusioned tanker owners have abandoned oil transportation and switched to carrying bulk dry good traffic, in particular, iron ore, coal and corn. The rapid generation of the tanker surplus on the scale observed would not have been possible without the creation of new shipyards. The new yards, specially designed to accommodate the super breed of tanker, were built quickly particularly in Japan where the government provided considerable financial backing. Indeed, shipbuilding became looked upon as a growth centre for the economy as a whole as well as a source of rapidly expanding export orders. Between 1960 and 1970 Japan's output increased from 1.7 million to 10.09 million GRT and by 1975 it totalled 16.9 [see EIU (1977)]. By 1975 Japan was producing more than 50 per cent of world output and this apparent success stimulated other far Eastern competitors, especially in Taiwan and South Korea. Excess capacity in bulk carriage now exceeds some 12 million tons or approximately 10 per cent of total world transportation. Nor will surplus capacity be readily eliminated. The current world fleet is relatively young; whilst there is doubtless room for scrapping, the fact remains that 80 per cent of all vessels over 18,000 dwt are less than ten years old.

6.14 Two other influences played their part in generating excess capacity. One was the rise in competition from the Eastern bloc countries; Comecon is now responsible for some 12 per cent of world freight tonnage and handles 20 per cent of the world's seaborne cargo. As these figures suggest, the Comecon countries are price competitive in their quotation of freight charges, partly, it is alleged, because their need for foreign currency earnings over-rides cost factors. The other influence was the rapid pace of technological change in shipping, notably the introduction of containerisation, lighter-abroad ships, roll-on-roll-off ships and various types of specialised carriers. While the rapid obsolescence induced by technology has been to the benefit of shipyards, the increases in ship productivity exacerbated the problem of excess carrying capacity. Other innovations have included the application of nuclear power to merchant shipping. The *Otto Hahn*, Germany's first nuclear ship produced an operating deficit of DM7 million, 90 per cent of which has been borne by the

Federal government. The unwillingness of the government to continue support means that the vessel is now destined for scrapping.

6.15 German shipowners, who have shown themselves remarkably willing to adapt and diversify their activities in the wake of increased structural change, also face additional difficulties. Crewing regulations on German ships are such as to render her operation and labour costs nearly as high as the United States and virtually double that on Greek and British ships. Indeed, it was recognition of these higher costs associated with operating under the German flag which justified the initial assistance granted to shipowners. In addition, the upward pressure upon the DM has increased the difficulties of selling ships built in West German yards (not least to West German shipowners). The decline of the US dollar has also caused a fall in shipowners' profits. This is because 80 per cent of all freight charges are quoted in US dollars and thus the net revenue of German shipping lines falls in proportion with the comparative decline of the US dollar against the D. Mark. Moreover, it is has long been the convention to quote insurance cover in US dollars, and hence implicitly the replacement value of the vessel. The continued decline of the US dollar thus implies a rising percentage of indebtedness against the insured asset which is unwelcome and indeed unacceptable to those providing mortgage cover.

6.16 In addition to the problems of oceangoing and coastal shipping, inland waterways are of considerable importance in the BRD. Inland shipping employs close on 30,000 people and it is a source of concern that future prospects for such traffic are decidedly bleak. The current recession, beginning in 1974, seriously reduced demand it is now estimated that at least 20 per cent of domestic inland tonnage is surplus to requirements. By far the greatest fear, however springs from the threat of competition from the Eastern European fleets following the completion of the Rhine-Main-Danube Canal scheduled for 1982. The Eastern shipping barges are mainly laid-up during the severe winter months but will now have the incentive to transfer to the Danube and other Western Europe waterways during the winter if they can cover only average variable costs. The increased competition in conditions of excess capacity will inevitably lead to a lowering of freight rates, especially if the Eastern bloc countries follow their oceangoing precedent and set rates primarily with a view to foreign exchange earnings and without regard to covering operating costs. At the present time, there appears to be no concerted government policy to cope with the difficulties of the inland shipping lines, despite the fact that the position of the inland boat owners is also threatened by the highly efficient but heavily subsidised German rail network. In contrast, the inland waterways of the UK are of comparatively minor importance.

6.17 The future prospects for shipping and shipbuilding in the two countries are far from encouraging. While the setting of conference rates for general cargoes provides a protection to shipowners from the full forces of competition, in the market for new ships a scarcity of new orders appears likely for a considerable period. In neither country has the shipbuilding industry adjusted to the new world situation. Even prior to the current crisis, the UK shipbuilding industry was maintained only by government subsidies and the nationalisation of the industry appeared to be as much a device for channelling greater public aid to the industry as a means of achieving 'orderly' contraction and regeneration. During its first year of operation, British Shipbuilders has made a loss of nearly £150 million. German yards have been even harder hit by the famine of orders as Table 6.10 shows. Forecasts by the Chairman of the German Shipbuilding Industry, Herr Bartels, that a 30 per cent reduction in capacity would now be necessary appears almost optimistic. Present orders suggest that the industry may be operating at around one third of capacity in 1979 with virtually no work at all available in 1980.

Table 6.10

WORLD SHIPBUILDING ORDERS, 1975-1977

(G.P.T, millions)

	31.12.1975	31.12.1976	31.12.1977
West Germany	4.2	2.4	1.1
UK	4.9	2.9	2.2
Japan	31.4	18.2	9.9
Sweden	6.5	4.0	2.1
France	4.9	3.0	2.0
Brazil	3.6	3.2	2.9
USA	5.0	4.7	3.6
Spain	4.3	3.8	1.9
World	82.3	55.4	36.7

Source: Verband der Deutschen Schiffbau industrie e.v.

D. The objectives of government support policies towards shipping and shipbuilding

6.18   The rationale for maritime support policies have been similar in the UK and West Germany. The differences are primarily those of emphasis reflecting the different conditions affecting the shipping and shipbuilding industries in each country and the different priorities accorded to objectives. In the case of shipping the purposes of the support policies can be listed as follows:

i.   *To maintain and increase the contribution of the industry to the balance of payments.* As the revenue from overseas business is in foreign currency earnings and the business of domestic importers and exporters would fall to foreign fleets if not carried by domestic shipping companies, almost the entire earnings of shipping companies may be viewed as a positive contribution to the balance of payments. For the UK it is considered vital to preserve the international position of its shipping fleet in order to maintain the contribution of the industry to the invisible account of balance of payments. In West Germany support for the domestic fleet is directed towards limiting and reducing the adverse foreign exchange balance represented by shipping. Because of the heavy dependence of UK shipowners on third country trade, UK support of its shipping fleet must be cautious because of vulnerability of the fleet to any retaliation from other countries in the form of cargo preference. West Germany, on the other hand, because of its large share of world trade, might be expected to derive substantial benefit from a protectionist shipping policy. The fact that the German government and German shipping industry have consistently supported the maintenance of freedom of entry to international shipping is an indication of commitment to the concept of workable competition. At the same time the German government has sought to pursue the interests of its domestic fleet through the negotiation of bilateral shipping agreements with certain other countries.

ii.   *To offer security to foreign trade.* The economies of both UK and West Germany are heavily dependent on foreign trade — for imports of food and raw materials and export earnings from manufactured goods. For Germany a large proportion of exports and imports travel by sea, and for the UK almost all foreign trade is by sea. For foreign trade to be wholly dependent for transportation on foreign registered vessels makes the national economy liable to disruption from political crises or commercial and labour relations problems entirely outside the control of that country. The claimed need for a national merchant fleet to provide security for foreign trade has been a particularly important objective of Germany's shipping policy. The desire to provide security for vital segments of Germany's foreign trade is reflected in the special assistance given to certain types of ship, notably large oil tankers.

iii.   *To enhance the competitiveness of export industries.* In the case of West Germany, the ability to deliver export goods quickly and efficiently is seen as essential to its export effort. Because of the high wage costs of German industry and rising international value of the mark, the competitiveness of German exports have become increasingly dependent upon quality, reliability and speed of delivery. Thus efficient shipping services are viewed as complementary to efficient export industries. For this reason government policy has been orientated towards making Germany's shipping fleet the most up-to-date and technically advanced in the world. For the UK on the other hand, the quality of shipping services is not a constraint on export performance. The UK's poor record in the prompt delivery of export orders stems from inefficiencies at the manufacturing level and, to a lesser extent, delays in dock handling.

The achievement of the goals of foreign exchange earnings from shipping and the maintenance of a national fleet to provide security to foreign trade require that national fleets are able to compete in a world freight market against 'flag of convenience' fleets with low wage crews and the subsidised fleets of the Comecon countries. For this reason both the UK and West Germany have felt it necessary to subsidise their national fleets, partly by concessions on indirect taxes to lower operating costs, but primarily by grants, tax relief and loans for the purchase of new ships. Assistance for new ship purchases lowers capital costs, may boost efficiency by having a modern fleet and can also be directed to benefit domestic shipbuilders. Support policies have also sought to maintain shipping companies against the strong fluctuations in profitability which result from the high level of fixed costs in the industry combined with variations in world trade. In West Germany the capital gains reserve and a carry-forward provision for losses are designed to counter the effects of the cyclical nature of shipping demand.

6.19   In terms of the percentage contribution of shipbuilding to GNP or in terms of the percentage of total labour force employed in the industry, shipbuilding is a minor industry. However, for a number of reasons, shipbuilding has been of considerable importance in the structural policies of both West Germany and Britain, and the reasons advanced for support are as follows:

i.   *Employment considerations.* In both UK and West Germany, shipbuilding is geographically concentrated. In UK the major locations are the estuaries of the Clyde, Tyne, Tees and Mersey and at Belfast. In West Germany the main centres are Hamburg, Bremen, Bremerhaven, Emden, Kiel and Lübeck. Changes in the employment in the industry have concentrated effects which are amplified by the importance of shipbuilding as a customer for steel, marine engines, cables and ships' fittings. The employment objective would appear to be the dominant motive behind UK support for its domestic shipbuilding industry and reflects the high levels of unemployment in the shipbuilding areas of the UK. The strength of the employment motive has led the government to continue to support certain shipyards even where the possibilities of reaching profitability in the long run have appeared to be extremely slim. Thus the Harland and Wolff and Govan (formerly UCS) companies have been heavily subsidised because of high local unemployment and consequential political backlash in the West of Scotland and Northern Ireland. By mid-1976 total loans and grants to Harland and Wolff amounted to £137 million — about £25,000 per employee. In West Germany employment considerations have not been paramount in influencing policy towards shipbuilding for unlike British shipbuilding, the industry has been expanding and the major shipbuilding areas do not suffer from high unemployment. However, in the current world shipbuilding crisis the likelihood of large scale bankruptcy and closures have resulted in the government's introduction of short-term support to prevent a sudden rise in unemployment and to allow an orderly adjustment of the industry to the new market conditions.

ii.   *Export earnings.* In UK and West Germany shipbuilding is a significant export industry. Between 1975 and 1977 exports as a proportion of the value of completed ships were 57 per cent for West Germany and 40 per cent for UK. Where government believes its currency to be overvalued in relation to foreign trade in manufactured goods, as has been the view both in UK and West Germany, there is an incentive for government to subsidise export-orientated manufacturing industries, particularly since direct subsidisation of exports would contravene GATT and the Treaty of Rome.

iii.   *The encouragement of growth industries.* Although in the UK the trend of shipbuilding output and employment has been slightly downward over the past two decades, world trade has steadily expanded over the period and the demand for ships has shown a strongly upward trend. Thus for most countries, including West Germany, shipbuilding has been regarded as a growth industry. Even in the UK modest growth in shipbuilding might take place if the yards could be modernised and reorganised and labour relations improve. The Geddes Report of 1966 suggested that a doubling of UK shipbuilding output would be possible if the necessary gains in efficiency could be attained. The idea that government finance for British shipyards was aimed at the investment and modernisation necessary to create long run prosperity has been a common justification for heavy public expenditure on the industry.

iv.   *The safeguarding of the industry against periodic recessions.* As a capital goods industry the shipbuilding industry is subject to volatile fluctuations in demand. Because profit margins are normally narrow due to international competition, production does not normally have to fall far below capacity operation before fixed costs cannot be covered. To maintain industry capacity, therefore, governments have accepted the need to provide finance to the yards to assist them during periods of recession.

v.   *Subsidisation of domestic shipbuilding in order to match the assistance given by other countries to their shipbuilding industries.* The growing competition of low-cost shipbuilding countries to the long-established shipbuilding countries and the general excess-capacity in shipyards during the current recession has encouraged an international subsidy race aimed at safeguarding national shipbuilding industries from the full brunt of the recession.

6.20   This 'subsidy race' displays the characteristics of the 'prisoners' dilemma'. For the shipbuilding nations as a whole, competitive subsidisation has resulted in a failure to reduce shipbuilding capacity and has added to the long-term adjustment problem of the industry while intensifying the problem of over-capacity in the shipping industry. Yet for national reasons each country is unwilling to limit subsidisation for fear that its domestic shipbuilding industry will be forced to bear a disproportionate share of the necessary reduction in world yard capacity. It is difficult to divide the shipbuilding nations into 'leaders' and 'followers' with regard to their subsidisation policies. On the basis of US estimates (see Table 6.11) the UK appears to offer particularly generous assistance to its shipbuilding industry, while Germany's support is comparatively small.

6.21   Limited subsidies to the shipbuilding industries which do not involve a distortion of competition between particular West German yards are thus viewed as entirely consistent with the BRD government's principles of maintaining workable competition in the industrial sector. Where West German firms compete in an international market then the maintenance of workable competition means that the BRD government must, at least partially, match the generous support given by other countries to their national shipbuilding industries. While the Federal government has been keen to limit its support to the shipbuilding industry and to ensure that assistance does not discriminate unfairly between different yards, financial assistance at state level has been of an ad hoc nature and has not followed any consistent principles.

Table 6.11

ESTIMATED GOVERNMENT FINANCIAL ASSISTANCE TO SHIPPING AND
SHIPBUILDING, 1970-75

	SHIPPING		SHIPBUILDING	
	Amount ($ millions)	% of revenue	Amount ($ millions)	% of revenue
Japan	208	4.3	88	0.9 − 2.0
UK	320	9.2	69	14.6
Norway	269	9.8	40	6.5
Sweden	128	8.4	33	3.8
Germany	99	4.3	61	2.6
France	121	9.0	179	24.1

Source: US Department of Commerce Report (1977), pp.1-2.

E. UK government policy towards the shipbuilding industry

6.22 Prior to nationalisation in July 1977, the shipbuilding industry was subject to more government inter-vention and received more government financial support than any other private sector industry. Calcu-lating the total amount of public subsidy to the industry involves considerable difficulty, for assistance has been provided through numerous departments and agencies in a variety of forms (including grants, loans, equity, tax relief, credit guarantees) the aggregation of which involves considerable difficulties. In the case of shipbuilding, however, the fact that most loans were never repaid and most equity finance went to yards whose commercial value was low, has meant that it has been possible to aggregate these forms of finance and treat them as grants. Table 6.12 shows the US Department of Commerce's estimate of govern-ment finance to the industry between 1965 and mid-1976. An alternative breakdown of government assis-tance to the industry for recent years is given in Table 6.13.

Table 6.12

PUBLIC GRANTS, LOANS, AND EQUITY PURCHASES UNDER THE SHIPBUILDING INDUSTRY ACT AND 1972 INDUST
INDUSTRY ACT (1965-JUNE 1976)

	Equity	Grants	Loans	Unexpended Provisions	Total
Private companies	—	6.3	16.9	—	23.2
Partly or wholly owned companies	26.9	17.3	46.4	29.0	119.6
Harland and Wolff	3.6	23.1	44.9	23.3	34.9
TOTAL	30.5	46.7	108.2	52.3	297.7

Source: US Department of Commerce Report (1977), pp.III-32.

The principal forms of assistance by government to the shipbuilding industry are described below.

6.23 *General regional assistance:* Throughout the post-war period shipbuilding has been a major beneficiary of UK regional support measures. Over 90 per cent of the industry has been eligible for investment grants, tax allowances and the regional employment premium. Between 1972/73 and 1977/78 regional develop-ment grants paid to shipbuilding amounted to £56.1m.

6.24 *Relief of indirect taxes:* Prior to 1963 the only selective support for the shipbuilding industry was 'Ship-builders' Relief' — a refund of indirect taxes amounting to 2 per cent of the gross value of ships completed.

6.25 *Financial support by the Shipbuilding Industry Board 1967-1972:* Government intervention into the industry backed by heavy financial support followed the publication of the report of the Geddes Com-mittee on the shipbuilding industry (1966). The report identified poor management, poor labour relations, inadequacies in marketing, purchasing, design and planning as the major problems of the industry and its principal recommendations were:

(a) a re-organisation of the industry into larger companies accompanied by greater specialisation by indi-vidual yards;

(b)   a comprehensive government policy involving greater financial assistance.

The 1967 Shipbuilding Industry Act established the Shipbuilding Industry Board (SIB) to encourage and finance re-organisation and modernisation in the industry along the lines recommended in the Geddes Report. The establishment of the Board marks the inauguration of a comprehensive structural policy towards the industry.

6.26   The loans and grants offered by the SIB were on a selective basis, the purpose being to encourage modernisation of shipyards and assist re-organisation. Some finance did encourage large-scale re-equipment, but in the main the finance was concentrated on the biggest loss makers, [Upper Clyde Shipbuilders (UCS), Harland and Wolff and Cammell Laird] for the purposes of providing working capital and covering losses. The Booz-Allen and Hamilton Report (p.88) estimated that only one third of SIB assistance was used for capital investment. Table 6.13 shows financial assistance to the industry from the SIB and government departments between 1967 and 1972. The table also indicates the remarkably high rate of subsidy to Cammell Laird, UCS and Harland and Wolff.

6.27   *Support under the 1972 Industry Act:* With the 1972 Industry Act the SIB was wound-up and since 1972 virtually all assistance to the industry has been within the framework of this Act (excepting payments to Harland and Wolff by the Northern Ireland Ministry). The principal schemes are as follows:

i.   Constructions Grant Scheme (1972-74) provided grants for the construction of new ships and mobile offshore installations at the rate of 10 per cent for 1972, 4 per cent for 1973 and 3 per cent for 1974. The final payments under the schemes were made in 1978.

ii.   Selective regional assistance: section 7 of the Act provides for selective financial assistance for projects which create or maintain employment in the assisted regions. Under this section £3m was supplied in loans and £3.3m in grants in the period up to 31 March, 1978.

iii.   Special assistance under Section 7. In addition to the measures described above, selective payments have been made since 1972 to the following yards.

—   **Govan Shipbuilders** — between June 1972 and March 1978 £63.5 million was advanced to the company, although much of this sum was in loans, these loans were converted to equity or grants.

—   **Cammell Laird** — loans of £19.4 million were advanced.

—   **Sunderland Shipbuilders** — after the acquisition of the company, together with the other shipbuilding interests of Court Line in 1974 for £16 million, further loans of £15 million were made to Sunderland Shipbuilders.

—   **Austin and Pickersgill** — loan of £9 million in 1975/76.

Special assistance to **Harland and Wolff** was provided by the Northern Ireland Ministry. By mid-1976 aid to the company had totalled £137 million.

iv.   Cost escalation insurance: In 1976 the government introduced a cost escalation insurance to cover shipbuilders against increases in costs on ship contracts.

v.   Shipbuilding intervention fund, 1977: In February 1977 a £65 million intervention fund was announced for the industry under the Industry Act. The scheme was to provide selective assistance to individual yards to enable them to quote competitive prices for particular orders (the principal objective is to be competitive with Japanese tenders). The major application of the scheme so far is the £28 million from the fund to gain the £115 million Polish ships order (this was in addition to the normal ECGD finance).

6.28   *Credit assistance for the buyers of ships:* In addition to direct assistance to shipbuilders, government schemes to assist the buyers of UK produced ships are aimed primarily at making British yards more competitive with those of other countries. Under the Export Credit Guarantee Scheme the government guarantees and subsidises loans made to foreign buyers for the purpose of buying ships from UK yards. The Home Credit Scheme was introduced in 1963 to provide similar financial terms to UK shipowners purchasing from domestic yards. The enabling legislation, the Shipbuilding Credit Act, was passed in the following year. Under the scheme loans are made by the clearing banks but lending above a certain limit is refinanced by the government and the difference between the rate of interest on the loans and commercial rates is covered by the government. Table 6.14 shows the growth of lending under the scheme.

Table 6.13

FINANCIAL ASSISTANCE TO UK SHIPBUILDERS, 1967-1972

		SIB Grants	SIB total payments	Payments from Government departments	Total assistance1 as per cent of sales
		(£m)	(£m)	(£m)	(%)
Appledore	0.35	0.35	1.10	—	2.2
Austin and Pickersgill			—	—	2.0
Cammell Laird		—	—	21.50	23.8
Doxford		—	0.1	—	2.0
Gavan/UCS		6.25	12.79	52.30	23.0
Harland and Wolff		7.04	15.04	26.64	21.8
Robb Caledon		0.10	0.51	—	2.4
Scott Lithgow		1.77	5.25	—	3.6
Swann Hunter		5.82	5.84	—	5.9
Vosper		0.09	0.10	—	n.a.
Yarrow		0.35	1.57	4.50	n.a.
Others		0.05	0.71	1.90	n.a.
TOTAL		21.16	42.93	116.84	n.a.

Note:

1   From G. Denton, Financial Assistance to British Industry in Corden and Fels (1976). This column relates to the years 1967 to 1971 and the assistance includes SIB payments, ad hoc assistance and shipbuilders' relief.

Source: Report by Booz-Allen and Hamilton (1973) — except for final column (see note 1).

6.29   Since 1975 the terms of export credit have been governed by the OECD Export Credit Understanding for Ships.

6.30   *Re-organisation and the extension of public ownership:*
A principal objective of the SIB was the re-organisation of the industry into fewer companies. In its Report for 1968/9 the Board announced that of twenty-seven of the shipbuilding companies covered by the Geddes Report, twenty-one had merged into seven groups and two had left shipbuilding. Table 6.15 shows the re-organisation over the period. But when, after re-organisation and SIB financed yards still faced bankruptcy, government often responded by offering further finance in the form of equity participation. The main reason for part or entire public ownership was the avoidance of unemployment. A popular view was that the introduction of public ownership would provide a better atmosphere for the resolution of disputes between management and labour over pay and working methods. In view of the poor managerial quality of some companies it was considered that government ownership would provide an opportunity for introducing more dynamic and up-to-date management methods. Public ownership was also seen as a way of improving co-operation between shipbuilding companies over R and D, design and purchasing.

6.31   The rescue of failing shipbuilding companies by equity purchases resulted in forms of public ownership that contrasted sharply with traditional approaches to nationalisation: public ownership was often partial with arms-length arrangements between government and management. The majority holding which government took in Fairfields Shipbuilding and Engineering Ltd in 1965 was followed by the company adopting radical methods of management and industrial relations. During the early 1970s as other shipbuilding companies ran into serious financial difficulties so government ownership expanded. Between 1970 and 1975 the government acquired:—

—   50 per cent ownership in Cammell Laird Shipbuilders Ltd.

—   100 per cent of Govan Shipbuilding Ltd.

—   47.6 per cent ownership of Harland and Wolff Ltd.

—   100 per cent ownership of Scotstown Marine Ltd.

—   100 per cent ownership of Appledore Shipbuilders Ltd.

—   100 per cent ownership of Sunderland Shipbuilders Ltd.

Table 6.14

UK HOME CREDIT SCHEME

	1972/73	1973/74	1974/75	1975/76	1976/77	1977/78
Proportion of vessel cost covered by guaranteed loan	80%	80%	70%[1]	70%	70%	70%
Maximum repayment period (years)	8	8	7[1]	7	7	7
Maximum interest rate (%)	7.0	7.0	7.5[1]	7.5	7.5	7.5
Guarantees, outstanding at year-end (£m)	601.9	642.4	795.9	895.5	932.4	884.4
Estimated annual benefit to borrowers[2]	16.3	28.2	71.2	76.5	71.6	51.9

Note: 1. From 1 July, 1974
2. Based on average difference between the rate of interest on guaranteed loans and the industrial bond yield.

Source: Industry Act, 1972. Annual Reports

Table 6.15

RATIONALISATION IN THE UK SHIPBUILDING INDUSTRY FROM 1965

EAST SCOTLAND

Henry Robb Shipbuilders
Caledonian Shipbuilding &   Robb Caldeon
   Engineering Co.   Shipbuilders
Burntisland Shipping Co*

LOWER CLYDE

Scott's Shipbuilding &
   Engineering Co.
Lithgows Ltd.   Scott Lithgow
Greenock Dockyard Co.

UPPER CLYDE

John Brown & Co.
Yarrow & Co.   Yarrow Shipbuilders
Connell & Co.   Upper Clyde
A. Stephen & Co.*   Shipbuilders
Fairfields   Govan Shipbuilders
Barclay Curle & Co.*

ULSTER

Harland & Wolff

TYNE & TEES

Vickers Ltd.
Swan Hunter & Wigham   British Shipbuilding
   Richardson   Ltd.
Hawthorn Leslie   Swann Hunter
J. Readhead & Sons   Shipbuilders
Furness Shipbuilding
Smith's Dock Co.

WEAK

Austin & Pickersgill
Bartram & Sons   Austin & Pickersgill
Wm. Doxford & Sons
J. Laing & Sons   Doxford & Sunderland Ltd.
J.L. Thompson & Sons

MERSEY

Cammell Laird & Co.

SOUTHAMPTON

J.I. Thorneycroft & Co. Ltd   Vosper Thornycroft

BARROW

Vickers Ltd. (Shipbuilding Group)

OTHERS

Blyth Dry Docks & Shipbuilding*
Appledore Shipbuilders Ltd.

*   finished shipbuilding between 1965 and 1972

—   100 per cent ownership of North East Coast Ship repairers Ltd.

6.32   In July 1974 the government announced in Parliament its intention of taking the whole of the shipbuilding industry into public ownership under a single national shipbuilding company. The Aircraft and Shipbuilding Bill was introduced in 1975 and passed in 1977. The purposes of nationalisation were:

(a)   to finance the industry so as to maintain employment and allow the industry to survive the shipbuilding recession;

(b)   to provide the investment funds required for the necessary modernisation of British yards;

(c)   to enable re-organisation in order to exploit scale economies in certain activities and improve management.

F.   UK government policy towards the shipping industry

6.33   While some of the financial aids paid to UK shipowners are unambiguously subsidies to the shipping industry, in the case of certain aids it is difficult to apportion the benefit between the shipowner and the shipbuilder. In the case of subsidies for ship purchases restricted to purchases from UK yards, the principal beneficiary will be the shipbuilder, since the effect of such subsidies is to bring down UK prices to those charged by lower-cost shipbuilding nations, thus shifting orders from foreign to domestic yards.

6.34   *Subsidies for ship purchases:* Under the 1966 Industrial Development Act, investment grants were introduced for expenditure on fixed assets by manufacturing industry. Section 5 of the Act introduced 20 per cent grants towards purchases of ships by UK owners which was increased to 25 per cent between 1967 and 1968. The programme was cancelled in 1971 as a result of the unexpectedly high cost of the grants and the general shift in government policy from investment grants to investment tax allowances. However, payments under the scheme continued after 1971 because of ships already on order. The grants were available to UK shipowners and UK subsidiaries of foreign shipowners for new vessels registered under the British flag. The objectives were the expansion of the UK fleet, the encouragement of modernisation and efficiency of the British fleet and increased orders for UK shipyards. The programme was remarkably successful in encouraging the expansion of the UK fleet, but a large part of new orders still went to foreign shipyards. Table 6.16 shows expenditure on investment grants for ships.

Table 6.16

INVESTMENT GRANTS ON UK SHIP PURCHASES

Financial Years	Expenditure (£ million)
1967-1968	22.7
1968-1969	48.1
1969-1970	75.7
1970-1971	66.1
1971-1972	115.6
1972-1973	97.5
1973-1974	105.0
1974-1975	59.5
1975-1976	46.4
1976-1977	21.0
1977-1978	4.9

Source: Industry Act 1972, Annual Reports.

6.35   *Depreciation Allowances:* Free depreciation became available to UK shipowners in 1965, the benefits being codified under the 1968 Capital Allowances Act and then revised in October 1970. As capital investment by shipping companies increased during the late 1960s and early 1970s so the write-off provisions have become increasingly valuable. One effect of the generous depreciation allowances has been to encourage non-shipping companies to become shipowners. Thus the Clearing Banks have formed subsidiaries to purchase ships and lease them to shipping companies. The subsidy element in free depreciation schedules is difficult to calculate but if the shipping company's total tax liability does not alter, the benefit occurs from the shifting forward of allowances. Table 6.17 estimates the subsidy element in the depreciation scheme.

6.36   *Home credit scheme:* The scheme is described in paragraph 6.28 above where it is noted that the intended beneficiary of the favourable credit terms is the UK shipbuilding industry. However, to the extent that the subsidised credit terms are greater than the minimum financial inducement necessary for the ship buyer to switch his order from an overseas to a UK yard, then he also benefits.

Table 6.17

ESTIMATED BENEFIT FROM FREE DEPRECIATION ON SHIPS

(£ million)

	Net fixed capital expenditure	*Estimated benefit[1]*
1971-1972	286.5	31.5
1972-1973	298.0	32.8
1973-1974	428.5	47.1
1974-1975	496.5	54.6
1975-1976	428.5	47.1
1976-1977	418.4	46.0

Note: 1. 11 per cent of capital investment — assumes 8 per cent cost of capital, 8-year straight-line depreciation compared with depreciation taken at end of first year.

Source: US Department of Commerce (1977) page III-25.

G. West German Government policy towards the shipbuilding industry

6.37 In comparison with other European countries, the level of financial assistance by government to the maritime sector has been low in the BRD (see Table 6.11). Also in contrast to the UK, German financial support has been concentrated upon shipping with relatively little support for shipbuilding. Since 1976, however, the seriousness of the fall in shipyard orders has resulted in much heavier financial support of the West German shipyards. Table 6.18 shows the US government's estimate of total financial assistance to shipbuilding between 1971 and 1975.

Table 6.18

TOTAL WEST GERMAN FINANCIAL ASSISTANCE TO THE SHIPBUILDING INDUSTRY

(DM million)

	1971	*1972*	*1973*	*1974*	*1975*
Modernisation funds, border loans, interest subsidies, KW & ERP loans, investory loss reserves, tax credits, R and D support	95.7	104.6	173.7	180.1	192.9

Source: US Department of Commerce Report (1977), pp.VI-18.

6.38 As with UK maritime aid, allocating the benefits of financial support measures between shipping and shipbuilding is not straightforward. In general, assistance to the shipbuilding industry is administered by the Federal Ministry of Economics, while assistance to shipping is by the Ministry of Transport. However, subsidies for new ship purchases which are limited to purchases from German yards will principally benefit the shipbuilding companies.

6.39 The Subsidy Reports list financial and tax allowances according to whom they are paid. The support for shipbuilding shown in the Reports is modest, but to it should be added subsidised credit available to purchasers from German yards, relief of indirect taxes to shipbuilders, and those aids paid to shipping companies which are to the benefit of shipbuilders (notably construction grants).

Table 6.19

PRINCIPAL FINANCIAL AIDS BENEFITING SHIPBUILDING IN THE BRD

(DM millions)

	1970	*1971*	*1972*	*1973*	*1974*	*1975*	*1976*	*1977*	*1978*
Grants for shipbuilders[1]	27.6	29.5	37.1	66.9	98.9	99.6	83.7	83.1	106.9
Construction grants1	87.3	81.9	56.3	60.0	60.0	118.3	150.1	155.0	255.0
Subsidy element in credit assistance for buyers[1]	156.5	156.5	156.5	303.5	303.5	303.5	329.4	329.4	329.4

Note: 1 = From Subsidies Reports
2 = From US Department of Commerce (1977) p.VI.43.

6.40 The general and selective schemes benefiting the shipbuilding industry of the BRD are described below. It should be noted that the conventions of the BRD government have been followed in distinguishing between aids to shipping and shipbuilding, and some of the major assistance to German shipyards (notably construction grants) are described in the section on shipping.

6.41 *Regional assistance measures:* The principal beneficiaries of regional assistance measures have been those shipyards located in the Eastern Border region. The Lübeck-based companies Flender Werft A.G., D & K Orenstein and Koppel A.G. and Schlichting Werft GmbH have received low interest loans (6 per cent) of about DM497.8 million. These were special ERP investment loans offered during the period 1966 to 1971. No further loans have been made since 1971. The subsidy element in these loans was calculated by the US Department of Commerce at DM15.2 million. (For a calculation of total shipbuilding aid, see Table 6.19).

6.42 *Credit assistance at favourable rates of interest:* The credit for foreign buyers has been supplied through 9 successive shipbuilding assistance programmes. Export credit is supplied through a special government credit institution, the Kreditanstalt für Wiederaufbau (KW). The financing is from the ERP programme and from the Federal Government. By estimating the difference in the average rate of interest on these loans and the market rate of interest, it is possible to estimate the subsidy element in these loans. The US Department of Commerce has calculated the subsidy element on budgeted funds as follows:—

(DM million)

1970	1971	1972	1973	1974	1975	1976	1977	1978
156.5	156.5	156.5	303.5	303.5	303.5	329.4	329.4	329.4

The acceptance of the OECD agreement on export credits for ships has limited assistance to shipbuilding more in West Germany than in most other OECD countries because of the lower rates of interest prevailing in West Germany than in countries with higher rates of inflation. The minimum rates of interest specified by OECD have not been far below actual market rates of interest in Germany.

6.43 Special assistance has been available to less developed countries for purchases from German yards. The programme is administered by the Ministry for Economic Co-operation which in 1976 and 1977 made available DM300 million for purchases from German industry. Loans to German shipowners from the ERP for ship purchases have been small. The loans are not limited to purchases from German yards although in practice most have been used for purchases from German yards. The amount of loan is shown in Table 5.21. Because the greater part of the German merchant fleet's ship purchases are from German yards, a large proportion of the aid schemes for German shipping companies provides an indirect benefit to German shipyards. This is particularly true of the construction subsidies and tax arrangements. The increase in the construction subsidy on new ships from 12.5 per cent to 17.5 per cent in 1977 was aimed primarily at protecting West German shipyards rather than assisting German shipping companies.

6.44 *Tax allowances:* These have taken the form of:

i. Customs Duty exemption — imports of materials for the building of oceangoing ships are exempt from customs duty. Since most of the inputs for Germany's shipbuilding industry are domestically produced, the benefit is trivial.

ii. Reserve funds against inventory losses — special reserve funds against inventory losses provide a tax benefit for shipyards. Between 1970 and 1974 the 9 largest West German shipbuilding companies increased their reserve funds by DM68.7 million of which (HDW) was responsible for DM39 million (US Department of Commerce, 1977 page VI—40).

6.45 *R and D support:* The Ministry of Science and Technology provides grants of up to 25 per cent towards selected R and D projects in the shipbuilding industry. Among the projects supported have been gas transporters, ice breaking ships and cargo carrying catamarans. The US Department of Commerce Report (1977) pp. vi—43) estimates that between 1970-1975 R and D support amounted to about DM4.5 million per year. The Federal Government's finance for R and D into shipbuilding would appear to be a little less than that of the UK Government.

6.46 *Yard modernisation assistance:* Low interest loans to shipbuilders have been available from (ERP) funds. These loans are available to all industries, but allocation to shipbuilding has been particularly important.

6.47 *Public ownership:* The Largest German shipyard, HDW, is 75 per cent owned by Salzgitter, the steel conglomerate owned by the Federal Government, and 25 per cent owned by the State Government of Schleswig-Holstein. The arrangement does not appear to have resulted in any preferential treatment of HDW by Federal or State governments, although HDW's balance sheet has benefited from Salzgitter's exemption from having to pay a dividend on its shareholding.

6.48 *Aid through State Naval Contracts:* Military contracts have been used to assist individual yards during the present crisis. Thus the Ministry of Defence brought forward orders for five ships to assist the industry — notably the Blöhm and Voss yard which was facing bankruptcy in 1977 prior to the government order. In 1976-1977 HDW took DM1260m of Defence Ministry orders, equivalent to 18 per cent of its sales.

6.49 *Assistance from State Governments:* In addition to Federal support for the shipbuilding industry there has been substantial support by state governments in the shipbuilding areas for their local industries. The principal shipbuilding states are shown in Table 6.20 following.

Table 6.20

DISTRIBUTION OF GERMAN SHIPBUILDING INDUSTRY BY STATE

(by production value 1977)

Schleswig-Holstein	29.7 per cent
Hamburg	17.8 per cent
Lower Saxony	15.8 per cent
Bremen	32.7 per cent
North Rhine-Westphalia	2.0 per cent

Source: *Deutscher Schiffbau 1977.* Verband der Deutschen Schiffbauindustrie e.v.

State government support was increased through a joint project which linked Länder support of the shipbuilding companies to the larger Federal programme. The 1977 Federal government budget DM450 million was earmarked for construction grants. To supplement this sum the coastal states (Hamburg, Bremen, Lower Saxony and Schleswig-Holstein) agreed to supplement this fund with state grants for projects not backed or insufficiently backed by the Federal government. (Verband Deutscher Reeder, Seeschiffahrt 1977 p.18). In addition selective assistance to local shipbuilding companies has been given by all five of the main shipbuilding states. This assistance has taken a variety of forms. Hamburg shipyards have benefited from state ownership of the shipyard land and heavy public investment in infrastructure at the freeport (interview at Economics Ministry, Bonn. September 1978).

H.   West German Government Policy towards the Shipping Industry

6.50 As has been explained above, West German policy towards its shipping industry has been to make the West German fleet competitive in international trade with the fleets of lower-cost nations, to make the German merchant marine the most modern and the most efficient in the world, to increase the proportion of Germany's trade carried in German ships for strategic reasons, to increase Germany's control over her own foreign trade and to assist the balance of payments. It is notable that German shipping assistance has been more selective than that of Britain. Aid has been restricted to particular types of ships and different rates of assistance have been paid according to types of ship. Financial assistance has been designed to encourage modernisation of the fleet through a more rapid scrapping and replacement of vessels. The principal aids are listed below.

6.51 *ERP loans to German shipping companies:* These have been much less significant than the finance given to foreign buyers. The loans have had a maximum of DM5.9 million per loan which covers only purchases of small ships. Table 6.21 shows the terms of the loans.

Table 6.21

ERP FINANCING ASSISTANCE TO GERMAN SHIPOWNERS

(DM millions)

	1971	1972	1973	1974	1975	1976
Authorised loans	23.1	23.1	45.0	45.0	45.0	45.0
Per cent financing	70.0%	70.0%	70.0%	70.0%	70.0%	70.0%
Interest rate	6.0%	6.0%	6.5%	7.5%	7.5%	7.5%

Source: US Department of Commerce Report (1977, pp.VI–8).

6.52 *Special Depreciation of Ships:* Additional depreciation against tax is allowable on new ships to the amount of 30 per cent of the purchase cost over 5 years in addition to the normal depreciation by a straight line method. The 30 per cent additional depreciation for 1971 to 1974 was increased 40 per cent for 1975 to 1978. The effect on depreciation of a ship is shown in Table 6.22 following.

Table 6.22

DEPRECIATION UNDER THE SPECIAL DEPRECIATION PROGRAMME

(per cent)

	1	2	3	4	5	6	7	8	Total after 8 years
Straight line depreciation	8.33	8.33	8.33	8.33	8.33	8.33	8.33	8.33	66.64
With special depreciation (1971-1974)	14.33	14.33	14.33	14.33	14.33	4.05	4.05	4.05	83.80
With special depreciation (1975-1978)	16.33	16.33	16.33	16.33	16.33	2.62	2.62	2.62	89.51

Source: US Department of Commerce Report, 1977, pp.VI—10

6.53 The tax advantages of shipowning have encouraged other firms and individual investors to become ship-owners, leasing the ships to operating companies. The average annual value of the depreciation provisions have been estimated by the US Department of Commerce at DM78.7 million for 1973 to 1975.

6.54 *Other tax benefits:* Some additional tax benefits have been:—

i. Taxes on gains from ship sales may be deferred for two years and are not levied at all if the capital gains are used for the purchase of a new ship during the two year period (Table 6.22).

ii. Preferential tax rate on foreign earnings. Up to the end of 1973, 50 per cent of foreign earnings from shipping were taxed at half the normal rate (i.e. 37.5 per cent instead of 50 per cent). From 1974 80 per cent of foreign earnings were taxed at half the normal rate (30 per cent instead of 50 per cent).

6.55 *Construction subsidies:* Construction subsidies are grants paid to German shipowners to cover a proportion of the costs of new vessels whether ordered from German or foreign shipyards. From 1965 to 1974 the subsidy amounted to 10 per cent of new ship costs. In 1975 it was increased to 12.5 per cent. From 1976 the subsidies could be combined with other aid measures, e.g. interest relief, to a maximum total subsidy of 17 per cent. In 1977 a special subsidy of 5 per cent was added to the base subsidy of 12.5 per cent and the new subsidy of 17.5 per cent was continued in 1978. The procedure under successive programmes has been for the government to establish the total budget and the percentage rate of the subsidy, to invite applications for assistance, then to decide the proportion of planned tonnage acquisitions which can be covered by the subsidy. In addition to the standard subsidies on ship purchases, in 1974 a special subsidy of 15 per cent was introduced for very large tankers. The purpose was to expand the proportion of Germany's petroleum imports carried in German ships. The total value of grants to the shipping companies is shown in Table 6.23.

Table 6.23

GRANTS TO BRD SHIPPING COMPANIES FOR NEW SHIP PURCHASES

(DM million)

1970	1971	1972	1973	1974	1975	1976	1977	1978
87.3	81.9	56.3	60	60	118.3	150.1	155	255

Source: Subsidies Report, for 1978 German Tribune 15.5.77

6.56 *Preference in Trade:* In coastal trade between German ports, foreign flag ships are not permitted if German flag vessels are available at competitive rates. Also the BRD government's permission is required for cargo pooling arrangements with non-German shipping companies.

6.57 *Short term assistance to meet financial crisis:* The severity of the late 70s depression in the world ship-building industry and the particular problems of the German-owned shipping companies, e.g. their relatively high costs, has led the BRD government to provide special short-term assistance to avert the threat to the long-term existence of the fleet. The most noticeable factor in the shipping market in 1976 and 1977 was the extension of the highly depressed conditions in the tanker industry to the bulk-carrier sector. To avoid liquidity crises and mass sell-offs by German bulk carrier owners, the government provided Federal guarantees for loans against bulk carriers.

I. **Comparison and assessment of the structural policies towards shipping and shipbuilding**

6.58 The comparison of the policy measures of the two countries is of interest not just in relation to the industries considered here, but also because the differences in policy are representative of the different approaches to structural policy in the two countries. In the case of shipbuilding policies the heavier subsidisation and the more interventionist stance of UK policies is a reflection of the political differences of governments in the two countries towards economic policy, notably the priority attached to employment maintenance by the UK government. The shipping industries of the two countries provides an interesting contrast. Not only is the level of financial support similar between the two countries, but it is the government of the BRD which had been more interventionist and selective in its policies than that of the UK. This difference reflects to some extent the importance attached in the BRD to the strategic role of the German merchant fleet, particularly in relation to the country's export trade, whereas the primary consideration for UK industrial policy — regional unemployment — is absent in the case of shipping. The comparative lack of selective intervention by the UK government in its shipping industry can also be attributed to the concentration of UK industrial policies on the manufacturing sector of the economy.

6.59 In assessing the effectiveness of the structural policies towards the maritime industries several difficulties present themselves. The objectives of policy measures are not always apparent from policy statements. In particular, both in the BRD and the UK, governments have been reluctant to admit that shipbuilding aids have been primarily for the purpose of protecting domestic shipbuilding capacity and maintaining employment. The most substantial offers of finance for UK shipyards have supposedly been for the modernisation and re-equipping of shipyards to enable them to raise their productivity towards international levels. Yet it is clear that subsidies have been used primarily to cover current losses and provide working capital for the purpose of maintaining employment in the medium-term. In the BRD, grants for purchases of new ships are classified as subsidies to the shipping industry, although the intended beneficiaries are domestic shipyards.

6.60 The allocation of the benefits of maritime aids between the shipping and shipbuilding industries presents some difficult problems. Subsidies to foreign owners on purchases from domestic yards are intended for the benefit of domestic shipbuilders. Subsidies to domestic shipowners on purchases of ships whether from domestic or foreign yards benefit domestic shipowners. Subsidies to domestic shipowners which are tied to purchases from domestic yards will tend to benefit both owner and builder. In all three cases the division of benefit between purchaser and supplier is dependent upon the relative importance of the price and quantity effects of the subsidy.

6.61 As with all policy interventions, the problem of assessing the influence of policy is in identifying how industry performance would have differed had the policy not operated (Cf Chapter VII paragraph 7.13 below). Special difficulties arise in assessing the influence of structural policies because of the two-way relationship between performance and policy: it is the sub-optimal performance of the industry which creates the need for structural intervention and moulds the form of policy instruments, while the operation of the policies themselves will impinge upon industry performance. A view which merits particular attention in relation to shipbuilding policies is that the reaction of industry to policy intervention is such as to counteract the effects of the policy instruments with the result that government policies have had very little long-term impact on the industry.

6.62 *Shipbuilding policies:* At first glance, the predominant feature of a comparison between structural policies towards shipbuilding in the BRD and UK is the similarity of the policy instruments employed. In both countries a major form of aid has been credit assistance in the form of interest subsidies and credit guarantees for domestic and foreign ship buyers. Construction grants and relief of indirect taxes to shipbuilders are paid in both countries. The principal differences in shipbuilding policies lie in the relative importance of different instruments, the higher level of subsidisation in the UK and selectivity in the application of the policy instruments.

6.63 The far heavier degree of financial support for the UK shipbuilding industry is primarily a reflection of the greater 'needs' of the UK industry, assuming that neither government would be willing to allow the major part of its domestic shipbuilding industry to close completely. Tables 6.4 and 6.5 indicate the great differences in the performance of shipbuilding in the UK and BRD. Between the five year periods 1955-59 and 1973-77, the tonnage output of UK yards fell at an average rate of around 1 per cent. This compares with an average annual rate of growth of about 6 per cent for German yards and 10 per cent for world output. Of the world's leading shipbuilding nations, Britain was the only one to fail to achieve significant output growth before the current crisis. In both UK and BRD shipbuilding has been subject to strong cyclical movements and even the UK has had periods of output growth — notably 1969-71 and 1973-76. This great discrepancy in performance took place despite the large size and steady growth of the UK merchant fleet as compared with the reliance of German yards on overseas orders.

6.64 Decline resulting from lack of international competitiveness does not alone justify maintenance by means of government subsidies. Explanation of government's willingness to prevent the contracting of the UK shipbuilding must take into account the location of the major shipyards in areas of high unemployment (see paragraph 6.19), yet even this factor does not fully explain the remarkably high level of financial support for UK shipbuilding as compared with other industries in similar situations (e.g. textiles). An important factor is likely to be the strong influence which the industry was able to exert as a result of the concentration of the industry into a single company in each shipbuilding area (e.g. UCS — Clyde, Cammell Laird — Merseyside, Harland and Wolff — Belfast), together with the traditional importance of the industry as a major exporter and symbol of British industrial prowess, and the militancy of shipyard workers.

6.65 The concentration of UK shipbuilding aids on selective grants, loans and equity funding for individual yards, as compared with the concentration of BRD aids on general support for the industry, partly reflects the importance of the employment objective in the UK. The least-cost means of achieving short-run employment targets is not to distribute aid generally to the industry, but to concentrate support on those yards facing closure. UK policy has followed this approach with the heaviest proportional support going to the financially weakest and commercially least-successful yards — notably Harland and Wolff, UCS and Cammell Laird. Whether such policies are the most economical means of maintaining employment over the longer term is questionable. To investigate the effectiveness of UK as compared with West German policy measures, it is necessary to investigate more closely performance in the two countries.

6.66 The success of the German shipbuilding industry, at least up until the current crisis, has been in spite of the handicaps of very high labour costs and a rising international value of the mark. The competitive strength of the German shipyards appears to be more the result of managerial competence rather than of government policy. The high labour costs of the German companies has been offset by specialisation on particular vessel types where quality construction, technical expertise and high levels of capital per worker could be exploited to their fullest advantage. Government subsidies have assisted the shipyards in meeting world competition but have been insufficient to shield the industry from price competition from low-cost producers. Nor have they had the effect of concentrating resources in particular sectors of the shipbuilding industry or in different companies. Where the Federal government did move from general support measures to more selective assistance, for instance in encouraging the construction of very large tankers, the inducement to participate in this highly competitive sector of the market which was experiencing a short-lived boom, was undoubtedly detrimental to the industry.

6.67 The effectiveness of the heavy and selective support of shipbuilding by the UK government must be judged not solely in terms of the success of government in preventing the closure of any major shipyard between 1967 and 1978, but also in the effectiveness of UK policy in solving the basic structural problems of the UK shipbuilding industry and providing a secure basis for future existence and development. The sources of poor performance of the UK industry have been the subject of a number of detailed studies (e.g. Geddes Report 1966, Booz-Allen and Hamilton Report, 1973). Three principal factors have been identified:

(1) Low labour productivity. UK employment in the industry since 1972 has exceeded that of Germany, despite the fact that Germany's output has been about 60 per cent greater in tonnage terms, and even greater in value terms. Comparisons have shown German labour productivity in terms of production tonnage and value per employee to be about three times the UK level. Nor has UK labour productivity increased significantly over time. An analysis of productivity during the period 1967-1971 showed that the increase in average output per employee in UK yards was entirely the result of increased vessel size. (Department of Trade and Industry, 1973, p.154).

(2) Poor delivery performance. The major reasons for the poor international reputation of UK shipbuilding and the preference of UK shipowners for purchases from foreign yards is the unreliable delivery record of UK yards. Between 1967 and 1971 of total UK ship completions:

— 48 per cent were delivered on or before the contracted date;
— 13 per cent were up to one month late;
— 18 per cent were 2-3 months late;
— 12 per cent were 3-6 months late; and
— 9 per cent were over 6 months late.

(Department of Trade and Industry 1973, pp.102-103). The principal causes of this poor delivery record have been identified as poor production planning and industrial relations disputes.

(3)   Low level of capital investment. Despite heavy (government financed) investment at certain yards, the level of investment in fixed capital has been low in UK yards relative to West Germany and to other shipbuilding nations.

6.68   Government policies since the 1960's have done little to solve these aspects of the poor productive per-formance of UK shipyards. Although the inadequacies of management, work practices, industrial relations and capital equipment were highlighted by the Geddes Report, subsequent government policies have frequently provided an environment for the continuation rather than the elimination of these inadequacies. While major injections of public funds into ailing shipyards have frequently been conditional upon the abandonment of restrictive working practices and the adherence to established procedures for resolving industrial relations disputes, such conditions have not been effective. Where the offer of government rescue did encourage trade unions to abandon restrictive labour practices and accept flexible working arrangements, such concessions were often purchased with special bonus or productivity payments to workers, as occurred at Fairfields Ltd. [Broadway (1976), pp.21-22]. Where the greater part of government finance for the industry is used for keeping unprofitable yards in business, then the incentives for management and workers to increase efficiency and profitability are blunted and, as the theory of X-inefficiency would suggest, the tendency is for average costs to rise above their minimal point. The failure of government policies to resolve the deep-seated problem of UK shipbuilding is clearly identified in the 1979 corporate plan for British Shipbuilders Ltd. The report notes that the yards are 'among the least productive in the world' with output per employee 50 per cent below typical Western European ratios and delivery performance has deteriorated sharply over the period 1973-1978.

6.69   This lack of impact of government policy on efficiency and productivity may seem surprising in view of the extent of structural re-organisation stimulated by government intervention. Since the Geddes Com-mittee's formation in 1966 the UK shipbuilding industry was reduced from 28 to 6 companies, which were amalgamated into a single corporation with the establishment of British Shipbuilders in 1977. Despite the amalgamations and managerial re-organisations at the highest level, there have been few yard closures and little attempt to exploit benefits of specialisation, for example, by the re-location of orders. The history of Upper Clyde Shipbuilders provides a clear example of how sweeping organisational and managerial changes can have only limited effect at production level [see Broadway, (1976)].

6.70   Measured against the objective of maintaining employment in the industry, structural policy has been fairly effective. In the absence of government assistance the shipyards of the Upper Clyde, Belfast and the Mersey would almost certainly have faced closure by the early 1970's, while in the current crisis it is doubtful whether more than a few yards could survive. At the same time, however, there is a clear conflict between the maintenance of employment in the short and medium-term and providing the foundation for self-sustaining viability which can secure employment in the long-term. It would appear that by providing selective support to unprofitable shipyards, the government has maintained almost intact the size, structure and distribution of the UK shipbuilding industry, but in doing so it has only delayed the necessary ration-alisation of the industry. It might also be argued that structural policy in discriminating in favour of the least profitable yards (and therefore impeding the progress of certain more profitable and progressively-managed yards) has conflicted with the objective of securing employment in the industry in the long-term.

6.71   *Shipping policies:* The effectiveness of the policies towards the shipping industries of the BRD and UK are more similar than in the case of shipbuilding. The differences that exist are the reverse of the differences in the shipbuilding industries of the two countries. Thus it is the UK that has had the larger and more inter-nationally successful shipping industry while the German fleet has been concerned mainly with the foreign trade of the BRD. Comparing policies, it is the Federal government which has adopted more interventionist policy instruments aimed at inducing structural changes within the industry.

6.72   The growth of the German fleet has been modest during the 1970s. The BRD's share of the world merchant fleet has fallen, and only a small proportion of foreign trade of the BRD is carried by the home fleet. The competitive disadvantages faced by the German fleet must be borne in mind, namely high wages costs, rising value of the DM and competition from COMECON fleets. While the performance of the German merchant marine must be considered reasonably satisfactory in such a competitive international market, the ability of the UK fleet to maintain its international position over the post-war period and to expand rapidly over the decade 1966-1976 is more impressive. This is particularly so in view of the fact that the UK fleet has achieved its growth largely through expanding its share of trade between countries, as growth of UK trade provided no basis for expansion of business. In 1974, 63 per cent of the receipts of the UK shipping industry were provided by cross-trading.

6.73 Aid to shipping has involved similar measures in both countries, tax concessions and subsidies for the purchase of new ships being the principal instruments. In both countries aid has been more limited than that to shipbuilding, particularly in the UK. Indeed it could be argued that the support given to shipbuilding has increased the difficulties of the shippers by encouraging the growth of excess shipping capacity. Subsidies to foreign shipping companies for the purchase of new ships have been particularly damaging to the domestic shipping industries. The shipping industry of the BRD has complained that 'as yet, shipyards are in effect the sole beneficiaries since the grants reduce their internationally uncompetitive prices' (Verband Deutscher Reeder, Annual Report for 1977).

6.74 Financial aid by both governments has been mainly in the form of general measures available to the industry as a whole with a comparative absence of selective assistance. In contrast with shipbuilding, and indeed most other industries, the support measures of the BRD have been more selective than those of the UK. The Federal government has identified particular structural objectives in relation to shipping which have been implemented by means of financial incentives. Incentives for new ship purchases and scrapping aids have encouraged modernisation of the fleet and incentives have been provided for the maintenance and expansion of particular types of shipping, for example, special inducements for tankers and the guarantees made available in September 1977 to maintain bulk carriers in the merchant fleet. The success of replacement in the BRD shipping industry is indicated by the low average age of the fleet (see Table 6.24).

Table 6.24

AVERAGE FLEET AGE IN YEARS

	1970	1971	1972	1973	1974	1975
Japan	9	7	7	6	7	7
UK	12	11	11	10	10	10
Norway	10	8	8	8	8	8
Germany	11	10	9	6	7	7
France	12	11	11	10	10	10
World	17	13	13	12	12	12

Source: US Department of Commerce Report, 1977 pp.1-13

6.75 The chief characteristics of UK aid to shipping are the relatively low level of support and the absence of selective intervention that is discriminatory between companies. The level of aid as a percentage of revenue has been on a comparable level to that received by the fleets of other nations but has been far below the level of support for shipbuilding. The absence of direct intervention by government with policies which are selective by companies is unusual for the UK industry faces intense international competition and strongly cyclical demand. Where shipping companies have run into financial difficulties there has been little effort by government to provide emergency support. Thus when the Court Line became insolvent, the British government allowed the sale of its shipping interests while nationalising its shipbuilding subsidiaries. The contrast between UK policy towards shipping and towards shipbuilding reflects in part the greater prosperity of the shipping industry but also the relatively weaker political pressures on government for support to the shipping industry. It has frequently been observed that UK economic policy has been heavily influenced by the electoral ambitions of government and by pressures from sectional interest groups. One result has been for industrial policy to be strongly affected by unemployment. Because the UK shipping fleet is widely distributed (unlike shipbuilding which is highly geographically concentrated), the constituency system of Parliamentary representation means that political pressures for financial assistance are weaker for shipping than for shipbuilding. Similarly, the geographical dispersion of the shipping industry means that an increase in unemployment in the industry tends to have a smaller electoral impact than an increase in unemployment in shipbuilding. The international character and environment of the UK shipping industry also means that it is less likely to appeal to the national government for a solution to problems than will the shipbuilding industry. This is particularly true of British shipping companies whose dependence on cross-country trade encourages a vigorously independent attitude towards national governments.

J. Conclusions

6.76 Study of policies in the UK and BRD towards the shipping and shipbuilding industries provides some interesting comparisons, not just between the two countries, but in the case of the UK between the two industries as well. Given the difficulties of identifying the relative importance of the different objectives of the governments in supporting their maritime industries and the difficulties of evaluating the precise effects of the policy interventions, it is not possible to draw clear conclusions on the effectiveness of different policy tools. Nevertheless, inferences may tentatively be drawn, some of which may be applicable to industries other than shipping and shipbuilding.

6.77 First, the examination of the impact of the policy measures of the two governments on the shipping and shipbuilding industries invites caution as to the ability of structural policies to achieve the long-term policy goals of employment maintenance, growth and balance of payments contribution. The history of UK policy towards the shipbuilding industry is particularly relevant in this context. Despite heavy and increasing financial support for the industry between 1967 and 1978, measurable economic benefits appear small. The inferior performance of UK shipbuilding in relation to the BRD and other shipbuilding nations would seem to be the result of inadequate investment, inadequate research, poor financial and cost controls, inadequate production planning, poor marketing and chaotic labour relations. These same problems appear to be as prevalent in 1978 as in 1966 despite over a decade of intense government interventions accompanied by structural reorganisation and to enormous injections of public funds.

6.78 So far as short-term policy objectives are concerned, government intervention and heavy financial support have achieved one important goal. As a result of government policy the company structure of UK ship-building has been re-organised and the heavy support has achieved its objective of maintaining industry employment, though only in the short-term. As far as long-term performance is concerned the objective of increasing international competitiveness by new investment and greater efficiency has been a remarkable failure. The greater part of grants and loans for investment have been used to finance losses and provide working capital and where substantial new investment has taken place, e.g. Harland and Wolff, Sunderland Shipbuilders, and the results have been disappointing. It could be argued that the short-term maintenance of employment in inefficient firms has inhibited progress in the industry which has only increased the size of the long-term performance improvements in industry but structural policy may be counter-productive. An assumption behind UK shipbuilding policy has been that publicly financed re-equipment of yards and support for losses in the short-run can enable more efficient production methods to be introduced which will enable the companies to move towards being self-supporting in the longer term. The experience of UK shipbuilding fails to support this assumption and evidence from the most heavily assisted yards lends support to the contrary hypothesis that short-term inhibits managerial change and encourages the maintenance of inefficient work practices at all levels in the employment hierarchy.

6.79 Secondly, the experiences of the industries allows a comparison between the relative effectiveness of general support measures available to the industry as a whole and more interventionist policies which aim to support particular activities or particular companies. Both countries have directed financial support at both the industry generally and at particular firms and activities. While the former should not affect resource allocation within the industry, the latter is designed to reallocate resources between products or between firms. Although selective support policies have the ability of achieving government objectives more directly and possibly with less waste of expenditure, an essential requirement of such policies is that the government can correctly identify the sectors of the market or the companies where increased resources are required in order to achieve the policy objectives. If the policy objective is the maintenance of employment in the short-term, then a selective policy of providing emergency support to companies in danger of insolvency is likely to be a less costly means of achieving any employment objective than a general support for the whole industry. If, on the other hand, the objective is to encourage growth and profitability in the industry by taking full advantage of market opportunities, there is no *a priori* reasons why the government's decisions on the allocation of resources should be more efficient than those of the market and company managers. Indeed, attempts by both the British and West German governments to direct resources into particular areas of the shipping market seem in retrospect to have been misguided. Both British and German governments encouraged the domestic shipbuilding industries to expand their production of large tankers just before the world slump in this sector of the market.

6.80 Thirdly, the comparison of the maritime aids and interventions by the governments of the UK and BRD reflects the different political structures and constraints existing in the two countries. The propensity of British governments to intervene selectively to support particular industries and enterprises arises in part from the electoral sensitivity of governments which is the product of a finely-balanced two-party system where changes in government can arise from changes in the majority party in a relatively small number of parliamentary constituencies. The influence exerted on government by a few particularly large trade unions may also increase sensitivity to unemployment. The contrasting government structure in the BRD means that the political forces impinging on the policy process are different and it is possible that economic policy is less subject to short-term political pressures. First, the Federal structure of government may result in weaker direct pressure on the Bund for selective interventions. Second, the greater formalisation and openness in the process of economic policy formulation (as indicated by the role of the Export Council, the influence of the independent economic research institutes and the more formal tripartite arrangements with industry and unions through the 'concerted action' programme) may tend to shield government from sectional interests. Finally, the adherence by the post-war governments of the BRD to a set of principles embodied in the philosophy of the social market economy and formally established in policy guidelines (the 1966 and 1968 *Principles of Sectoral Policy*) provides a sharp contrast to the virtually unlimited powers of industrial intervention which the UK government conferred upon itself in the 1972 Industry Act.

CHAPTER 6 : REFERENCES

Broadway, F. (1976) *Upper Clyde Shipbuilders. A study of government intervention in industry . . . the way the money goes, Centre for Policy Studies, London.*

Business Statistics Office *Business Monitor*, PQ370, HMSO

Competition from East Bloc Fleets. (1976) *Inter Economics.* Contributions from B. Kroger and H. Kern.

Denton, G. (1976) Financial assistance to British Industry. (In W. M. Corden and G. Fels, *Public Assistance to Industry*, Macmillan.

Department of Trade and Industry (1973) *British Shipbuilding, 1972. A report to the Department of Trade and industry by Booz-Allen & Hamilton International BV, HMSO.*

Department of Industry (1974) *Public Ownership of shipbuilding and associated industries: Discussion Paper.*

Department of Industry *Research of Development Requirements Boards Reports*, 1973–4, 1974–5, 1975–6, 1976–7, HMSO.

Economic Intelligence Unit (1977) Shipping and Shipbuilding in Western Europe. *Economic Trends*, No. 50.

H. P. Drewry (Shipping Consultants) Ltd *Support for the World Shipbuilding Industry*, London.

US Department of Commerce (Maritime Administration, Office of Policy & Plans) *The Maritime Aids of the Six Major Maritime Nations*, Washington

Verband Deutscher Reeder *Shipping 1977 and 1976.* Hamburg.

Verband der Deutscher Schiffbauindustrie ev *Die Subventionlerung des Schiffbaus in den Konkurrenzländern*, Hamburg.

Verband der Deutscher Schiffbauindustrie ev (1976) *German Shipyards for Inland Waterway Vessels and Small Ships.* Hamburg.

Verband der Deutscher Schiffbauindustrie ev *Deutscher Schiffbau 1976 and 1977*, Hamburg

CHAPTER 7

THE APPRAISAL OF STRUCTURAL ECONOMIC POLICIES

Q: What constitutes success? Is it just that you have found a home for money?

A: The Treasury people sometimes accuse us of that. . . No we do not say a scheme is a success because
we have spent a lot of money, but it may be necessary to spend a lot of money in order for a scheme
to be a success.

Department of Industry evidence to the Committee to Review the Functioning of Financial Institutions (The Wilson Committee) p. 121, 1977.

A. Introduction

7.1   So far this study has concentrated on the evolution and description of structural economic policies and the
intellectual underpinnings of such policies has been confined to the economic arguments which have supported the rationals for specific kinds of intervention. However, an important public issue is that of know-
ing whether the policy measures actually introduced are not only appropriate for the objectives in view but
are in some sense efficient. Techniques have to be devised to identify projects which are worthy of state
support but in advance of their introduction. To policy makers faced with many competing claims on the
government budget, at the very least some lip-service has to be paid to standard methods of project appraisal if only to satisfy critics in tthe legislature and elsewhere.

7.2   Once particular structural measures are in operation, a further concern of policy makers is to monitor their
effects. Interest in monitoring may be simply to ensure that stated policies are being implemented by
measures which have legislative sanction and structural policies are no exception in this respect. However,
the purpose of monitoring may be to observe whether or not, in the light of experience, a particular measure was the appropriate one, including observation of any possible unintended 'side-effects'. Thus it may
be the case that an economic analysis, ex-post, may generate information which will be useful in deciding
whether, if a given policy objective is still relevant, the existing instruments should continue in use or
be replaced by others.

7.3   The development of suitable appraisal techniques has been slow, reflecting the complexity of the policy
issues rather than any lack of intellectual agility or effort on the part of economists. For this reason it has
been thought appropriate to devote sections II and III of this Chapter to expanding on this point for it
has an important bearing on the choice of actual appraisal measure. In subsequent sections an account is
given on the use of techniques of appraisal applied to structural policy instruments, and also by the political
and administrative structure of government.

B. The 'ex-ante' economic approach to appraisal

7.4   *Cost-benefit analysis.* In selecting projects for public support, 'traditional' economic appraisal has been
derived mainly from welfare economics. Welfare economics provides the rationale for government action
which is designed to improve the allocation of resources in circumstances where the market fails to do so.
'Market failure' may arise from a number of causes, among them:

i.   Imperfections in the goods and factor markets resulting from monopolistic and restrictive practices; and

ii.   The identification of goods and services for which there is a demand but which the market cannot or will
not provide — the 'externality' argument.

The economic analysis associated with (i) has been directed towards identifying such imperfections, but
structural policies are not generally associated with their removal. (It might be argued that support for
small firms is sometimes justified on the grounds that it is designed to improve freedom of entry into
imperfect markets.) In this context, (ii) is of more importance and there are many examples where structural aid is designed to take account of the externality problem. Regional aid, for example, designed to
promote investment in particular areas is sometimes justified in terms of an externality argument because
redirection of industry away from congested urban areas may reduce social costs and create social benefits
through the external economies which accrue to other firms in the assissted area. A pertinent example for
this study is that of aid to new technology which may benefit sectors other than the one in which it is
directly applied. If those who could employ the technology cannot exclude non-beneficiaries then they
will lack the incentive to do so.

7.5   The accepted technique for identifying projects which are worthy of support, within the ambit of allocative efficiency, is usually some version of cost-benefit analysis. This is a well known technique which need not be described in detail [for a useful and practical approach to cost-benefit analysis, see Sugden and Williams (1978)]. It is sufficient for the present purpose to indicate how it differs from the normal financial appraisal undertaken by a private decision maker, say a firm, in deciding whether or not to undertake a project. Such appraisal will usually recognise that in making a reckoning of profitability, costs and returns experienced now and in the near future are considered as more valuable than those obtained in the more distant future so that a method of comparison has to be devised which enables costs and returns at different points of time to be compared, as exemplified by DCF (discounted cash flow) procedure. A procedure such as DCF implies that the user can express costs and benefits in money values and that only those imposed on the user and benefits enjoyed by him are relevant. In projects undertaken or supported by government, financial appraisal would have at best limited relevance and at worst could be highly misleading. The very concept of external economies implies that a much wider view has to be taken about benefits and costs even if efficient allocation is the only objective. Further, it may be difficult if not impossible to attach money values to benefits and costs in situations where the output of the project is not priced. Finally, once the assumption is dropped that allocative efficiency is the only relevant criterion, the acceptance of a project need not necessarily have to depend on whether the (discounted) benefits exceed the (discounted) costs. It is obvious that the welfare function of government may contain 'arguments' other than efficient allocation, notably the distributional effects of public or publicly supported projects. Cost-benefit analysis is a technique which may have its origins in financial appraisal but it has to operate on a much less restricted and more difficult canvas.

7.6   The general methodology of appraisal found in cost-benefit analysis (CBA) would seem to offer a useful approach for assessing structural aid policies. However, it turns out that, except in the very general sense that any assessment requires the identification of the 'opportunity cost' of policies, CBA is very difficult to apply. There are a number of reasons why this is so:

i.   Though CBA can take account of objectives other than allocative efficiency, it is often difficult to obtain technical agreement on how these objectives are to be formulated and expressed in money values. The problem is compounded when an attempt is made to apply a financial yardstick to the objectives which structural policies are meant to promote. How can anything other than a subjective valuation be used to assess the benefits from avoiding de-industrialisation?

ii.   Unlike the use of CBA for government provision of services which embody investment decisions, the *ex ante* assessment of structural policies in the form of selective aid involves calculations of the behaviour of private firms who are the instruments through which the policy in question is to be achieved. The data gathering problems may be considerable and if there is a time limit on getting the policy into operation, as found in 'rescue' operations, this exercise may be excessively crude. Furthermore, if firms are being dealt with at arm's length, a further 'cost' imposed on the assessors is that of analysing the quality of data. The data may be 'massaged' so as to maximise the chances of receiving aid;

iii.   In any calculation of future benefits and costs of the kind found in CBA, problems arise about the appropriate way of treating risk and uncertainty. However, whatever method is used, in structural policies characterised by selective aid to a number of firms account has to be taken of the particular attitudes of individual firms to these factors which may be conditioned by the particular form and amount of the aid on offer. In consequence the relation between an injection of aid and the desired result in terms of investment, output, or employment may be particularly difficult to forecast;

iv.   There is an implicit assumption that, even if the difficulties just listed could be overcome, selective aid to policy instrument operating independently of others and with a distinct role in meeting macro-economic policy objectives. In practice, particularly in the UK, selective aid has often been part of a package deal encompassing agreements of tariffs, quotas, government contracts and other instruments of policy which in effect overshadow the normal functioning of market incentives. Financial aid has sometimes taken the form of side-payment to induce firms to comply with government decisons such as those concerning incomes and prices policies. In CBA the movements in financial flows which structural policy measures are designed to influence are meant to convey information about the way in which firms adjust within the market economy to the stimuli of selective aid programmes, and by which alternative aid packages might be evaluated. However, if subsidies, grants and loans are more in the nature of side-payments it becomes very difficult to reflect policy objectives in such flows and to isolate the effects, and therefore the effectiveness, of structural policy measures.

7.7   *Cost effective techniques.* Cost effectiveness analysis (CEA) sidesteps some of the above mentioned difficulties because it requires that a pre-determined objective or objectives can be taken as given. It then compares alternative ways of meeting the stated objective and normally the "least expensive" will be judged the most efficient. Let us assume that aid is granted to industry for the dual purpose of providing employment and aiding the balance of payments through import substitution. (These two objectives provided the justification for British Government aid to British Leyland.) In principle, it is possible to evaluate the first objective in terms of cost per job which then may be compared with possible alternative policies. Likewise, the foreign currency saving may be compared with alternative savings achieved through similar policies in other sectors of the economy. A certain programme might be judged efficient with regard to one objective but not the other, in which case a value judgement is required to determine the order or priority, but clearly, if a given aid programme were judged to be inferior to the alternative on both counts, it should not logically be chosen. The weakness of the cost effectiveness approach is that it requires a prior ordering of objectives — in effect a welfare function — which implies a pre-determined political decision with all the attendant difficulties of getting politicians to agree on such an ordering and sticking to it. CEA's great virtue, however, is that by dealing in terms of alternative policies and programmes its implicity highlights the force of the budget constraint. The cost of aid channelled to one sector is the resources withdrawn from another — regardless of the means of finance.

7.8 It follows that any given measure of selective aid to a specific sector or industry to pursue a particular objective will face, in the aggregate, a certain degree of 'crowding out'. In practice, it becomes virtually impossible to identify those sectors where crowding out occurs, particularly in cases where the financing is provided through general budgetary measures. If employment is the objective, for example, it is important to ensure that aid is channelled to a relatively labour intensive activity, (when all effects, direct and indirect, are taken into account) which is (net) export intensive. In principle, it is not unduly difficult to identify sectors which would qualify according to these criteria when analysed in purely static terms. For policy purposes, however, the great difficulty is that, over time, different industries face disparate growth rates and growth potential. One may sympathise with the desire to assist the adjustment process of an industry experiencing inevitable decline, but it is probably self-defeating to support an industry no longer enjoying a comparative advantage, for the long term aggregate impact upon macro-economic objectives is likely to be negative. An additional criterion for deciding the location of selective aid, therefore, would appear to be its relative income elasticity of demand, and the prospects of international competiton from others more advantageously placed. In contrast to the United Kingdom, this principle of 'sailing towards where one's comparative advantages lie' seems firmly accepted in the BRD. Notably, aid to shipping is concentrated upon the high technology end of the market in which competition from countries such as Korea, Singapore, and Vietnam, is still in its infancy.

7.9 The difficulties in applying CBA and CEA does not mean that they are to be ruled out as appraisal tools. Nevertheless, even in cases where they may be regarded as major components in an appraisal exercise, the information base for such appraisal must be much wider than that implied by these tools. In viewing whether a particular structural measure will produce the desired result, government policy must be set alongside the planning strategy of the firms to whom support is to be offered. The question must be posed: will firm X or even firm Y, given its planning objectives and capacity for maximising them subject to risk and uncertain yt, respond in a predictable and quantifiable way to the receipt of aid of £x or DM y. To answer it requires that, as a minimum, a full investigation becomes necessary of corporate plans and this must call for a range of expertise extending far beyond the normal prfessional capacities of economists, particularly in assessing such factors as the quality of financial reporting and entrepreneurial skill of the potenti l;recipients.

C. Monitoring and 'ex-post appraisal

7.10 The economist has no professional status when it comes to the formulation of proposals for monitoring the operation of structural policies if the object of monitoring is simply to ensure that public money is spent in accordance with the relevant legislation authorising the use of funds for such policies. Nevertheless, where legislation allows administrators a good deal of discretion in the choice of firms to be supported, legislative bodies themselves, such as the Select Committees of the House of Commons or of the BRD, will wish to 'monitor the monitors' in order to observe if their intentions are being carried out and public money is going only to those firms and industries for which any particular aid or subsidy scheme was supposed to be designed. Where there is a budget constraint on aid or subsidies, such bodies will wish to form a view about the methods of selection of firms in receipt of public funds. In principle at least, the dialogue between legislators and administrators will have to take some account of *ex-ante* economic appraisal which has taken place or might have been instituted. Linking such appraisal to the specifications of legislators and administrators, as one might expect, is not an easy task. Clearly, it requires a willingness of economists to adapt their analyses to take account of objectives other than the ultimate benefit to consumers, which dominates welfare economics, and a willingness of legislators and administrators to specify those objectives in a form which makes it possible to produce a meaningful appraisal. As Wiseman (1975) has shown, while legislators may reasonably complain if they are denied the necessary information of the intended and actual effects of selective aid schemes, they cannot expect officials to specify objectives for them.

7.11 The economist's role is more clear-cut as an examiner of the effects of aid and subsidy programmes in achieving stated ends. This form of *ex-post* appraisal seems to be particularly important in the case of structural policies, not only because of their increasing scope in recent years but also because of the relative lack of experience in their use. This is not to say that such appraisal does not run into particular difficulties of its own.

7.11 An example chosen from the long and continuing debate on the effects of regional policies in the UK will indicate some of the difficulties of *ex-post* appraisal. The general methodology adopted by economists and statisticians has been to select certain indicators for measuring the 'success' of a policy designed to improve the relative economic position of poorer regions. An attempt is then made to measure changes in these indicators as have occurred as a result of known policy measures and to compare how these indicators would have moved given some other policy alternative. The usual policy alternative chosen is a 'passive' policy rather than the assumed use of some alternative policy instruments. [For political 'blessing' for this approach, see The Select Committee on Expenditure Report on Regional Development Incentives (1963).]

7.13 When this approach is used in practice it turns out to run into formidable problems:

i. There may be debate about the choice of success indicators but, even if these are agreed, there are likely to be difficulties in obtaining accurate measures of their movements on a regional basis, and, as such indicators have to be measured through time, definitions may change over the relevant time period.

ii. Measurement of the cause-effect relationship between specific policies and results is fraught with difficulties. Employment is often taken as an indicator of 'success' but it may be affected by a whole range of policies not specifically directed towards improvement of regional trends. In addition, even if some clear link can be established between some regional measure and employment trends, problems of interpretation are presented by the need to recognise the existence of time-lags which may themselves vary through time. If the evaluation of the policy depends on the time-incidence of employment, then accounting for time lags becomes crucial.

iii. While economic historians are still locked in argument about the validity of a 'counterfactual' approach in appraising the results of policies [cf. Lee (1977)], it has been commonly accepted as applicable in modern economic and econometric investigation. Thus in the examination of the effects of regional policies no dispute has been engendered by the use of a 'policy-on., 'policy-off' comparison but honest technical disagreement is highly likely in defining the dimensions of the counterfactual situation. If a regional policy is characterised by grants to firms in particular regions, then, were these grants not to exist, there would be an implied change in the size and structure of the central government budget. There is not enough information generated from the instruction 'assume a policy-off situation' to indicate what the change might be and how it would affect the economy at large and regional trends in particular. [For friendly disputation on these matters, see Moore and Rhodes (1975) and Mackay (1975)].

7.14 The technical difficulties besetting ex-post appraisal of this kind, as with CBA and CEA, have the unfortunate effect of casting doubts on the status of economists in appraisal work. Anyone who has been closely engaged in such work soon realises that this offers the temptation to politicians and to administrators to ignore the results, particularly if these happen to support criticisms of policy measures to which they are committed. In addition, there is a further temptation in the form of raising the status of the complementary skills necessary to make economic appraisals, such as analysis of engineering, accounting and scientific data. For example, in appraisal of the effects of government aid to promote innovations, the effect of such innovations on the production process obviously cannot be determined by economists, but by applied scientists and engineers. The technological evidence may offer only partial guidance on the eventual economic effects of innovations but scientists and engineers working for government are often asked to exceed their brief and to pronounce on the economic potential of new processes though they may have no knowledge of the relevant markets for the fianl products. Casual empiricism suggests that their enthusiasm for particular innovations leads them to over-emphasise both the economic benefits and non-economic benefits, such as national prestige. Politicians and administrators, too, cannot resist this kind of optimism, preferring to risk estimates of benefits which can be precisely wrong rather than accepting economists' estimates which may be only vaguely right.

D. Structural policy appraisal in the UK

7.15 If the intentions of successive governments towards economic appraisal were to be judged by the growth in resource inputs, then it could be argued that economic appraisal is meant to be taken seriously. With the growth in selective aid measures in the 1970's there was a considerable expansion in the economic personnel and their range of duties in the relevant British Ministries, notably the Departments of Trade and Industry. However, the use of cost-benefit analysis and cost-effectiveness analysis pre-dates this period. With the growing interest of governments in expanding the range and quality of welfare services in the late 1960's, attention was concentrated on combining this growth with improved efficiency in government spending in order to combat any latent growth in tax resistance as the size of the public sector relative to the private sector expanded. By the time structural policy measures, other than long-established regional aid programmes, were developed, the Treasury had firmly established itself as the arbiter in technical matters of appraisal. The Treasury Management Accounting Unit set up in the late 1960's has acted as a source of information for government departments on each other's applications of CBA and CEA, has insisted on taking the lead in promoting discussion on technical issues and on persuading economists in other departments to clear their methods and results with the Unit. Where the Treasury as paymaster is closely involved in the formulation if industrial policies, and latterly this role has assumed more importance within it, it is in a strong position to take the lead on technical appraisal. After the announcement of the New Industrial Strategy (cf. Chapter 4) and the appointment of a further Second Permanent Secretary to the Treasury to head its prosecution, senior economists from the Departments involved met regularly and frequently, under the Chairmanship of the Head of the Government Economic Service, to work out in detail how economic appraisal of the strategy programmes was to be carried out.

7.16 The main issue raised by British experience is the reluctance of government officials to reveal how selective aid is appraised and what such appraisal would reveal. No legislation requires them to make such appraisals and the only information which need be provided about offers of selective aid is the publication of the nature and the amount of aid in the government publication *Trade and Industry*. The result of this reluctance has been a long and sometimes bad-tempered tussle between the Parliament and Whitehall. For example, in the 9th Report on the White Paper on Public Expenditure 1976–77, the House of Commons Expenditure Committee complained bitterly that they had no information on the perceived needs underlying the various selective aid programmes, the nature of the policy objectives, the extent to which it was believed that the objectives are attained and the assumptions underlying needs and costs. The Committee concluded that in the absence of such relevant information in was not competent to discharge its duties as the Parliamentary 'watchdog' on spending.

7.17 The problem of how much information to reveal is clearly regarded by any government in power as depending on the political advantages to be gained from doing so. It cannot be assumed that Government Committees chaired by Opposition members of the House of Commons are solely concerned with some form of objective assessment of expenditure programmes and governments see no reason why such committees should be provided unasked with material which might cast doubt on the feasibility and effectiveness of government programmes. So far as selective aid is concerned, however, the reasons given for restricting the information flow have been supposedly technical ones:

i.   'The amount of information which we make available is not of itself sufficient to carry out a detailed analysis, because some information which would be required which relates to the on-going performance of the company is not unreasonably regarded by those companies as confidential to them and it would have adverse effects on them if it were made public'. [Evidence submitted to the Expenditure Committee (Trade and Industry Sub-Committee), 8th Report of the Expenditure Committee 1977–78, pp. 44–45]

ii.   It is often claimed in official replies to Committees that it would not be in the public interest, as distinct from the interest of individual companies, to divulge the reasoning and assumptions underlying economic appraisal of specific selective aid programmes. For example, the revelation of assumptions made about future inflation rates and exchange rates might lead to adverse 'announcement' effects.

iii.   The 'Principle of Unripe Time' has been invoked in the case of those support programmes which emanate form the Industry Act of 1972 and the Industrial Strategy programme. It is claimed that major support programmes will take a long time before the desired results will be achieved, though what the time scale is meant to be is not revealed.

iv.   Finally, in what may be regarded as a rather remarkable admission, the absence of information may spring from pure ignorance. In a Memorandum submitted by the Department of Industry to the Expenditure Committee, there appears the following statement:

'Inevitably, because the various forms of regional and sectorial support are regarded as part of a general approach to industrial and regional needs they overlap and it is, therefore difficult to identify with precision the effects of particular measure of support.' (Eighth Report 1977–78).

7.18 Though reluctance to reveal appraisal methods and results emanates from a desire to protect their political masters or because of technical desiderata, officials do on occasion make statements based on some economic analysis of selective aid. However, if we were to judge the quality of such analysis from such statements then one could hardly form a very favourable impression. Two examples demonstrate this point. In the *Eighth Report from the Expenditure Committee* (to which reference has laready been made), it is asserted by the Department of Industry in its Memorandum to the Committee that the effectiveness of Regional Development Grants may be demonstrated by the progressive increase in the share of manufacturing activity going to the poorer areas of Scotland, Wales and the North – which increased from less than 22 per cent in 1951 to over 30 per cent in 1975. Our previous discussion of *ex-post* appraisal methods in Section C of this Chapter soon makes clear now misleading such a statemen can be. This claim ignores completely the problem of how to calculate the trend which would otherwise have occurred if Regional Development Grants had not been made. The statement also abstracts from the resource cost of the programme. The second example is taken from the Expenditure Committee's examination of the projections of selective aid appearing in the annual Blue Book on Public Expenditure in the same Report. In the Blue Book (Cmnd. 7049–1 and Cmnd 7049–2, 1977), estimates of future selective assistance to individual firms, industries and undertakings administered primarily by the Departments of Industry and the Department of Energy show a marked decline from 1978–79 onwards as indicated below:

	1978–79	1979–80	1980–81	1981–82
Selective Aid (£m at 1977 Survey Prices)	166	150	101	62

However, these projections are based entirely upon existing support policies and commitments (which possess finite termination dates) and make no provision for future salvages of companies which find themselves in the circumstances of a British Leyland. Moreover, with regard to that latter company, the official figures are based upon the amount of support then currently promised and not on an estimation of what *may* ultimately be needed if the company is to be rendered viable. Undoubtedly, there are difficulties in adjusting the figures for essentially unpredictable events yet the existing figures must be looked upon as extremely suspect and in all probability a vast under-statement as long as present industrial policy is pursued.

7.19 As already indicated and as can be confirmed by other evidence [see, for example, N. Gardner(1975)] the economic appraisal methods used in government are highly sophisticated when placed alongside official statements of this kind. Must one therefore conclude that such methods are totally disregarded by administrators and politicians? This issue is quite important, for the resource inputs employed in economic and statistical appraisal are quite considerable. It is very difficult, even with experience in undertaking such appraisal work to find a clearcut answer. It can at least be said that, as a minimum, even the most single-minded Permanent Secretary or doctrinaire minister requires a suitable data base and a reasonably coherent analytical framework within which to present a case for selective aid to a particular sector or firm, and expects economists and statisticians to provide it.

7.20 A minister may be able to avoid detailed investigations by Parliamentary Committees but in dealing with the Treasury and its ministers who have to take an overall view of public expenditure and with Treasury officials whose stock-in-trade is rigorous appraisal of all programmes, the brief supplied by his own economists and administrators must be able to stand up to rigorous scrutiny. There are two circumstances, however, where *ex-ante* economic appraisal of selective aid is likely to be ineffective, both of them derived from the Cabinet's view of what is to their political advantage. The first concerns 'rescue cases' i.e. firms likely to cease trading unless they receive government support. If such cases occur in politically sensitive areas, notably marginal constituencies, then quick action will be called for. There simply may not be time for proper appraisal to be undertaken in which aid requirements are matched with estimates of the likelihood of the firm's survival. Reliance will have to be placed on the off-the-cuff reaction of financial analysts rather than on the considered view of cautious economists which, by the time it is formulated, may be otiose – the firm may have disappeared!

7.21 The second occurs in case where what may be termed the 'intangible' non-economic benefits weigh heavily in the policy preferences of the government. In principle, while, as indicated in Section B of this chapter, specific benefits cannot be reduced to an economic calculus, this should not rule out the necessity for the kind of appraisal methods used by economists, particularly in circumstances where governments are working to a budget constraint. Following Gardner (1975), let us assume that a proposal for launching aid to an aerospace project is under consideration in which the proximate aim is to minimize the Exchequer cost. A calculation is then made of the probability of full recovery within a given period of time of the sum to be granted to the firm undertaking the project. (This entails some highly sophisticated methods of analysis which need not concern us here.) Let it be further assumed that the project would show a loss. The economist could claim that if it were decided to go ahead with the project, then the expected value of the loss offers a minimum valuation of the 'non-economic' benefits perceived by the government in approving the project, i.e. at the margin it would prefer to use Exchequer funds in the form of an aerospace subsidy than any alternative use of the funds, given a budget constraint. It is to be noted that, for simplicity, this example ignores other dimensions of economic appraisal which could be incorporated in the analysis such as making allowance for export performance and import savings. However, even this kind of formulation which avoids the economist having to pass judgement on governmental decisions, while allowed to take place, has not reconciled politicians, administrators and other technical advisers in government to this form of appraisal. To politicians it appears to tie their hands, for it is rarely politically advantageous to reveal the weighting they attach to policy objectives, when these may have to change. *A fortiori*, placing a minimum valuation on non-economic objectives will simply add to their troubles. To administrators, economic appraisal which attempts to incorporate non-economic objectives, even in this circumspect way, appears to trespass on their territory. It offers a rival approach to the exercise of their judgement and experience in advising ministers on how to act, though clearly any sensible economist will respect the administrator's knowledge of, say, the relevant (aerospace) sector in calculating the probabilities of recovery of funds. The economist's and administrator's approaches need not therefore be competitive but complementary. Other technical advisers who may have been closely concerned with the scientific development of innovations which firms might adopt with government support may be in the delicate position of evaluating the prospective performance of their own brain children. They are not likely to be sympathetic to appraisal methods which raise the possibility that their children might be strangled at birth. The position of all three of these groups of critics of economic appraisal can easily be rationalised because of the admission by economists themselves that *ex-ante* and *ex-post* appraisal are subject to a high degree of uncertainty.

7.22 On balance, then, it appears that economic appraisal of selective aid has much less influence on government decision making in the UK than economic analysis and related policy measures associated with the pursuit of the more traditional forms of macroeconomic intervention. In both activities it has always been agreed by economists in government that obtaining and maintaining influence in policy matters requires that senior economists become directly involved in the final critical stages of policy formation. The very analytical difficulties of appraisal of the effects of selective aid programmes already adumbrated in Section B and the sensitiveness of the political issues arising from the obtrusiveness of selective aid measures are important offsets to the influence of status and of personality which might otherwise be enough to ensure that the economist is seen as well as ready by Ministers in pursuit of policies.

E. Structural appraisal in the BRD

7.23 For many years there has been an explicit commitment in BRD delegated legislation to the necessity for 'Erfolgskontrolle' (lit. 'success control' and broadly interpreted by German writers as meaning project appraisal) in the disbursement of government funds. Such appraisal can be interpreted very widely to cover *ex-ante* appraisal, monitoring in the traditional sense already described, and *ex-post* appraisal, and does not refer exclusively to techniques developed primarily by economists. CBA and CEA analyses are only recent additions to the categories covered by 'Erfolgskintrolle'. We may take as a landmark in German economic discussion the appearance of a work edited by Recktenwald (1970) on CBA and programme budgeting in which of the 26 primarily analytical articles which appeared, only 3 were contributed by German writers. Formal recognition of the contribution of CBA (interpreted in a very wide sense to include CEA) followed very quickly. In paragraph 7.2 of the Bundeshaushaltsordnung 1973 (the Federal Budget Ordinance 1973) it was announced that CBA should be applied to 'suitable measures of considerable financial importance' (geignete Massnahmen von erheblicher finazieller Bedeutung). An associated administrative regulation elaborated the circumstances in which CBA might effectively be used. By 1976 it was considered appropriate to investigate how far the Ordinance of 1973 had been invoked but, of the 50 or so CBA studies completed, very few fell within the rubric of the ordinance itself and none of these it seems, were within the field of 'Strukturpolitik'. Nevertheless, active interest has developed in appraisal methodology, judging at least by the experience recorded in professional administration journals (e.g. *Handbuch der Verwaltung*) which have filtered through from official sources [cf. Meyer zu Drewer (1978)]. The Ministry of Finance apparently continues to keep a tally of CBA studies and acts, like the British Treasury, as a clearing house for information on methodology and results.

7.24 Although paragraph 7.2 BHO has legal force, there does not appear to be any clear policy about when this ordinance is to be invoked and by whom. As is clear from its content, and from the quotation already given, it is framed in rather vague terms and it does not specify who may invoke it. In consequence, either ministries in charge of projects which might be subject to CBA invent their own rules regarding its implementation, e.g. by scrutinizing investment projects estimated to cost more than a certain amount, or wait until they have to succumb to outside pressure from financial 'watchdogs' such as the Ministry of Finance, the Audit Offices of the Federal Government or the Bundestag. At the same time, though paragraph 7.2 BHO has no binding force and pressure to invoke it must come from outside, this does not prevent legislation designed to promote new expenditure from indicating by cross reference to 7.2 BHO that it is expected that appraisal work will be carried out.

7.25 Though there is little published information on how appraisal work is conducted and what practical influence it may have on structural policy and public officials consulted have an understandable reluctance to bend the rules governing confidentiality, it is possible to give a general idea of the influence of such work on selective aid policies. First of all it should be noted that the Sechster Subventionsbericht [6th Subsidy Report (1977)], discusses how 'Erfolgskontrolle' can be specifically applied in the appraisal of subsidy measures. The subsidy reports already contain elaborate appendices which record the following information in respect of subsidies or tax reliefs:

(a) The nature of the project.

(b) Whether it represents: (i)   maintenance aid;
                                 (ii) adjustment aid;
                                 (iii) growth aid; or
                                 (iv) aid for other purposes.

(c) Past expenditure and budgeted expenditure for coming financial year.

(d) Whether in the form of grants or loans etc.

(e) A written statement of: (i)   its objectives;
                                (ii) legal basis; and
                                (iii) claimed results and prospects of continuation.

For example, recalling the discussion on shipbuilding subsidies, it is interesting to note that under our heading (e) the number of ships and tonnage completed by firms receiving subsidy is given together with the amounts of loan and subsidy finance received over the period 1965–73. There then appears the quite categorical statement: "The subsidies have undoubtedly contributed to the fact that the German merchant fleet now belongs to the most modern and most efficient (fleets) in the world" (Sixth Report, p. 147, cf. also 6.50 above). The Sixth Report, however, admits that this kind of information and *ex-post* appraisal is no more than a point of departure for more rigorous analysis. The point of entry of CBA and CEA is seen to be, interestingly enough, when policy aims change and subsidy measures then require to be reappraised. (This observation is clearly conditioned by the legislative procedures which must be followed by on-going subsidisation which is subject to regular scrutiny by the Bundestag.) One learns that both CBA and CEA are increasingly being used in appraisal of agricultural subsidy policy, transport, and regional structural policy. It appears that the great bulk of these studies is carried out by outside experts rather than internally and the Sixth Subsidy Report gives in detail an example taken from the appraisal of environmental measures (pp. 33–35) in which a 'plain man's guide' to the application of CBA is given. In short, the Report endeavours to give an answer to contemporaneous criticism by such economists as Zimmerman (1977) who have complained that, while recognizing that reports of this sort must be of necessity apologetic in character, they have not explained the basis of the evaluation of programmes.

7.26 As the BRD subsidy programme was not originally envisaged as a major development of Strukturpolitik but as, at most, a set of supplementary selective aids which, with the exception of growth aid, were of a temporary nature, it is not surprising that methods of appraisal, as distinct from monitoring, have not been the subject of a dailogue the Bundestag through its committees and the Federal administration. This is the main contrast one can make with the British position. It may also be the case that potential worries among professional economists and others conversant with appraisal work may have been defused by the reliance placed upon the use of outside experts to conduct them. However, there are sufficient doubts about the likelihood that selective aid will be phased out in the BRD to warrant a continuing interest in the question of 'Erfolgskontrolle'. For example, the Commission for Economic and Social Change (Kommission für wirtschaftlichen und socialen Wandel), several of whose members supported an active Strukturpolitik, particularly in the form of selective aid to new technology and regional aid, recommended the setting up of a special Council for Structural Problems which would conduct, *inter alia*, evaluation of sectoral aid schemes alongside alternative forms of state action to achieve the same ends (see their Report p. 134).

Further, all its members, who represented very diverse points of view, agreed to recommend that Bundestag committees should have more technical resources at their disposal in order to provide them with better information on the methods and results of project appraisal (p. 565). But it is also recognised that the present state of the art of appraisal extended neither to the production of agreed evaluation criteria nor to complete knowledge of the economic and social consequences of government aid programmes.

7.27 Very recently, the need to parallel the continuation of subsidies with improved appraisal methods has been recognised by the Ministry of Finance in their comments on the Seventh Subsidy Report (see Bulletin des Presse- und Informations amt der Bundesregierung vom 3.8.1979). At the same time it is admitted that 'the difficulties of appraisal begin . . . with the fact that the aims are not sufficiently precise; and, they end with the fact that there is a decided lack of usable instruments of measurement that can discern the degree of achievement in reaching the goals in view.' (p. 872). Reluctantly perhaps, one must say Amen to that.

F. Summary and Conclusions

7.28 This chapter has shown that those responsible for the formulation and execution of selective aid policies have had to search for methods of *ex-ante* and *ex-post* appraisal to supplement the more conventional monitoring devices which are used to ensure that government disbursements on selective aid are provided for authorised purposes. It is therefore recognised that efficiency in selective aid policy involves something more than a costing of proposals, the preparation and authorisation of a budget and a system of budget control. As a minimum, alternative aid programmes to achieve stated ends are necessary and, once alternatives are investigated, some form of CEA is required. Furthermore, the effects of the chosen alternatives in achieving given policy aims require some comparison between what has actually happened compared with some alternative situation, though administrators are obviously reluctant to compare actual outcomes with hypothetical ones. The potential impact of economic appraisal, *ex-ante* and *ex-post*, should therefore be considerable if not decisive in the development of selective aid programmes.

7.29 Our survey of what happens in practice must bear out the conclusion that the actual impact of economic appraisal has been small. The reasons are not difficult to find. The most important one is clearly the suspicion in the mind of administrators and politicians of the lack of professional commitment among economists, including those who support the use of CBA and CEA techniques, to important components of selective aid programmes. This characteristic of economic thought has already been documented in Chapter 3. The gist of the economists' argument is simply that, within the broader spectrum of economic policy, selective aid policies are likely to be less effective than traditional macro-economic policies supplemented, perhaps, by state encouragement to factor mobility, in achieving macro-economic aims. This judgement carries the implication that politicians in power must work with a much restricted range of policy measures and thus are given fewer opportunities to dramatize their role as the progenitors and operators of specific policy instruments [cf. Peacock (1977)], a role which sometimes also appeals to administrators. Casting doubt on selective aid policies, therefore, hardly enhances the popularity of sceptical economists. A related reason is associated with the sheer technical difficulty of generating conclusions precise enough to satisfy politicians and administrators from the standard appraisal techniques. Furthermore, where sensitivity tests of possible outcomes of industrial projects supported by aid programmes indicate that alternative assumptions about costs and benefits make no difference to the final result, it rarely seems to happen — though this is merely casual empiricism — that the results produce positive support for projects on purely economic grounds. A final judgement favourable towards the institution of an aid programme or its continuance on grounds of its 'success' has then to be derived from the judgement of others who are prepared to rush in where most economists worth the name would fear to tread.

REFERENCES TO CHAPTER 7

Deutscher Bundestag (1977) *Sechster Subventionsbericht*, Section IV

Gardner, N. (1976) 'Economics of Launching Aid' in Whiting (*op. cit.*)

House of Commons Expenditure Committee (1977–78) Eighth Report

Kommission für wirtschaftlichen und sozialen Wandel (1976) *op. cit.* Chapter XIII

Lee, C. H. (1976) *The Quantitative Approach to Economic History*, Martin Robertson, Chapter 4

Mackay, R. R. (1976) Discussant's comment in Whiting, (*op. cit.*)

Meyer zu Drewer, Hans (1978) 'Erfahrungen mit Nutzen-Kosten-Untersuchungen in der Verwaltungspraxis des BML' in *Planung, Durchführung und Kontrolle der Finanzierung von Landwirtschaft und Agrarpolitik*, BLV Verlagsgesellschaft München

Moore B. and Rhodes J. (1976) op. cit.

Peacock, Alan (1979) 'Giving Economic Advice in Difficult Times' in Peacock, Alan (*op. cit.*)

Recktenwald, Horst (Editor) (1970) *Nutzen-Kosten-Analyse und Programmbudget*, J.C.B. Mohr, (Paul Siebeck) Tübingen

Sugden R. and Williams, A. (1978) *The Principles of Practical Cost-Benefit Analysis.* Oxford

Wiseman, J. (1976) 'An Economic Analysis of the Expenditure Committee Reports' in Whiting (*op. cit.*)

Zimmerman, Horst (1977) 'Die Informations funktion des Subventionsberichts,' *Finanzarchiv*, 35 pp. 451 – 468.

CHAPTER 8:

SOME QUESTIONS RAISED BY STRUCTURAL ECONOMIC POLICIES

A. Introduction

8.1   This report has endeavoured to determine the dimensions of structural policy and has attempted to justify concentration on selective aid measures used in the BRD and UK as its main component (Chapter 1). The economic background to the perceived need for structural policies reveals considerable disagreement about the nature of the evidence of structural change and its interpretation (Chapter 2). Economic analysis of the logic of economic policy provides at most reluctant support for selective aid measures (Chapter 3) of the kind which have actually developed in both countries (Chapter 4). The different emphasis of selective aid policies reveals a much greater degree of acceptance in the BRD of structural changes which follow from economic growth and the nature of support for the computer industry illustrates this theme (Chapter 5). Likewise, in the case of declining industries, notably shipbuilding (Chapter 6), the UK has chosen to be much more selective in its policies, requiring negotiations with individual companies and with the unions determined to preserve jobs at any cost. When it comes to the problem of assessing and monitoring the performance of structural aid measures, only lip service is paid in both countries to methods of appraisal derived from economic analysis (Chapter 7) which is hardly surprising once it is realised that economic criteria of selective aid performance have had limited relevance to policy decisions and how difficult it is in any case to apply standard methods of economic appraisal (such as cost-benefit and cost-effective analysis) to measure the effects of aid measures.

8.2   The general conclusions drawn from our analysis is that if structural policies are judged in terms either of the narrower criteria of the economist or the wider criteria which take account of political objectives, they have yet to prove their worth as substitutes for other policy instruments designed to achieve the same ends. It would need a fuller investigation beyond the present one to justify this categorical statement but it is doubtful if even the most recondite statistical and econometric tests would enable one to firm up what must be an impressionistic judgement. As demonstrated in paragraphs 7.12 to 7.14, technical appraisal which might be used to produce a more conclusive result is beset by methodological as well as practical difficulties. As has been shown, the practical application of selective intervention runs into operational snags which change the data on which the marrying of objectives and instruments of policy are based. It is not denied that this sort of difficulty is endemic in any attempt to apply the logic of economic policy to practical situations. Thus the use of macro-economic policy instruments has to allow for the fact that adverse public reactions to budgetary changes may force politicians to revise their strategy because remaining in power may be more important to them than promoting long-term economic stabilisation. However, this kind of feedback problem seems if anything to be more virulent and potentially at least more damaging to the policies themselves in the case of selective aid measures. In the rest of this report, we illustrate this conclusion largely by reference to our previous analysis.

B. The logic and practice of structural policies reconsidered

8.3   *Objectives and trade-offs.* Structural policies are justified in terms of their influence on the general aims of macro-economic policy and not, as found in textbooks, in terms of specific welfare criteria which primarily emphasise allocational objectives. At the risk of labouring a point made at several stages in this work (c.f. paragraphs 1.15 to 1.17, paragraphs 3.2 and 3.24) there are major problems in persuading governments to make too explicit statements of aims and trade-offs, and to express these in quantifiable terms, at least to the public at large. A major reason for this (c.f. 1.16) is to reduce the political 'feed back' which is generated by reactions to the failure to achieve stated targets. In the case of structural policies which imply the disaggregation of specific targets by industrial sector, such as employment, output and export performance, this emphasis on vagueness will suit administrators for otherwise they become much more closely identified with sectoral intervention and more easily exposed to the risk of failure. It is much easier to obtain wide consensus about the proposition that a government is against sin that about the ranking and scale of measurement of its virtuous pursuits. However, if it is not clear, or not made clear, what the objectives translated into target variables really are then it is obviously difficult to specify the appropriate instruments to influence them.

8.4   *The policy model reconsidered.* However clearly or obscurely the objectives and trade-offs are formulated, the choice of appropriate policy instrument depends on their supposed influence on the economy. A policy model of the economy has to be produced in which both the targets and the instruments are specified. There is some measure of agreement about the dimensions of such a model. For any individual country it must represent a scenario of its possible economic development which indicates, inter alia, its growth potential, the expected conjunctural path, the broad structural changes in the economy and the pattern of foreign trade. Furthermore, it is generally agreed, as implied in the last sentence, that the scenario considers the medium and long-term developments of the economy because the influence of policy instruments, such as selective aid measures, will be relatively slow. One immediately sees that the combination of disaggregation of economic variables and emphasis on the remoter future, as compared with short-term macroeconomic models, presents a much stiffer test to economic forecasters. The greater likelihood of forecasting errors must increase the risks attached to the making of appropriate policy choices, a point given particular stress in relation to structural policy by the German Council of Economic Advisers (See Sachverständigenrat zur Begutachtung der gesamtwirtschaftlichen Entwicklung 1976/77, paragraphs 313—315).

8.5 However, within this broad framework which determines the requirements for a policy scenario, very different sequences of economic events may be depicted, depending on the precise economic models which is used to detect them. As we have seen in paragraphs 2.7 to 2.13, 'structuralists' have emphasised the paramountcy of the manufacturing sector as the engine of growth and to a general improvement in the control which growth allows in achieving other objectives such as reducing inflation and balance of payments deficits. Therefore a scenario of future economic development which manifests de-industrialisation is a warning that structural readjustment may be necessary if growth is to be maintained. At the same time, the acceptance of this thesis, which has been questioned in 2.13 and 2.14, does not promote agreement as to how the manufacturing sector is to be made to become this engine of growth. The Kaldorian view (c.f. Kaldor (1977)) has placed most emphasis on manufacturing economies of scale and the achievement of self-sustaining growth by selective tax and subsidy measures that simultaneously improve the demand for manufacturing products and induce a shift of factors, including both labour and capital, into the supply of manufactured goods. An alternative thesis, which has partly influenced the British New Industrial Strategy (see 4.36) rejects the proposition that increasing the capital/labour ratio in manufacturing is the complete answer and emphasises the need to improve the efficiency of factor inputs. However, this counterthesis has not been accompanied by a tight-knit argument, in favour of a particular set of policy measures. In the BRD, for instance (c.f. 3.19 and 3.20), emphasis might be laid on the use of competion policy on a wide front as a method of improving factor efficiency, whereas in the UK the refusal to bring restrictive practices in the labour market within the ambit of competition policy would rule out a similar line of approach. In short, the indicators of specific policy measures derived from study of the performance of the economy, point in every direction, reflecting wide technical disagreements among economists.

8.6 *The structural policy instruments.* Let it be conceded that objectives and trade-offs can be firmly established and that the government is able to predict how its own objectives might change through time. Let it be further conceded that an agreed view can be reached about the relation between the desired rate of economic growth and the structural changes in the economy which will follow from it. Furthermore, let it be assumed that the technical relation is known between any particular subsidy and tax measure and its influence on the output of each industrial sector so that, in principle at least, the structural change which would equate the desired with the actual rate of growth could be achieved, but, to introduce some realism into the argument, within a budget constraint covering the entire range of selective measures. (As must be clear from the argument in Chapter 2, these concessions go far beyond what our previous evidence and analysis can allow.) It seems highly probable that the appropriate use of selective aid measures would require a very high degree of flexibility with constant adjustments of aid to the different sectors which could at times be positive and at times negative. There would also have to be a high degree of coordination of selective aid measures and of coordination between such measures and fiscal and monetary policy.

8.7 Experience indicates that this degree of flexibility and coordination encounters major political difficulties. Even where, as in the BRD (c.f. paragraph 4.6), explicit allowance is made for combining a selective aid policy which is growth-promoting together with support to alleviate the effects of structural change on those employed in sectors likely to decline in the long run, it has been politically impossible to fulfil the stated intention of making maintenance aid a very limited and decreasing element in subsidy policy (for data see Table 4.3). So far as coordination is concerned, the argument may be prefaced by a point made in paragraph 3.16. Selective aid measures engender competition among government Ministers because these measures dramatise more effectively than general measures Ministers' political role and enhance their reputation as policy activists. They are not likely to be willing to have their hands tied in negotiations for aid finance from the Treasury by the need to coordinate their activities with one another. Though such statements cannot be documented, it is interesting to observe that selective aid policy has done nothing to promote the amalgamation of major Ministries in either the BRD or UK and where amalgamation has been introduced, as with the UK Department of Economic Affairs (1964—67) and the Department of Trade and Industry (1970—74) with the clear intention of improving policy coordination, it has been short-lived.

8.8 The recognition of the fact that giving effect to structural adjustments will encounter opposition both within and outside government is the origin of an administrative accompaniment to structural measures designed to resolve differences by 'involvement. in the planning process. The idea of 'concerted action' is familiar from the well known attempts in the BRD to make macro-economic policies 'stick' by joint meetings of employers and trade union representatives together with the Council of Economic Advisers. In the UK, on the other hand, the idea has become an integral part of the New Industrial Strategy (c.f. paragraphs 4.36) instituted in 1975 in which, as we have seen (paragraph 8.4) the removal of supply constraints by structural policies is the dominant theme. If dirigisme is ruled out as a method for ensuring the flexibility and coordination which a structuralist approach demands, then a possible alternative is to seek a cooperative solution. Policies have to be presented to, assessed by and agreed among those most affected by their operation. Those closely engaged on the technical sidelines can have nothing but admiration for the speed and skill with which the administrative machinery was created to ensure cooperation which is well described by two of its principal administrative architects in the Department of Industry — Alan Lord, then Deputy Secretary and Ann Mueller, then Under-Secretary [see Lord (1977) and Mueller (1977)]. Within a few months, sector working parties (SWPs) were established in all major branches of manufacturing industry under the aegis of the National Economic Development Office (NEDO) which eagerly grasped this new opportunity to expand its role as a kind of benign ringmaster, more in keeping with its former glory in the 1960s, chivvying along the SWPs to ponder, assess and recommend policies of their own but hopefully consistent with the general objective of improving industrial efficiency. The essence of the administrative achievement lies in the rapid extension of the older Economic Development Committees (the little 'Neddies') to cover a much wider range of industrial sectors (the SWPs) and in getting agreement to a combined membership of unions and management together with representatives of the appropriate Government sponsoring department and of NEDO itself.

8.9 It is all too easy in the initial flurry of excitement engendered by a carefully orchestrated administrative operation of this kind to forget its ultimate purpose. Improvement of industrial efficiency can only take place as a result of decisions which result in a 'downward shift' in average cost curves for industrial products or in some form of product innovation which shifts demand curves to the right. These decisions depend on agreements between management and workers at firm and, more likely, at plant level. On the other hand, profitability of a firm can depend on a whole range of other factors which may be within government control such as exchange rate policy, protection from import penetration and the panoply of selective aid measures themselves. It is hard to see why firms either alone or in concert should wish to go through the agony of inducing unions to alter their work practices and taking risks in product development when other, softer, options are not ruled out of discussion in consultative bodies. The fact-finding activities of the SWPs may have improved our knowledge of the economic position and problems of individual sectors of manufacturing industry and some SWPs have indulged in a modicum of self-criticism when international comparisons have revealed comparative inefficiency. Even those who economists have been *parti pris* have openly expressed their sceptism of the possibility of self-criticism leading to the fixing concrete targets for industrial sectors and to the specification of the action necessary at firm level. Thus D. K. Stout, as Economic Director of NEDO, has produced documentary evidence which clearly indicates that SWPs have used their opportunity of interface with government departments to step up their claims for subsidies rather than be shamed by the evidence of inefficiency into improving performance at plant level. Several SWPs have made open bids for selective import controls to protect their members. As Stout adds: '. . . the main criticism is that it is hard to see how the speed of improvement in productivity and non-price competitiveness (and hence in trade performance) which can be brought about in this way can be fast enough to counteract protectionist pressures' [Stout (1979) and, for similar sentiments, Balogh (1979)].

8.10 Though it is normally claimed that the Industrial Strategy programme can only be judged by results which can only emerge in the 1980s, the risk that the programme will never be much more than a jaw-boning exercise, highlights an earlier point about the polarisation of views on economic policy in the UK (paragraph 3.16). Though agreed on the diagnosis that manufacturing industry suffers from 'generalised inefficiency' alongside foreign competitors, and that cooperative action under the aegis of the NEDO is unlikely to succeed, there is no agreement about alternative courses of action. On the other hand, there are those who maintain that the only alternative is *dirigisme* of the kind associated with Planning Agreements (c.f. paragraph 4.36) by which firms simply have to accept radical changes in their objectives and their planning organisation in return for selective aid. On the other hand, there are those who would prefer to see the abandonment or containment of selective aid programmes, other than those to promote labour mobility, and their substitution by a vigorous 'workable' competition policy nationally and internationally, e.g. through EEC action.

8.11 Rather than speculate on which of these approaches are desirable or feasible, a matter which has already been much discussed in the UK and BRD (see Chapter 3), it is felt that a useful way to conclude this study is to consider what light it might throw on the development of structural policies in the future.

C. The possible future of structural policies

8.12 *The national context.* The way in which structural policies have developed in response to policy objectives and; the economic and political environment in which these objectives are sought suggest that in both the UK and BRD, they are likely to persist, though the emphasis on its different components may change.

i. The expectation of slower growth in Western industrial countries and the persistent difficulties associated with controlling inflation mean that governments under pressure to maintain the growth in living standards have to compete in raising productivity. With growing dependence on foreign trade, raising the real income multiplier will depend on export performance and the reduction in demand for importables, and this cannot be done simply by maintaining the growth in domestic aggregate monetary demand. What is interesting about this scenario is the impetus it has given to organised labour in both the BRD and UK to support not only increases in the proportion of annual output resources to be devoted to investment but also 'steering of investment' (Investitionslenkung) through state agencies to the 'most productive' channels. There are many facets to be discussion of investment steering in both countries. In the UK, on the whole, the TUC has supported two major measures for intervention in the capital market. The first consists of greater state control over the supply of finance to industry and the second the control of the use of firms' undistributed profits through their transfer to a Swedish-type state investment fund [c.f. TUC Evidence to the Wilson Committee (1977)]. In the BRD, the discussion of 'Investitionslenkung' began in the 1960s as part of a much wider debate about the relative merits of 'market socialism. and 'the social market economy. which lasted until the mid-1970s [see, for example, Zinn (1973) and Steger (1973)]. By the time concrete proposals had been extracted from the academic debate, as presented to the SPD Party Congress in 1977, they looked very similar to those of the TUC and had even attracted the sympathy of prominent writers on economic policy [see Fels (1978)]. Both schemes are clearly influenced by the revival of ideological objections to the 'social market economy. which have more public appeal as memories of the Nazi 'Verschmelzung von privater Macht und Zentralverwaltungswirtschaft. (see paragraph 1.16) fade and the performance record of the social market economy seems to have become more tarnished. 'Investitionslenkung' may therefore become a serious contender for inclusion in the weaponry of structural policies, if only because it has not been tried as a means of improving productive efficiency, whereas it has been traditionally associated with stabilisation programmes. If so, then the technical debate will centre in a revival of the age-old problem as to whether central planners can 'out-forecast' the market in a way which ensures that investment decisions will maximise growth in output and employment.

ii. As observed above, 'supply-oriented' growth policies, however organised, take time to work and are primarily directed towards increasing the value of only one important variable, real output, which is of concern to the working population. Workers are obviously concerned with the immediate rather than the remote future and with how far their employment opportunities will be affected along the time path towards the longer-term goal. Further, supply-oriented growth policies raise fears about the extent to which real output improvements may be obtained by labour-saving measures or imply rapid shifts of occupation as the economic structure alters. The price to be paid by governments under pressure to improve long-term productivity under the threat of international competition, is likely to be an 'active' short-term employment programme. Both the BRD and the UK were operating temporary employment subsidies schemes in the mid-1970s but on the expectation, as the word 'temporary' implies, that such subsidies would encourage employers in industries most affected by depression to retain labour (as in the British case) or encourage firms to take on unemployed labour (as in the German case) in advance of their requirements during the expected upswing [For a full account of the West German scheme, see Schmid (1979)]. Both the BRD and UK schemes, therefore, were not designed with large-scale structural problems in mind, and both, even allowing for the effects of the increase in employment on the reduction of demands for state unemployment benefit, were relatively costly to the central government budget. Faced with continuing budget constraints and with the general expectation that improvements in long-run growth and stability will not automatically improve general employment opportunities, it seems likely that government employment policies will become more selective. Equity considerations alone would indicate, as in the Carter Administration programme in the USA [c.f. Palmer (1978)] that subsidies should be concentrated on 'target' groups encountering particular difficulties in obtaining employment initially and in remaining in employment during a major part of working life. This would further suggest that structural change may only be one element governing the choice of employment programmes, much more emphasis now being placed on such target groups as the long-term low income unemployed, particularly the young. Again one must stress that as soon as governments enter the business of offering selective support, familiar problems cannot be avoided — the incentive given to create further pressure groups with a vested interest in particular programmes, the appraisal of the policy instrument as a tool of selection strategy, and the coordination — in this case between education and training and employment programmes — of policies.

8.13 *The international context.* A dominant feature in the discussion of future economic trends in industrialised countries has been the continuing importance of success in international markets. The growth in the importance of international prosperity is frequently illustrated by the ratio

$$\frac{\text{Value of Exports} + \text{Value of Imports}}{\text{Gross National Product}}$$

all at current prices, and although this is a crude measure, it is sufficient for our purposes. The ratio for the UK has risen from 37.45 in 1965 to 58.11 in 1976, and in the BRD from 34.50 in 1970 to 41.20 in 1978. However, as shown in Chapter 2 (c.f. paragraph 2.20 and Table 2.5) the period is characterised in the British case by a pronounced fall in international competitiveness in manufactures, whereas this is not the case in the BRD. Nevertheless, the same worries beset both countries about the future of their competitiveness against a background of growing competition from Eastern European and Asian countries. It is not surprising, therefore, that structural measures, particularly in the UK, have in the past been trade-related. Apart from 'traditional' forms of support for exports such as export credit and deterrents to imports such as tariffs, as soon as assistance is given to particular sectors or firms, account can be taken of its place in world markets. It has already been demonstrated how important export markets have been to shipbuilding in both the BRD and UK (c.f. paragraph 6.19) and how crucial an element this has been in the argument for support, though adjustment aid has been given in both countries in a way which claims to avoid the breaking of international trade agreements.

8.14 The shipbuilding case highlights a problem of growing concern to individual trading nations, namely the extent to which national adjustment aid measures may be neutralised by similar measures taken by competitors (c.f. paragraph 6.20). Yet, given the continuing and perhaps increasing 'openness' of industrial economies which makes international competitiveness a major influence on growth and employment prospects, there will be a strong temptation to such countries to extend the use of selective aid, though ostensibly not designed to influence the balance of payments directly, particularly if they are already bound by longstanding international agreements such as those embodied in GATT. Not surprisingly, the renegotiations of the GATT agreement and OECD Declarations have now taken on board the problem of creating an 'international order for public subsidies' [c.f. also Malmgren (1977)]. An alternative approach is implicit in the growing interest in industrial policy expressed by the EEC. This is to 'internalise the (negative) externalities' produced by international competition in selective aid, if need be by the transfer of major areas of industrial policy to the EEC. While such a move might reduce subsidy competition among EEC members as trading partners, it does nothing to promote an international order for structural measures, except possibly in reducing the costs of bargaining if EEC countries can operate as a cohesive trading bloc.

D. Conclusion

8.15 The study of structural economic measures is instructive if only because it demonstrates how policy instruments which may be initially derived from technical judgements and are then translated into administrative acts become politicised. This presents the economic analyst with a dilemma. If he wishes to build a testable model which is meant to offer guidance on the economic effects of a particular measure, account must be taken of the reactions of those whose actions are influenced by selective aids, for example, and how these feed back to and affect the actions of political decisionmakers. The problem becomes even more complicated, as indicated in the final paragraphs of this study, when account is taken of the effects of structural measures in one country on the policies of another. It is very difficult in any event to give much content to economic models of the international bargaining process, and particularly difficult when, as has been argued, the precise economic effects of selective aids are often difficult to trade. If, on the other hand, an attempt is made to evaluate selective aids, further difficulties soon emerge. Technical economics discussion has sought to appraise the various forms of adjustment aid principally with reference to welfare economics with its emphasis on the failure of the market to optimise the allocation of resources, yet it is rarely the purpose of such measures to perform that task. If one asks the question, did the structural measures achieve what governments sought to achieve with them, then skills other than those derived from economics are needed — those, for example, of the private detective! — In order to induce sponsors to reveal their preferences. This report does not resolve these dilemmas, but may have a contribution to make simply in having recognised their existence. Perhaps a little more than that may be claimed for it tries to show that even if it can be assumed that policymakers really intend to minimise the resource costs (of which the budgetary cost is a crude measure) of selective aid measures and really seek to maximise long-run economic objectives rather than short-term political ones, it cannot be demonstrated that measures designed to influence the structure of the economy or to mitigate the effects of rapid changes in that structure can by themselves achieve that object. If such measures can only be made to work if they are buttressed by much more radical forms of intervention such as state direction of investment and detailed state approval and monitoring of individual company plans, it may well be asked whether these particular remedies are not worse than the disease.

REFERENCES TO CHAPTER 8

Balogh, T. (Lord) 'Comment' in Blackaby op. cit. pp. 196–201.

Fels, G. (1978) 'Eine mittelfristige Strategie muss jetzt auf der Angebotsseite ansetzen', *Die Welt*, 3 October.

Kaldor, N. (Lord) (1977) 'Capitalism and Industrial Development: Some Lessons from Britain's Experience', *Cambridge Journal of Economics*, pp. 193–204.

Lord, Alan (1977) *An Approach to Industrial Strategy*, Sir Ellis Hunter Memorial Lecture No. 7, York.

Malmgren, Harald (1977) *International Order for Public Subsidies*, Thames Essay No. 11, Trade Policy Research Centre.

Mueller, Ann (1977) 'Industrial Efficiency and UK Government Policy' in *Industrial Efficiency and the Role of Government* (edited by Colette Bowe), HMSO, pp. 260–277.

Palmer, John L. (1978) 'Employment and Income Security' in *Setting National Priorities, the 1979 Budget.* (Edited by Joseph Peckman), the Brookings Institution, pp. 61–90.

Schmid, Gunther *(1979)* 'The Impact of Selective Employment Policy: The Case of a Wage-Cost Subsidy Scheme in Germany 1974–5', *Journal of Industrial Economics*, June, pp. 339–358.

Steger, U. (1973) 'Okonomische Probleme der Investitionslenkung in der Markwirtschaft', *Wirtschaftsdienst*, No. 10.

Stout, D. K. (1979) 'Deindustrialisation and Industrial Policy' in *Deindustrialisation* (edited by Frank Blackaby), Heinemann and National Institute of Economic and Social Research, pp. 171–196.

Trades Union Congress (1977) Evidence to the Wilson Committee, *Committee to Review the Functioning of Financial Institutions : Evidence on the Financing of Industry and Trade*, Vol. 2, HMSO, pp. 73–109.